Shakespeare

Othello

A CASEBOOK

EDITED BY

JOHN WAIN

Revised Edition

MACMILLAN

First edition 1971
Reprinted nine times
Second edition 1994

Published by
MACMILLAN PRESS LTD
Houndmills, Basingstoke, Hampshire RG21 6XS
and London
Companies and representatives
throughout the world

ISBN 0–333–53353–4 hardcover
ISBN 0–333–53354–2 paperback

A catalogue record for this book is available
from the British Library.

This book is printed on paper suitable for recycling and
made from fully managed and sustained forest sources.

10   9   8   7   6   5   4
04   03   02   01   00   99   98

Printed in Hong Kong

CASEBOOK SERIES

JANE AUSTEN: *Emma* (Revised) David Lodge
JANE AUSTEN: *'Northanger Abbey' & 'Persuasion'* B. C. Southam
JANE AUSTEN: *'Sense and Sensibility', 'Pride and Prejudice' & 'Mansfield Park'*
B. C. Southam
BECKETT: *Waiting for Godot* Ruby Cohn
WILLIAM BLAKE: *Songs of Innocence and Experience* Margaret Bottrall
CHARLOTTE BRONTE: *'Jane Eyre' & 'Villette'* Miriam Allott
EMILY BRONTE: *Wuthering Heights* (Revised) Miriam Allott
BROWNING: *'Men and Women' & Other Poems* J. R. Watson
CHAUCER: *The Canterbury Tales* J. J. Anderson
COLERIDGE: *'The Ancient Mariner' & Other Poems* Alun R. Jones & W. Tydeman
CONRAD: *'Heart of Darkness', 'Nostromo' & 'Under Western Eyes'* C. B. Cox
CONRAD: *The Secret Agent* Ian Watt
DICKENS: *Bleak House* A. E. Dyson
DICKENS: *'Hard Times', 'Great Expectations' & 'Our Mutual Friend'* Norman Page
DICKENS: *'Dombey and Son' & 'Little Dorrit'* Alan Shelston
DONNE: *Songs and Sonnets* Julian Lovelock
GEORGE ELIOT: *Middlemarch* Patrick Swinden
GEORGE ELIOT: *'The Mill on the Floss' & 'Silas Marner'* R. P. Draper
T. S. ELIOT: *'Prufrock', 'Gerontion' & 'Ash Wednesday'* B. C. Southam
T. S. ELIOT: *The Waste Land* C. B. Cox & Arnold P. Hinchliffe
T. S. ELIOT: *Plays* Arnold P. Hinchliffe
HENRY FIELDING: *Tom Jones* Neil Compton
E.M. FORSTER: *A Passage to India* Malcolm Bradbury
WILLIAM GOLDING: *Novels 1954–64* Norman Page
HARDY: *The Tragic Novels* (Revised) R. P. Draper
HARDY: *Poems* James Gibson & Trevor Johnson
HARDY: *Three Pastoral Novels* R. P. Draper
GERARD MANLEY HOPKINS: *Poems* Margaret Bottrall
HENRY JAMES: *'Washington Square' & 'The Portrait of a Lady'* Alan Shelton
JONSON: *Volpone* Jonas A. Barish
JONSON: *'Every Man in his Humour' & 'The Alchemist'* R. V. Holdsworth
JAMES JOYCE: *'Dubliners' & 'A Portrait of the Artist as a Young Man'* Morris Beja
KEATS: *Odes* G.S. Fraser
KEATS: *Narrative Poems* John Spencer Hill
D.H. LAWRENCE: *Sons and Lovers* Gamini Salgado
D.H. LAWRENCE: *'The Rainbow' & 'Women in Love'* Colin Clarke
LOWRY: *Under the Volcano* Gordon Bowker
MARLOWE: *Doctor Faustus* John Jump
MARLOWE: *'Tamburlaine the Great', 'Edward II' & 'The Jew of Malta'* J. R. Brown
MARLOWE: *Poems* Arthur Pollard
MAUPASSANT: *In the Hall of Mirrors* T. Harris
MILTON: *Paradise Lost* A. E. Dyson & Julian Lovelock
O'CASEY: *'Juno and the Paycock', 'The Plough and the Stars' & 'The Shadow of a
Gunman'* Ronald Ayling
EUGENE O'NEILL: *Three Plays* Normand Berlin
JOHN OSBORNE: *Look Back in Anger* John Russell Taylor
PINTER: *'The Birthday Party' & Other Plays* Michael Scott
POPE: *The Rape of the Lock* John Dixon Hunt
SHAKESPEARE: *A Midsummer Night's Dream* Antony Price
SHAKESPEARE: *Antony and Cleopatra* (Revised) John Russell Brown
SHAKESPEARE: *Coriolanus* B. A. Brockman

STRODE'S COLLEGE
LIBRARY

CONTENTS

ACKNOWLEDGEMENTS

The editor and publishers wish to thank the following for permission to use copyright material:

S. T. Coleridge, 'Marginalia on *Othello*' and 'Report of a Lecture at Bristol', from *Shakespearean Criticism*, ed. T. M. Raysor (J. M. Dent & Sons Ltd, London, and E. P. Dutton & Co. Inc., New York); A. C. Bradley, extract from *Shakespearean Tragedy* (Macmillan & Co. Ltd); T. S. Eliot, extract from 'Shakespeare and the Stoicism of Seneca', from *Selected Essays* (Faber & Faber Ltd, London, and Harcourt, Brace & Co., New York); G. Wilson Knight, 'The *Othello* Music', from *The Wheel of Fire* (Methuen & Co. Ltd); William Empson, 'Honest in *Othello*', from *The Structure of Complex Words* (Chatto & Windus Ltd, London, and New Directions Publishing Corporation, New York); F. R. Leavis, 'Diabolic Intellect and the Noble Hero', from *The Common Pursuit* (Chatto & Windus Ltd, and New York University Press); Nevill Coghill, extracts from *Shakespeare's Professional Skills* (Cambridge University Press); John Bayley, for the extract from 'Tragedy and Consciousness', from *Shakespeare and Tragedy* (Routledge and Kegan Paul, 1981), by permission of Routledge; Christopher Norris, for the extract from 'Post-Structuralist Shakespeare', from *Alternative Shakespeares*, ed. John Drakakis (Methuen, 1985), by permission of Routledge; Anthony Brennan, for the extract from 'Iago, the Strategist of Separation', from *Shakespeare's Dramatic Structures* (1986), by permission of Routledge; Karen Newman, for the extract from 'And Wash the Ethiop White', from *Shakespeare Reproduced*, ed. Howard and O'Connor (Methuen, 1988), by permission of Routledge.

Every effort has been made to trace all the copyright-holders but if any have been inadvertently overlooked the publishers will be pleased to make the necessary arrangement at the first opportunity.

7

GENERAL EDITOR'S PREFACE

The Casebook series, launched in 1968, has become a well-regarded library of critical studies. The central concern of the series remains the 'single-author' volume, but suggestions from the academic community have led to an extension of the original plan, to include occasional volumes on such general themes as literary 'schools' and genres.

Each volume in the central category deals either with one well-known and influential work by an individual author, or with closely related works by one writer. The main section consists of critical readings, mostly modern, collected from books and journals. A selection of reviews and comments by the author's contemporaries is also included, and sometimes comment from the author himself. The Editor's Introduction charts the reputation of the work or works from the first appearance to the present time.

Volumes in the 'general themes' category are variable in structure but follow the basic purpose of the series in presenting an integrated selection of readings, with an Introduction which explores the theme and discusses the literary and critical issues involved.

A single volume can represent no more than a small selection of critical opinions. Some critics are excluded for reasons of space, and it is hoped that readers will pursue the suggestions for further reading in the Select Bibliography. Other contributions are severed from their original context, to which some readers may wish to turn. Indeed, if they take a hint from the critics represented here, they certainly will.

A. E. DYSON

INTRODUCTION

Othello seems to have been written in 1604, and first performed at Court on 1 November of that year. It was printed in the First Folio in 1623, but there was a separate edition, in Quarto, brought out by one Thomas Walkley in 1622. Walkley presumably knew, by that date, that the First Folio, which offered a 'collected' Shakespeare to the public for the first time, was just about to appear, and perhaps rushed out his edition of the play to make a last-minute profit. But the text he used has several interesting differences from the one used by Heminges and Condell. It omits 160 lines, adds a few and is not Bowdlerized; an Act of Parliament in 1606 forbade oaths on the stage, and the Folio text complies with this, but the Quarto does not, and perhaps goes back to an earlier manuscript. Editorial work on the text of the play has thus been full of problems from the beginning; the editor of the Second Quarto (1630) uses the First Quarto with some corrections derived from the First Folio.

For an editor, then, *Othello* has always been one of the most difficult of the plays, and to this day it bristles with unsolved textual problems and disputed readings. For the interpretative critic, on the other hand, it would seem to be one of the simplest of Shakespeare's major works. Compared with the dazzling complexities of *Hamlet*, the cloudy sublimities of *King Lear* or the delicate poetic symbolism of *A Winter's Tale*, there seems to be, in *Othello*, nothing much to dispute about. The play makes its terrific impact on us, we respond deeply or shallowly according to whether we have deep or shallow natures and there's an end of it. Or so, at least, I thought before I began the reading necessary for this book. Although the play had always been one of my favourites, I had not read much criticism of it, since I am one of those people who turn to criticism only when they feel themselves in difficulty. And with

Othello I was conscious of no difficulty; I had a consistent interpretation of it which satisfied me.

I

Othello, as I saw it then and still see it now, is a tragedy of misunderstanding. No one among the characters understands anyone else; nor are they, for the most part, very strong on self-understanding either. If Othello understood Desdemona, he would know that she is simply not the kind of girl who would, during their very honeymoon, start a love affair with his first officer. If Desdemona understood Othello, she would know that he does not yet see her as a real girl, but as something magical that has happened to him, and that he will run mad if anything should happen to make him believe that her white magic has turned to black. If Emilia understood Iago she would know that he is not merely a coarsely domineering husband who has forced her into endless petty compromises for the sake of peace and a *modus vivendi*, but also, on a side hidden from her, a fiend who delights in torture. But then Iago does not, until it happens, know this about himself. Unaware of the power of love, he cannot imagine the suffering into which he will plunge Othello by plausibly slandering Desdemona, and therefore cannot imagine the holocaust at the end. Nor can he foresee the transformation that will occur in himself. The great temptation scene (III iii) is so convincing because it shows Iago's fall as well as Othello's. At the beginning of that scene they are both sane men; at the end, they are both mad, and both in the grip of the same madness. Hence the dreadful tragic irony of

> – Now art thou my lieutenant.
> – I am your own for ever.

Iago, the matador, succumbs to the excitement of his combat with the bull. One mistake, and those deadly horns will rip him to pieces. From that point on, he abandons all thought of motives and works from contingency to contingency. Of course Desdemona must die, for if she lives it will come out, one day, that Iago was lying, and Othello will hunt him down if it takes the rest of his life. Cassio must die for the same reason. Likewise Roderigo, who also knows too much. (And, like everyone else in the play, understands too little.) Iago's original intention, however much he may dress it up in a patchwork of motives, is to do as much harm to Othello and Cassio as his stunted little imagination can suggest. That harm turns out to be as far beyond his original conception as Othello's love for Desdemona is beyond his vulgarian's notion of love as 'a lust of the blood and a permission of the will'. Once he realizes the gigantic suffering he has unleashed, and the destructiveness that goes with it, he cannot halt or even slow down: it is too late. But Iago continues on course for reasons other than self-preservation. He is intoxicated; he has bull-ring fever. He is the perfect type of all those insignificant little men – they turn up every week, in the murder cases – who all at once feel the urge to destroy another human being, and get drunk on the realization that this large, important action is suddenly, incredibly, in their power.

II

If this view is correct, and *Othello* is a tragedy of misunderstanding, how does this arise? Why do the characters misunderstand each other? In each case, Shakespeare has provided, it seems to me, a sufficient answer. Desdemona, already young and inexperienced, has been over-protected by her father, so that she has even less knowledge of life and people than she might have. Iago misunderstands because, when it comes to anything that concerns the more generous emotions, he is a brute and a fool. Roderigo misunderstands because, in any case rather stupid, he is persuasively misled by Iago. Othello is taken in by Iago not only because Iago is a good actor (a fact which Shakespeare has already planted in II i) but because Iago has previously shown himself trustworthy and is so regarded by everyone; and also because, for all his power and importance in Venice, he is an outsider. Venice needs him, uses him, rewards him, but does not entirely take him in. His acceptance is partial; there are certain limits to it, which, though they are not spoken of, are quite clear in everyone's mind. Brabantio, to take the most notable example, has been glad to have Othello as a guest in his house, has in fact 'loved' him, but feels betrayed when Othello marries his daughter. (The justification for Othello's and Desdemona's secrecy, for the clandestine wooing and midnight elopement, is obviously that if Othello had asked in a normal way for Desdemona's hand in marriage, Brabantio would have refused, forbidden him the house as he had already forbidden Roderigo, and thereafter had the girl watched day and night.)

This, of course, raises the question of Othello's colour. I agree with Mr Louis Auchincloss that Othello is not regarded by the aristocratic Venetian characters as a social inferior: 'They regard him as Victorian Englishmen might have regarded some splendid Maharajah. . . . The Venetian aristocrats will not admit him to their inmost society, and they certainly do not want their daughters to marry Moors. But then they probably would not marry their daughters outside of fifty families along the Grand Canal.'[1]

Still, Brabantio thinks his daughter must have been bewitched to make her want to do anything as 'unnatural' as marrying a black man, and throughout the play the characters who dislike Othello tend to make it an additional point against him that he is dark-skinned. Those who like him tend to make no fuss about his colour one way or the other; while there is nobody, however pro-Othello, who says that he is all the more admirable *because* of his race, for the early seventeenth century had not heard of 'negritude'.

Those who fall under the spell of Othello's personal magnetism, who see, as Desdemona puts it, his visage in his mind, do not find anything unattractive in his racial characteristics. In the murder scene Desdemona does indeed find him terrifying

as he rolls his eyes and gnaws his nether lip, details which
seem to be hints to the actor to play the scene like a full-
blooded African; but, since he is about to murder her, the poor
girl might be forgiven for being frightened of him. What is
important about Othello's racial difference from the other
characters is not that it makes him terrifying or disgusting – it
manifestly doesn't, except to people with a grudge against him
already – but that it is the outward symbol of his isolation.
Throughout the play, whether in the close-knit social fabric of
Venice, or in the garrison-town atmosphere of Cyprus, he is
surrounded by people who are different from himself in every
way, just as he was on that far-off day that comes back to his
mind in the last few seconds of his life, when in the Turkish
city of Aleppo he intervened to protect a visiting Venetian
businessman who was being beaten up in the street: a street
full of people whom he chose to defy and dominate, whereas
the Venetians were people he had chosen to serve. In each case
it was a *choice*, a conscious decision of the will, not the blind
natural instinct that makes a man fight for his own hearth and
his own gods. Othello willed himself into a relationship with
Venice, and the will is terribly limited in what it can achieve.
Hence his insecurity; hence his touching pride in the way he
has carried out his side of the bargain ('I have done the state
some service'); hence the fact that Desdemona's love, which
gives him an intimate, living link with Venice and promises to
break down his outsiderdom, is central to his whole being, so
that when he thinks it withdrawn he despairs of going on with
anything, even his trade of fighting ('Othello's occupation's
gone'); hence his bewilderment before Iago's commonplace
cunning, the bemused suffering of the bull in the bull-ring.

III

Such were my thoughts about *Othello*; and, serenely reading
and watching the play according to these notions, I imagined
that the critics, when I came to study them, would on the

whole, and with modifications here and there, give support to
the interpretation I found so unquestionable. Far from it.
What awaited me was the usual experience that comes to one
who reads criticism in bulk. It was like walking placidly down
a quiet corridor, opening a door and suddenly coming upon a
crowd of people arguing at the tops of their voices. One faction
was praising Othello, attributing to him a generous share of
every virtue under the sun; another was busily destroying his
character, offering a view of him as a coarse, vain, lustful and
brutal ruffian who would be very apt, Iago or no Iago, to
murder his wife on some delusory grounds. Hands were held
up in horror at the wickedness of Iago, some of those most
shocked professing at the same time an involuntary tremor of
admiration at his unsurpassed brilliance and the coolness of
his villainy; in another corner, he was dismissed as a mere
creature of the plot, a shallow liar and braggart who could
never have taken in anyone less stupid and self-centred than
his master. Others, again, dwelt on his wrongs and murmured
that revenge was, after all, a kind of wild justice. At the
mention of Desdemona's name, some eyes filled with tears of
pure adoration; others became narrow and suspicious. Not
only the characters, but the play as a whole, came in for totally
different interpretations. The idea of magic is central to it.[2]
The idea of magic is not central to it.[3] It is a Christian tragedy
– Othello's fall is a version of Adam's, while the fate of
Desdemona is an inversion of Eve's.[4] Its plot is incredible.[5] Its
plot has 'surrealistic rightness'.[6] It is part of the response to
James I's heroic poem, 'Lepanto'.[7] It is a diagram of Spanish
political history, with Othello as Philip II and Iago as his
enemy, Antonio Perez.[8] 'Perhaps the greatest work in the
world', trumpets one voice;[9] but another growls, 'A bloody
farce without salt or savour.'[10]

The character of Othello himself has provided a focus
for ramified disagreement. To Swinburne, Othello was 'the
noblest man of man's making'; T. S. Eliot, on the other hand,
spoke rather sourly of his 'cheering himself up' and came out
with that celebrated critical *mot* about 'Bovarysme'. And the

dispute goes on. Nevill Coghill, in these pages, shows convincingly that Eliot's view could never be convincingly manifested by an actor and is therefore unlikely to have been intended by a consummate dramatic artist like Shakespeare; on the other side, Robert B. Heilman comes very close to restating the Eliot position when he says:

Othello is the least heroic of Shakespeare's tragic heroes. The need for justification, for a constant reconstruction of himself in acceptable terms, falls short of the achieved selfhood which can plunge with pride into great errors and face up with humility to what has been done. All passion spent, Othello obscures his vision by trying to keep his virtues in focus.[11]

The classic inheritor and developer of the Swinburne line is A. C. Bradley; of the Eliot line, F. R. Leavis. In their respective essays, the two possible attitudes towards 'the noble Moor' stand revealed without qualification or misgiving. To read the two essays together, and try to achieve some mediation or synthesis between them, is a fascinating critical exercise. For the disagreement affects, as it is bound to, every facet of the play and every character. Since Bradley takes Othello to be entirely blameless, he has to explain why anyone should hate him so much as to destroy him. He accordingly sites the main complexity of the play within Iago's character, and devotes about half of his total space to an analysis of it, conducted with that characteristic Bradleian scrupulousness and intensity. To Dr Leavis, this preoccupation with the inner reaches of Iago's mind is hardly more than a simple waste of time; as he sees it, Iago, though 'sufficiently convincing as a person', is 'subordinate and merely ancillary . . . not much more than a necessary piece of dramatic mechanism'. Othello's tragedy, to Leavis, is essentially precipitated by Othello's own shortcomings – by his egotism, and by his love of Desdemona which is merely sensual and possessive and does not extend to any real knowledge of who and what it is that he is loving. ('It may be love, but it can be only in an oddly qualified sense love of her'.) To Leavis, Othello's habit of self-idealization, his simple heroic way of seeing himself in widescreen images, served him well

enough in a life of martial adventure, but would never have
fitted him for the reciprocity of marriage, so that 'the tragedy is
inherent in the Othello–Desdemona relationship'. When
things go wrong, when pressure builds up, Othello's inade-
quacies are revealed like the cracks in a dam. 'The self-
idealization is shown as blindness and the nobility as here no
longer something real, but the disguise of an obtuse and brutal
egotism.'

Leavis's view would make the play largely a criticism of
Othello's character. Certainly it is true that Othello's blindness, his vulnerability to Iago's suggestions, arise from that
statuesque largeness of outline which makes him unwieldy in
manoeuvre. He *is* an egotist; we see it in his coolly callous
treatment of Brabantio, or in the account of his wooing which
he gives to the Senators – an account which makes it sound as
if *she* wooed *him,* and doesn't at all square with Desdemona's
later protestation that Cassio

> came a-wooing with you, and so many a time,
> When I have spoke of you dispraisingly,
> Hath ta'en your part.

Othello's life has not been such as to allow him the luxury of
fine discrimination and *nuance.* Since his arms had seven
years' pith, he has lived in an atmosphere where to hesitate, to
have second thoughts or inner reservations, was to be killed by
enemies who were prepared to be simple and decisive. Such a
life breeds egotists. And Othello's egotism is egregious enough
to make Iago's work fairly easy. [12] But to say this and to wash
our hands of him, to echo Leavis's 'the essential traitor is
within the gates', is to dodge the emotional impact of the play,
to deny somehow that the tragedy is tragic. And this, surely,
falsifies the experience we can testify to have undergone. We
know that we have witnessed the overthrow of a strong and
generous man; our hearts have been wrung as they would not
have been wrung by the sight of a preposterous egotist (whatever his countervailing good qualities) getting his deserts. To
me, Bradley is closer to the heart of the play, for all his over-

elaboration and his side-issues; he recognizes that the tragedy
lies in the assassination of love by non-love; he may go on too
much about Iago, but he understands the essential truth about
him, that he was less than a complete human being because
love had been left out of his composition, left out so completely
that he did not recognize it or suspect its existence. (Even
Roderigo, who perceives very little, understands things that
Iago does not understand; he knows that Desdemona is 'full of
most blessed condition'; he loves her, and his love instructs
him in her true nature.) Bradley puts it very well: '[Iago] was
destroyed by the power that he attacked, the power of love;
and he was destroyed by it because he could not understand it;
and he could not understand it because it was not in him.'
Othello, egotist as he is, unpractised at understanding other
people as he is, retains the possibility of development because
he knows what it is to love. And it is only the loveless heart
that cannot learn.

Leavis's view, then, seems to me a brilliant (and characteristically trenchant) account of what Othello *is*; but Shakespeare's
tragedy is tragic because it takes account, by implication, of
what Othello *may become*; and this too Bradley sees, when he
tells us that Othello in middle age 'comes to have his life
crowned with the final glory of love'. Part of that crowning, we
are surely meant to perceive, would be the easing of Othello's
rigid stance towards life, the diminution of his egotism in the
joy of knowing and loving another person.

IV

However that may be, Leavis and Bradley represent the two
principal ways in which the character of Othello, and consequently the tragedy, have been viewed. With regard to Iago,
they agree at least in finding him repulsive. Whether on a large
scale or a small scale, he *is* the villain, the 'demi-devil'. And
yet, it seems, even Iago has had his apologists. As early as
1790, a 'Gentleman of Exeter' published an essay called 'An

Apology for the Character and Conduct of Iago', based on the incontrovertible fact that Iago has a good reputation, as man and soldier, before the story opens, and arguing that if he were really wicked it would surely have been noticed in his twenty-eight years. In the nineteenth century two critics, the Englishman Heraud and the American Snider, found themselves believing that Iago has actually been cuckolded by Othello; this would give him a powerful motive for revenging himself, and thus makes his conduct, though still wicked, that of a man and not a mysterious fiend. Several twentieth-century critics have followed these two in finding Iago's suspicion a reasonable one; John W. Draper, after assembling satisfactory evidence that Elizabethan notions of honour made the cuckold a universally despised figure and that any man threatened with this fate would understandably seek his revenge, asks: 'Is Iago then so black a villain? Is he not a commonplace Renaissance soldier, "honest as this world goes", caught in the fell grip of circumstance and attempting along conventional lines to vindicate his honour? Indeed, if honesty and honour be something of the same, is he not from first to last "honest Iago" '?

Even if we find it incredible (as I do, for one) that Othello has, at some earlier stage, made love to Emilia, there remains the fact that Iago thinks he may well have done, and thinks, moreover, that a lot of people believe he has ('it is thought abroad that 'twixt my sheets He has done my office'). Whether Iago has any grounds for this suspicion or whether he is just being neurotic, the belief is strong enough to 'gnaw his inwards' like 'a poisonous mineral', so that in one of his later soliloquies (III iii), when he is rejoicing in the torment he is causing Othello, he can revert to the same imagery and say,

> Dangerous conceits are in their natures poisons
> Which at the first are scarce found to distaste
> But, with a little act upon the blood,
> Burn like the mines of sulphur,

and knowing what he is talking about. On this view, his motive would be to make Othello go through the same agony as himself. Thus Mario Praz, who sees Iago as 'incensed by the public report that Othello has cuckolded him', points out that the story of his revenge has 'parallels in many cases of retaliation instanced by Italian *novelle*'.

Once more a polarity reveals itself; as in the case of Othello, critics divide into two camps. On the one hand there are those who take it that Iago does not really understand his own motivation, and when he claims to do so, in his soliloquies, he is merely rationalizing. Coleridge's phrase, 'the motive-hunting of a motiveless malignity', is much quoted in this camp. Hazlitt, a little later, saw Iago in a similar light, as an aesthete of evil. He denies that Iago is without motivation, for 'Shakespeare . . . knew that the love of power, which is another name for the love of mischief, is natural to man. He would have known this . . . merely from seeing children paddle in the dirt or kill flies for sport.' To Hazlitt, Iago is 'an amateur of tragedy in real life; and instead of employing his invention on imaginary characters or long-forgotten incidents, he takes the bolder and more desperate course of getting up his plot at home, casts the principal parts among his nearest friends and connections, and rehearses it in downright earnest with steady nerves and unabated resolution'. (My own view, that his immediate motives for hostility are clear enough but that the full range of possibilities only comes into view with action, and calls out an unexpectedly fiendish side to his own nature, clearly makes me a satellite of this critical body.) On the other hand there are the critics who see Iago's motives rather as he professes to see them himself. To Kenneth Muir, 'The secret of Iago is not a motiveless malignity, nor evil for evil's sake, nor a professional envy, but a pathological jealousy of his wife, a suspicion of every man with whom she is acquainted, a jealous love of Desdemona which makes him take a vicarious pleasure in other men's actual or prospective enjoyment of her at the same time as it arouses hatred of the successful Moor and it may even be suggested, a dog-in-the-manger attitude that cannot bear to think of Desdemona happy with any man, and especially with a coloured man, a man he hates.'[13]

V

To my mind, the most successful of the attempts to mediate between these two schools is the strenuous chapter on 'Honest in *Othello*' in William Empson's *The Structure of Complex Words* (1951). The gist of this chapter is reprinted here, but readers should note that the argument is much easier to follow if it is put back in the context of the book. A word is 'complex' when it has a cluster of possible meanings, the smaller ones not so much fighting the 'head sense' as sheltering under it and taking on its protective colouring so as to live their own lives in safety. To interpret a complex word correctly is to understand fully the passage, and often the whole work, in which it occurs. Clearly this kind of criticism, though its procedures are 'verbalist', is no mere matter of lexicography or semantics: it is concerned with sorting out feelings, and life-styles, and social attitudes (different senses of a word tend to be dominant among different classes).

Empson gets to work on 'honest' with two richly suggestive chapters on the development of the word from its mediaeval use ('deserving the receiving social honour'). About the middle of the sixteenth century, he traces the beginning of a vague slang use for purposes of general approval among friends. An 'honest' man came to mean 'one of us, the type we like'. Since the simpler and older Chaucerian sense might now have unintentionally comic undertones, it quickly died off, leaving a new 'head sense': 'truthful, not stealing, promise-keeping'. The contrapuntal play of these two senses gave scope for irony, since an 'honest' man, one who owned up to his motives, however discreditable, might be selfish and unreliable and yet 'honest' in the sense of not being a hypocrite, therefore truth-telling. This alternative sense became very powerful during the Restoration, with its anti-Puritan feeling and its cult of (especially aristocratic) independence. One has the impression, in fact, that the use of 'honest' to mean 'one of us' travels upwards from the lower to the upper classes during the seventeenth century. (Certainly if Shakespeare caught it at the

moment when it began its upward trajectory he could use it to
convey a great deal of the range of feeling of someone as touchy
as Iago.)

Empson continues his biography of the word 'honest' until
he reaches the wonderfully rich but stable cluster of meanings
indicated by this passage:

> A Victorian gentleman, while Gladstone was being discussed, could
> remark (in his pompous manner) 'honest Jones, our butcher, thinks
> the man a windbag', and this could chiefly mean that he was himself
> in doubt. Gladstone might be above Jones's head, or Jones might
> have sturdy common-sense: in any case what you needed here was a
> certain breadth. A slow and rather dumb readiness to collect the
> evidence, a quality that Jones probably has, is in view, however much
> Jones may be a fool.

Armed with this kind of insight, Empson proceeds to
interpret the character of Iago, and his function in the play, by
means of the reverberations of the word 'honest' as he applies
it to himself and has it applied to him by others. His essay is in
fact a close and sensitive piece of character-analysis, almost
Bradleian, though in a very different idiom from Bradley's; it
shows us an Iago who is certainly wicked and not to be
defended, but also human and credible. Iago's class-jealousy is
alerted by the patronizing overtones in the word 'honest'; he
feels, probably quite rightly, that Cassio was important to
Othello in a way that he could never be – notably as an
intermediary in Othello's wooing – and this led directly to
Cassio's being promoted over his, Iago's, head; so that Cassio,
in addition to being 'a mathematician' (i.e. better educated), is
also a charmer who is unfairly rewarded for his gentlemanly
manners. This same plausibility is the reason why Iago fears
Cassio with his nightcap, as well as Othello, and gives him a
powerful set of motives for trying to bring the two of them into
collision. Empson's account also offers us an Iago who is
'honest' in the sense that, for a surprising amount of the time,
he really is uttering his true opinions, and one of the things
that irritate him is the way people always assume, when he
comes out with some misanthropic remark, that it is only his

fun, whereas his cynicism really does have roots deep in his destructive emotions.

And so the theories of Iago's character mount up, until one is reduced once again to that bewildered and yet exhilarated condition in which one exclaims that Shakespeare's work has the baffling richness of life itself. The list of interpretations could be extended, but perhaps one more is enough. In 1938, Laurence Olivier played Iago, opposite the Othello of Ralph Richardson, as a repressed homosexual whose motive was an unrecognized passion for Othello. The production was not a success, largely, one gathers, because most people in the audience could not make out what Olivier was supposed to be conveying; but the theory itself marched on, and was given a full-scale exposition by a writer in the *Psychoanalytical Quarterly* in 1950.

VI

And Desdemona? Surely there is agreement about her? Bradley, for his part, is unashamedly a worshipper: 'Desdemona, the "eternal womanly" in its most lovely and adorable form, simple and innocent as a child, ardent with the courage and idealism of a saint, radiant with that heavenly purity of heart which men worship the more because nature so rarely permits it to themselves . . .' It is true, he admits, that she is not clever; where an earlier critic, Mrs Jameson, had credited her with 'less quickness of intellect and less tendency to reflection than most of Shakespeare's heroines', but thought she made up for it by having 'the unconscious address common in women', Bradley says firmly that Desdemona 'seems deficient in this address, having in its place a childlike boldness and persistency, which are full of charm but are unhappily united with a certain want of perception'. No doubt he considers it part of Desdemona's innocent childishness that she is inclined to be economical with the truth. Heraud in 1865 had already noted that 'Her passion was romantic, and there exists fiction in whatever is romantic. She suffers from illusion and loves to be deluded. If she is selfdeceived, she likewise deceives others. . . . From timidity of disposition she frequently evades the truth, when attention to its strict letter would raise difficulties.'

If Heraud was strict, John Quincy Adams, sixth President of the United States, had already been far stricter. To him, Desdemona was little better than 'a wanton':

Her conversations with Emilia indicate unsettled principles, even with regard to the obligations of the nuptial tie, and she allows Iago, almost unrebuked, to banter with her very coarsely on women. This character takes from us so much of the sympathetic interest in her sufferings, that when Othello smothers her in bed, the terror and the pity subside immediately into the sentiment that she has her deserts.[14]

I am a Bradleian here; what Desdemona reveals in the 'willow' scene with Emilia is, to me, a touching innocence about sexual matters, accentuated in the presentation by the fact that Othello's brutality has left her in a state of shock in which she has sought refuge in the pre-pubertial emotions. I suppose what the President meant by that remark about her 'unsettled principles' is that she asks Emilia in a wondering tone if it is really true that some women break their marriage vows, instead of simply stamping her foot and refusing to hear about it; and also because, in a kind of free-association way, she brings in the name of Lodovico and says he is 'a proper man'. W. H. Auden, in his essay 'The Joker in the Pack' (1963), seizes on the same point: in this scene, he says, Desdemona

. . . speaks with admiration of Ludovico and then turns to the topic of adultery. Of course, she discusses this in general terms and is shocked by Emilia's attitude, but she does discuss the subject and she does listen to what Emilia has to say about husbands and wives. It is as if she had suddenly realized that she had made a *mésalliance* and that the sort of man she ought to have married was someone of her own class and colour like Ludovico.

These interpretations would not, I think, stand up to stage production. It would be very difficult to get the actress playing Desdemona to render her wandering, shocked, child-like remarks about adultery as a 'discussion'. Or to convey that she thinks of the ruin of her Eden as something merely unsuitable, a '*mésalliance*'.

VII

I found, then, that there was a great deal of disagreement about this apparently straightforward play, and that much of it was relevant, perceptive debate and not mere argufying. In fact, *Othello* has been the subject of lively dispute ever since its own century. Thomas Rymer's amusing and pugnacious *A Short View of Tragedy* (1693) gave the play a hostile scene-by-scene analysis, rejoicing in every improbability, and generally seeing it as a compendium of faults. The whole performance is too long for inclusion here, but we join him as he begins on Act IV and follow him to the end. This, at least, gives the flavour of Rymer's ferocious cross-examination (he was a lawyer who studied the drama as a hobby); merely to quote his general conclusions about the play, as most selections do, is to make him look a fool, and he was actually a sharp-witted man with an axe to grind. English drama, in the last years of the seventeenth century, stood at an important cross-roads; the period of silence during the Commonwealth, when the theatres were closed by law, had been long enough to obscure the tradition that flourished from the days of Elizabeth to those of Charles I. There was no particular reason why the English drama should revert to its old ways, and Rymer was for starting again with a truly 'classical' theatre that should rival the French. To do this it was necessary to get rid of Shakespeare, whose plays, old-fashioned as they were, continued to fill the theatre and thus keep Elizabethan conventions alive in the minds of audiences. *Othello*, on Rymer's own admission, was a great favourite, so he turned all his guns on it, as Tolstoy was later to do, from not dissimilar motives, on *King Lear*. Of the two pieces of monumental wrong-headedness, I prefer Rymer's, which is at least amusing and, in its own way, very acute.[15]

Rymer finds the plot of *Othello* incredible. (Some of his objections turn up again in an essay by Robert Bridges, written in 1906 and published twenty years later.)[16] He has also two objections which would not, I think, occur to anyone nowadays. They stem from his neo-classical position. The first is that the behaviour of Iago and Othello is untrue to life because it is not 'soldierly'. The second is that the play has no moral.

Let us take these in order. The Renaissance derived most of its critical theory from Aristotle's *Poetics*, and there (1451 b 1) it found the doctrine of generality. 'The difference between the poet and the historian,' Aristotle tells us, 'does not lie in the fact that they express themselves in verse or prose . . . but in the fact that the historian speaks of what has happened, the poet of the kind of thing that *can* happen'. Some Renaissance critics took over this idea in the clumsy and restrictive form that all soldiers in literature must be soldierly, all kings must be kingly, all women womanly, all senators wise. Hence, to Rymer, Iago is 'a close, dissembling, false, insinuating rascal, instead of an open-hearted, frank, plain-dealing Souldier, a character constantly worn by them for some thousands of years in the World'. Next, the moral. Rymer wants the Aristotelian quadrivium of 'Plot, Character, Thought and Expression'; he thinks that a lofty play should give the audience some nugget of general wisdom to take home and examine, and the story of Othello seems too idiosyncratic for this. 'What,' he demands, 'can remain with the Audience to carry home with them from this sort of Poetry, for their use and edification?' and concludes satirically that it boils down to 'a warning to good housewives to look well to their linen'.

Both these objections were answered with characteristic firmness by Dr Johnson. In the great essay which forms the Preface to his edition of Shakespeare (1765), Johnson took pains to vindicate, Shakespeare's truth to 'nature' against the narrow conception of 'nature' urged by such English writers as Rymer and John Dennis in his *An Essay on the Genius and Writings of Shakespeare* (1712), as also by Voltaire in *L'Appel à toutes les nations d'Europe* (1761):

Dennis and Rymer think his Romans not sufficiently Roman; and Voltaire censures his kings as not completely royal. Dennis is offended that Menenius, a senator of Rome, should play the buffoon; and Voltaire perhaps thinks decency violated when the Danish usurper is represented as a drunkard. But Shakespeare always makes nature predominate over accident; and, if he preserves the essential character, is not very careful of distinctions superinduced and adventitious. His story requires Romans or kings, but he thinks only on men. He knew that Rome, like every other city, had men of all dispositions; and wanting a buffoon, he went into the senate house for that which the senate house would certainly have afforded him. He was inclined to show an usurper and a murderer not only odious, but despicable; he therefore added drunkenness to his other qualities, knowing that kings love wine like other men, and that wine exerts its natural power upon kings. These are the petty cavils of petty minds; a poet overlooks the casual distinction of country and condition, as a painter, satisfied with the figure, neglects the drapery.

As for Rymer's objection that *Othello* has no 'moral', teaches no wisdom, there will probably always be critics who will agree with him. (Wilson Knight's preliminary admission that *Othello* is 'a story of intrigue rather than a visionary statement' is, in its restated way, Rymerian.) But here again, Johnson was in no doubt, as we see from Boswell's account of their conversation (*Life*, 12 April 1776):

I observed the great defect of the tragedy of *Othello* was that it had not a moral; for that no man could resist the circumstances of suspicion which were artfully suggested to Othello's mind.

JOHNSON. 'In the first place, Sir, we learn from *Othello* this very useful moral, not to make an unequal match; in the second place, we learn not to yield too readily to suspicion. The handkerchief is merely a trick, though a very pretty trick; but there are no other circumstances of reasonable suspicion, except what is related by Iago of Cassio's warm expressions concerning Desdemona in his sleep; and that depended entirely upon the assertion of one man. No, Sir, I think *Othello* has more moral than almost any play.'

Johnson's line-by-line comments on the play, in his edition, show his usual perspicuity and humanity. They have, unfortunately, been crowded out of this over-crammed volume, but should be consulted either in Walter Raleigh's selection (*Johnson on Shakespeare*, 1908) or W. K. Wimsatt's *Samuel*

Johnson on Shakespeare (New York, 1960), or, better still because complete, in the Yale edition of Johnson's *Works*. Neither
Raleigh nor Wimsatt gives, for instance, the delicious note on
'I have rubb'd this young quat almost to the sense', nor the
magisterial explication of:

> Patience, thou young and rose-lipp'd cheribin
> Ay, here, look grim as hell.

But Raleigh does at least give us Johnson's heartfelt note on
Act V scene vi: 'I am glad that I have ended my revisal of this
dreadful scene. It is not to be endured.'

VIII

All in all, *Othello* has provoked so much good critical writing
that I have found the problem of space an insoluble one. In
particular, the reader will find here no sustained discussion of
Shakespeare's handling of his source, the unvarnished story
of garrison intrigue and murder given in Giraldi Cinthio's
Hecatommithi (1565); Kenneth Muir's masterly short treatment in his Shakespeare's Sources (vol. I, 1957, pp. 122–40)
will provide the essential information, but the relationship of
this play to its source is one of the most interesting in all
Shakespeare's work, and should be borne in mind continually.
Again, there is no discussion here of the text and its problems.
The Cambridge 'New Shakespeare' volume, edited by Alice
Walker and J. Dover Wilson (1957), provides an authoritative
discussion of the matter, but the interested reader should
follow also Nevill Coghill's argument in *Shakespeare's Professional Skills* (a book we have already pillaged twice), for Mr
Coghill brings the experience of years of theatrical production
to support his contention that the 1622 Quarto gives us the
play as performed, and the 1623 Folio represents Shakespeare's own revisions after seeing how it worked out in performance.

A sense of the theatre will always be an asset in our effort to understand Shakespeare, and for that reason I should have liked, also, to include some of the interesting *dramatic* criticism that has survived, in which the critic not only reveals his attitude to the play but gives the flavour of some fine actor's performance, as Lamb recalled the Iago of Roland Bensley,[17] or Hazlitt conveyed the excitement of Kean's Othello,[18] or as, in our own time, John Russell Brown coolly anatomized the heady, voodoo magic of Olivier's Moor.[19] But even if there had been space to include these, our narrow bounds would have been burst immediately by the huge inflow of criticism which, in the last twenty-five years, has started from the assumption that performance and study are both equally necessary to a Shakespearean text, and of equal status: that the spectator in the theatre, and the reader in the armchair, are both essential enjoyers and judges of the play, and that the really interested person will be one and the other at different times.

That is one change we notice in the criticism produced in the 1970s and 1980s; another, and even greater, is an enormously increased attention to theory at the expense of practice. Criticism is always generated by excitement, and the excitement that generates the most recent criticism seems often to be excitement about the speculative thrust that produces new theories and the drama of the clash between rival theories, rather than excitement about the individual work of literature (which is now always referred to as 'text', as if to convey that in the new world of professionalism there are no books or plays or songs, only texts). A good place to study this kind of criticism is in a collection of essays, *Alternative Shakespeares*, published in 1985 under the editorship of John Drakakis, who declares in his Introduction that 'Criticism is now an openly pluralist activity, with proponents of particular positions contesting vigorously the intellectual space which it has occupied.' Criticism never was, of course, anything but pluralist; in any culture the body of generally received opinion about the dominant literary masterpieces of that culture, whether they are by Homer, Dante, Shakespeare, Tolstoy or whomever, has been syncretic, woven of endless variation and interchange. The 'vigour' that John Drakakis finds tonic is, of course, the vigour with which rival theories are 'contested'; it's all great fun, obviously. As he remarks a little further on (p. 16):

the call has been for a radical departure based upon an extrapolation of certain of the theoretical implications of Saussurian linguistics, especially those areas concerned with the differential mechanisms of sign production, along with new developments in cultural materialism, psychoanalysis, Marxist social analysis and latterly, feminism.

All these intellectual tools – sometimes manifesting themselves as procedures and habits of mind, sometimes more simply as a matter of opinion and bias – are undoubtedly there in modern criticism as they are there in the modern political and social discussion. Perhaps, however, one can be forgiven for thinking that the passion generated by discussion of them is not primarily passion about Shakespeare. Many years ago T. S. Eliot gave an austere warning against 'the preposterous suggestion that criticism can become an autotelic activity.' The word 'autotelic' is a characteristic Eliotism; it properly belongs to theology and means sufficient to its own ends, not dependent on anything outside itself, from Greek *autos* (self) and *telos* (end or objective). Since that warning was uttered, the notion that criticism can become 'autotelic' has blossomed from a suggestion to an assumption and finally into an orthodoxy. When students enrol at a university to study literature it is assumed from the beginning that 'Critical Theory' is as important a part of their studies as the literature itself. In Europe generally, and especially in France, critical theorists such as Roland Barthes and Jacques Derrida are taken as seriously as poets, dramatists and novelists. Whether or not this is a sign of health in a national literature I haven't the space to discuss here, and there is not much point in stating a merely dogmatic opinion, though I imagine mine is fairly easy to guess. But whatever we may think of it, the notion that criticism can somehow be more important than the thing criticized, which in previous centuries would have seemed merely lunatic and in Eliot's day was a danger to be guarded against, is now an orthodoxy.

This is fair enough, though to say that it is fair enough does not necessarily bind one to accepting it hook, line and sinker. The present is a period like any other, and part of the usefulness of a collection such as this is to encourage readers to reflect that certain attitudes which seemed natural, inevitable indeed, to past ages have gone out of fashion and have been abandoned. With so much controversy in the air, Shakespearean criticism may seem at times to be a mere hubbub, a brawl distracting one's attention from what Shakespeare wrote. Admittedly Shakespeare's work, like that of any major writer, is far more interesting than anything any critic has said about it, but in practice the two tend to become inseparable. Our approach to a Shakespearean play can never in any case be 'pure', in perfect laboratory conditions, so that we are always influenced to some extent by light refracted through historical lenses; the fact that Johnson, or Coleridge, or Bradley, saw the play in a certain light is bound to affect our view of it if we have read those critics, and if we haven't read them we shall be deprived of the many useful insights they could have given us. There seems to be no way out of this one. People who say resolutely, 'I'm not going to read any criticism, I'm just going to respond directly to the play/poem/novel, without anyone intervening between it and me', end up with too narrow an approach, and (usually) not knowing enough, since most criticism conveys information as well as analysis.

Thus, Christopher Norris's examination of F. R. Leavis's examination of A. C. Bradley's examination of *Othello*, which from a certain traditionalist point of view would seem to spread too many layers of interpretation over the text, derives its value precisely from this willingness to be multi-layered. Modern theorists such as Jacques Derrida, whose starting-point is in linguistic philosophy, set themselves to disentangle the implicit philosophical and theoretical assumptions that have underlain Western culture, and which traditional criticism skates over or denies, or merely implicitly shares. The

result is not much like 'literary appreciation'; it is more of a
hard delve into the buried ideas and beliefs on which a civiliza-
tion builds its structures, which is why the pioneer structuralist critics borrowed so willingly from anthropology. Many of
the 'ideas and beliefs' brought to light by modern critical
analysis are overtly political. The Marxists have always
claimed that literature was politics under another name, but
they have more recently been joined by other groups. The
Feminists, no less than Marxists, see literature as politics.
Thus Karen Newman's essay combines an historical approach
little regarded in the past, taking account of the repressed
history of the colonized and exploited people with a contemporary vigilance about the play's treatment of women; these
issues are treated not only through the characterization but
through the texture of the language, which Dr Newman sees as
partly hiding and partly revealing the possibilities of these new
readings.

Here again, as in the reception of Shakespeare's work generally, internationalism has taken over. It is no longer assumed
that because Shakespeare is the greatest English poet, a great
national possession like the Crown Jewels or *Habeas Corpus*,
therefore the British view of him is the natural and authoritative view. As the New Criticism of the 1950s originated in
America, so the new wave of theories, structuralism, post-
structuralism, deconstructionalism and the others that come
and go before one has time to count them, have their roots in
an attempt by French theorists (Derrida, Foucault and Barthes)
to apply the procedures of modern linguistic philosophy, itself a
movement some sixty years old, to the analysis of literature.
Their cause was taken up in some American universities (Yale,
notably) and from there has found its adherents in England.

This movement will have its virtuosi, like any other, and will
pass away from the earth, like any other, and will leave its
permanent traces behind, like any other. If I personally don't
believe that the changes it heralds will be final and permanent
so that things 'will never be the same again', that is partly
because I have been accustomed throughout my life to seeing

schools of criticism as products of, rather than the creators of, their historical periods; and also because I believe that one of the prime tenets of this school of criticism – that the individuality of the author has no significance, that literary works ('texts') might just as well write themselves, that the significance is put into them by social and historical forces operating through 'the language' and there is no decision-making role for the author as individual man or woman – I believe this view to be extravagantly absurd. But then I am writing after the events of 1989/90 when Václav Havel, a playwright whose works were banned by the government of his country and who was put in prison for writing them, but who nevertheless had the courage to persist in writing them and the vision to interpret the contemporary world in the way he did, has not only been released from his cell, not only been honoured and admired by people who have flocked to see new productions of his works, but has been elected president of his country. Obviously the Czechs, for their part, don't believe that the individual author has no significance, any more than they believe, as one wing of modern criticism evidently does, that literature is primarily concerned with language and the subtleties of its various modes of operation. They seem to think it is produced by actual living men and women and is concerned with life, which is what I also believe.

The recent movements in criticism have undeniably had one excellent result, however sceptical one may feel about them; they have put the more traditionalist practitioners on their mettle. Thirty years ago there was a good deal of loose 'appreciative' writing, not very highly charged with meaning, that would not be tolerated today. The rough competition of the arena is good for critics, particularly for academic critics who are not driven by the cruder considerations of writing for the week's rent and the next meal.

But whatever the motivation, criticism we must have, because criticism airs issues and makes us look freshly at masterpieces; and what masterpieces are greater than Shakespeare's? An imagination as profound and an art as supple as his, add up to an important reality, as important as a large-scale historical event or an inescapable physical presence like a mountain range. We must help one another to understand it, and criticism is just another name for that help.

JOHN WAIN

NOTES

1. Louis Auchincloss, *Motiveless Malignity* (Boston, 1969) p. 7.
2. John Middleton Murry and, to some extent, R. B. Heilman.
3. David Kuala.
4. John E. Seaman, in *Shakespeare Quarterly*, XIX 81–5.
5. E. E. Stoll, *Othello, An Historical and Comparative Study* (1915) and later works.
6. Heilman.
7. Emrys Jones.
8. Lilian Winstanley, *'Othello' as the Tragedy of Italy* (1924).
9. Macaulay, *Essay on Dante* (1824).
10. Rymer, *A Short View of Tragedy* (1693).
11. *Magic in the Web*, p. 166.
12. Cf. G. I. Duthie, *Shakespeare* (1951), p. 165: 'The tragedy in *Othello* is caused by two forces working in conjunction: it is caused by an external force of evil deliberately bringing itself to bear on a noble figure which has within it a *seed* of evil.'
13. Critical works referred to in section IV: J. A. Heraud, *Shakespeare, his Inner Life* (1865); D. J. Snider, *System of Shakespeare's Dramas* (1877); John W. Draper, 'Honest Iago', *PMLA*, XLVI (1931); Mario Praz, 'Machiavelli and the Elizabethans', *Proceedings of the British Academy*, XIV (1928); William Hazlitt, *Characters of Shakespeare's Plays* (1817); Kenneth Muir, 'The Jealousy of Iago', *English Miscellany*, 2 (Rome, 1951). The views of the Exeter gentleman are summarized in the variorum *Othello*, ed. Furness (1886) pp. 408–9.
14. *Notes, Criticism and Correspondence upon Shakespeare's Plays and Actors* (New York, 1863).
15. For an illuminating discussion of Rymer's critical position, see Marvin T. Herrick, *The Poetics of Aristotle in England* (Yale and Oxford, 1930) pp. 57–62.
16. *The Influence of the Audience: Considerations Preliminary to the Psychological Analysis of Shakespeare's Characters* (New York, 1926).
17. 'On Some of the Old Actors', in *Elia* (1823).
18. *The Times*, 27 Oct 1817.
19. *Shakespeare's Survey*, 18 (1965).

PART ONE
Earlier Comments

Thomas Rymer

From *A SHORT VIEW OF TRAGEDY* (1693)

ACT IV

Enter Jago *and* Othello.

Jago. *Will you think so?*
Othel. *Think so,* Jago!
Jago. *What, to kiss in private?*
Othel. *An unauthorised kiss.*
Jago. *Or to be naked with her friend a-bed.*
　An hour or more, not meaning any harm?
Othel. *Naked a-bed,* Jago, *and not mean harm!* –

AT THIS gross rate of trifling, our General and his Auncient March on most heroically, till the Jealous Booby has his Brains turn'd, and falls in a Trance. Would any imagine this to be the Language of Venetians, of Souldiers and mighty Captains? no *Bartholomew* Droll cou'd subsist upon such trash. But lo, a Stratagem never presented in Tragedy:

Jago. *Stand you (a) while a part –*
　– Incave yourself,
　And mark the Jeers, the Gibes, and notable scorns,
　That dwell in every region of his face;
　For I will make him tell the tale a new,
　Where, how, how oft, how long ago, and when
　He has and is again to Cope your Wife:
　I say, but mark his gesture. –

With this device *Othello* withdraws. Says *Jago* aside:

Jago. *Now will I question* Cassio *of* Bianca,
　A Huswife –
　That doats on Cassio. –

39

> *He, when he hears of her, cannot refrain*
> *From the excess of Laughter. –*
> *As he shall smile,* Othello *shall go mad;*
> *And his unbookish jealousy must conster*
> *Poor* Cassio's *smiles, gesture, and light behaviour,*
> *Quite in the wrong. –*

So to work they go: And *Othello* is as wise a commentator, and makes his applications pat, as heart cou'd wish – but I wou'd not expect to find this Scene acted nearer than in *Southwark* Fair! But the *Handkerchief* is brought in at last, to stop all holes and close the evidence. So now being satisfied with the proof, they come to a resolution that the offenders shall be murdered.

> Othel. – *But yet the pity of it,* Jago! *ah, the pity!*
> Jago. *If you be so fond over her iniquity, give her Patent to offend. For*
>   *if it touches not you, it comes near no Body. –*
>   *Do it not with poison, strangle her in her Bed;*
>   *Even the Bed she has contaminated.*
> Oth. *Good, good; the Justice of it pleases; very good.*
> Jago. *And for* Cassio, *let me be his undertaker. –*

Jago had some pretence to be discontent with *Othello* and *Cassio*: And what passed hitherto was the operation of revenge. *Desdemona* had never done him harm, always kind to him and to his Wife, was his Country-woman, a Dame of quality: for him to abet her Murder shews nothing of a Souldier, nothing of a Man, nothing of Nature in it. The *Ordinary* of *Newgate* never had the like Monster to pass under his examination. Can it be any diversion to see a Rogue beyond what the Devil ever finish'd? Or wou'd it be any instruction to an Audience? *Jago* cou'd desire no better than to set *Cassio* and *Othello*, his two Enemies, by the Ears together, so he might have been reveng'd on them both at once: And chusing for his own share the Murder of *Desdemona*, he had the opportunity to play booty, and save the poor harmless wretch. But the Poet must do every thing by contraries, to surprize the Audience still with something horrible and prodigious beyond any human imagination. At this rate he must out-do the Devil to be a Poet in the rank with *Shakespear*.

Soon after this, arrives from *Venice Ludovico*, a noble Cousin of *Desdemona*; presently she is at him also on behalf of *Cassio*.

> Desd. *Cousin, there's fallen between him and my Lord*
> *An unkind breach; but you shall make all well.*
> Lud. *Is there division 'twixt my Lord and* Cassio?
> Desd. *A most unhappy one; I would do much*
> *To attone them, for the love I bear to* Cassio.

By this time we are to believe the couple have been a week or two Married: And *Othello's* Jealousie, that had rag'd so loudly and had been so uneasie to himself, must have reach'd her knowledge. The *Audience* have all heard him more plain with her than was needful to a Venetian capacity: And yet she must still be impertinent in her suit for *Cassio*. Well, this *Magnifico* comes from the *Doge* and Senators to displace *Othello*.

> Lud. – *Deputing* Cassio *in his Government.*
> Desd. *Trust me, I am glad on't.*
> Oth. *Indeed!*
> Desd. *My Lord!*
> Oth. *I am glad to see you mad.*
> Desd. *How sweet* Othello?
> Oth. *Devil!*
> Desd. *I have not deserved this.*
> Oth. *O Devil, Devil! –*
> *Out of my sight!*
> Desd. *I will not stay to offend you.*
> Lud. *Truly, an obedient Lady.*
> *I do beseech your Lordship call her back.*
> Oth. *Mistress!*
> Desd. *My Lord?*
> Oth. *What would you with her, Sir?*
> Lud. *Who, I, my Lord?*
> Oth. *I, you did wish that I wou'd make her turn:*
> *Sir, she can turn, and turn, and yet go on,*
> *And turn agen; and she can weep, Sir, weep;*
> *And she is obedient, as you say, obedient,*
> *Very obedient. –*
> Lud. *What, strike your Wife!*

Of what flesh and blood does our Poet make these noble Venetians, – the men without Gall, the Women either Brain or

Sense? A Senators Daughter runs away with this Black-amoor; the Government employs this Moor to defend them against the Turks, so resent not the Moors Marriage at present; but the danger over, her Father gets the Moor Cashier'd, sends his Kinsman, Seignior *Ludovico*, to *Cyprus* with the Commission for a new General; who, at his arrival, finds the Moor calling the Lady, his Kinswoman, Whore and Strumpet, and kicking her: what says the *Magnifico?*

> Lud. *My Lord, this would not be believ'd in* Venice,
>   *Tho' I shou'd swear I saw't; 'tis very much;*
>   *Make her amends: she weeps.*

The Moor has no body to take his part, no body of his Colour; *Ludovico* has the new Governor, *Cassio*, and all his Countrymen Venetians about him. What Poet wou'd give a villanous Black-amoor this Ascendant? What Tramontain could fancy the Venetians so low, so despicable, or so patient? this outrage to an injured Lady, the *Divine Desdemona*, might in a colder Climate have provoked some body to be her Champion; but the Italians may well conclude we have a strange Genius for Poetry. In the next Scene *Othello* is examining the supposed Bawd; then follows another storm of horrour and outrage against the poor Chicken, his Wife. Some Drayman or drunken Tinker might possibly treat his drab at this sort of rate and mean no harm by it; but for his excellency, a My lord General, to Serenade a Senator's Daughter with such a volly of scoundrel filthy Language is sure the most absurd Maggot that ever bred from any Poets addle Brain.

And she is in the right, who tells us,

> Emil. – *A Begger in his Drink*
>   *Cou'd not have laid such terms upon his Callet.*

This is not to describe passion. *Seneca* had another notion in the Case:

> *Parvae loquuntur curae, ingentes stupent.*

And so had the Painter who drew *Agamemnon* with his Face covered. Yet to make all worse, her Murder, and the manner of it, had before been resolv'd upon and concerted. But nothing is to provoke a Venetian; she takes all in good part; had the Scene lain in *Russia*, what cou'd we have expected more? With us a Tinkers Trull wou'd be Nettled, wou'd repartee with more spirit, and not appear so void of spleen:

> Desd. *O good* Jago,
>> *What shall I do to win my Lord agen?*

No woman bred out of a Pig-stye cou'd talk so meanly. After this she is call'd to Supper with *Othello, Ludovic, &* c.; after that comes a filthy sort of Pastoral Scene, where the *Wedding Sheets*, and Song of *Willow*, and her Mothers Maid, poor *Barbara*, are not the least moving things in this entertainment. But that we may not be kept too long in the dumps, nor the melancholy Scenes lye too heavy undigested on our Stomach, this *Act* gives us for a farewell the *salsa, O picante*, some quibbles and smart touches, as *Ovid* had Prophecied:

> *Est & in obscoenos deflexa Tragoedia risus.*

The last *Act* begins with *Jago* and *Roderigo*: Who a little before had been upon the huff:

> Rod. *I say it is not very well. I will make my self known to* Desdemona*: if she will return me my Jewels, I will give over my suit and repent my unlawful sollicitation; if not, assure your self I'll seek satisfaction of you.*

Roderigo, a Noble Venetian, had sought *Desdemona* in Marriage, is troubled to find the Moor had got her from him, advises with *Jago*, who wheadles him to sell his Estate and go over the Sea to *Cyprus* in expectation to Cuckold *Othello*; there having cheated *Roderigo* of all his Money and Jewels on pretence of presenting them to *Desdemona*, our Gallant grows angry, and would have satisfaction from *Jago*, who sets all right by telling him *Cassio* is to be Governour, *Othello* is going with *Desdemona* into *Mauritania*; to prevent this, you are to murder *Cassio*, and then all may be well.

> Jago. *He goes into* Mauritania, *and takes with him the fair* Desdemona, *unless his abode be lingred here by some accident, wherein none can be so determinate as the removing of* Cassio.

Had *Roderigo* been one of the *Banditi*, he might not much stick at the Murder. But why *Roderigo* should take this for payment, and risque his person where the prospect of advantage is so very uncertain and remote, no body can imagine. It had need be a *super-subtle* Venetian that this Plot will pass upon. Then, after a little spurt of villany and Murder, we are brought to the most lamentable that ever appear'd on any Stage. A noble Venetian Lady is to be murdered by our Poet, – in sober sadness, purely for being a Fool. No Pagan Poet but wou'd have found some *Machine* for her deliverance. *Pegasus* wou'd have strain'd hard to have brought old *Perseus* on his back, time enough to rescue this *Andromeda* from so foul a Monster. Has our Christian Poetry no generosity, nor bowels? Ha, Sir *Lancelot*! ha, St *George*! will no Ghost leave the shades for us in extremity to save a distressed Damosel?

But for our comfort, however felonious is the Heart, hear with what soft language he does approach her, with a Candle in his Hand:

> Oth. *Put out the light, and then put out the light:*
> *If I quench thee, thou flaming Minister,*
> *I can again thy former light restore.* –

Who would call him Barbarian, Monster, Savage? Is this a Black-amoor?

Soles occidere & redire possunt –

The very Soul and Quintessence of Sir *George Etheridge*!

One might think the General should not glory much in this action, but make an hasty work on't, and have turn'd his Eyes away from so unsouldierly an Execution; yet is he all pause and deliberation, handles her as calmly and is as careful of her Souls health as it had been her *Father Confessor. Have you prayed to Night,* Desdemona? But the suspence is necessary that he might have a convenient while so to *roul his Eyes,* and so to *gnaw* his *nether lip* to the spectators. Besides the greater cruelty – *sub tam lentis maxillis.*

But hark, a most tragical thing laid to her charge!

Oth. *That Handkerchief, that I so lov'd and gave thee,*
  Thou gav'st to Cassio.
Desd. *No, by my Life and Soul!*
  Send for the man, and ask him.
Oth. *By Heaven, I saw my Handkerchief in his hand. –*
  – I saw the Handkerchief.

So much ado, so much stress, so much passion and repetition about an Handkerchief! Why was not this call'd the *Tragedy of the Handkerchief*? What can be more absurd than (as *Quintilian* expresses it) *in parvis litibus has Tragoedias movere*? We have heard of *Fortunatus his Purse* and of the *Invisible Cloak*, long ago worn threadbare and stow'd up in the Wardrobe of obsolete Romances: one might think that were a fitter place for this Handkerchief than that it, at this time of day, be worn on the Stage, to raise every where all this clutter and turmoil. Had it been *Desdemona*'s Garter, the Sagacious Moor might have smelt a Rat; but the Handkerchief is so remote a trifle, no Booby on this side *Mauritania* cou'd make any consequence from it.

We may learn here that a Woman never loses her Tongue, even tho' after she is stifl'd:

Desd. *O falsly, falsly murder'd!*
Em. *Sweet* Desdemona, *O sweet Mistress, speak!*
Desd. *A guiltless death I dye.*
Em. *O who has done the deed?*
Desd. *No body; I my self; farewel:*
  Commend me to my kind Lord; O farewel!

This *Desdemona* is a black swan, or an old Black-amoor is a bewitching Bed-fellow. If this be Nature, it is a *lascheté* below what the English Language can express.

For *Lardella to make love like an Humble Bee* was, in *The Rehearsal*, thought a fancy odd enough.

But hark what follows:

Oth. *– O heavy hour!*
  Methinks it shou'd be now a huge Eclipse
  Of Sun and Moon, and that the affrighted globe
  Shou'd yawn at Alteration.

This is wonderful! Here is Poetry to *elevate* and *amuse*. Here is sound All-sufficient. It wou'd be uncivil to ask *Flamstead* if the Sun and Moon can both together be so hugely eclipsed in any *heavy hour* whatsoever. Nor must the Spectators consult *Gresham* Colledge whether a body is naturally *frighted* till he *Yawn* agen. The Fortune of *Greece* is not concern'd with these Matters. These are Physical circumstances a Poet may be ignorant in, without any harm to the publick. These slips have no influence on our Manners and good Life, which are the Poets Province.

Rather may we ask here what unnatural crime *Desdemona* or her Parents had committed, to bring this Judgment down upon her: to Wed a Black-amoor, and innocent to be thus cruelly murder'd by him. What instruction can we make out of this Catastrophe? Or whither must our reflection lead us? Is not this to envenome and sour our spirits, to make us repine and grumble at Providence and the government of the World? If this be our end, what boots it to be Vertuous?

Desdemona dropt the Handkerchief, and missed it that very day after her Marriage; it might have been rumpl'd up with her Wedding sheets: And this Night that she lay in her wedding sheets, the *Fairey* Napkin (whilst *Othello* was stifling her) might have started up to disarm his fury and stop his ungracious mouth. Then might she (in a Traunce for fear) have lain as dead. Then might be, believing her dead, touch'd with remorse, have honestly cut his own Throat, by the good leave and with the applause of all the Spectators: Who might thereupon have gone home with a quiet mind, admiring the beauty of Providence, fairly and truly represented on the Theatre.

> Oth. – *Why, how shou'd she be murdered?*
> Em. *Alas, who knows?*
> Oth. *You heard her say her self, it was not I.*
> Em. *She did so; I must needs report a truth.*
> Oth. *She's like a liar gone to burn in Hell.*
> *'Twas I that did it.*
> Em. *O, the more Angel she,*
> *And you the blacker Devil!*

Oth. *She turn'd to folly, and she was an Whore.*
Em. *Thou dost belye her, and thou art a Devil.*
Oth. *She was false as Water.*
Em. *Thou art rash as Fire,*
   To say that she was false: O, she was heavenly true.

In this kind of Dialogue they continue for forty lines farther, before she bethinks her self to cry Murder.

Em. – *Help, help, O help!*
   The Moor has kill'd my Mistress! murder, murder!

But from this Scene to the end of the Play we meet with nothing but blood and butchery, described much-what to the style of the *last Speeches and Confessions of the persons executed at Tyburn*; with this difference, that there we have the *fact* and the due course of Justice, whereas our Poet, against all Justice and Reason, against all Law, Humanity, and Nature, in a barbarous, arbitrary way, executes and makes havock of his subjects, *Hab-nab*, as they come to hand. *Desdemona* dropt her Handkerchief; therefore she must be stifl'd. *Othello*, by law to be broken on the Wheel, by the Poets cunning escapes with cutting his own Throat. *Cassio*, for I know not what, comes off with a broken shin. *Jago* murders his Benefactor *Roderigo*, as this were poetical gratitude. *Jago* is not yet kill'd, because there yet never was such a villain alive. The Devil, if once he brings a man to be dipt in a deadly sin, lets him alone to take his course; and now when the *Foul Fiend* has done with him, our wise Authors accomplish him and do the Devils drudgery.

Philosophy tells us it is a principle in the Nature of Man *to be grateful*.

History may tell us that *John an Oaks, John a Stiles,* or *Jago* were ungrateful. *Poetry* is to follow Nature; Philosophy must be his guide: history and *fact* in particular cases of *John an Oaks* or *John of Styles* are no warrant or direction for a Poet. Therefore *Aristotle* is always telling us that Poetry is σπονδαιότερον καὶ φιλοσοφώτερον, is more general and abstracted, is led more by the Philosophy, the reason and nature of things than History, which only records things

higlety piglety, right or wrong, as they happen. History might
without any preamble or difficulty say that *Jago* was ungrateful. Philosophy then calls him unnatural. But the Poet is not
without huge labour and preparation to expose the Monster,
and after shew the Divine Vengeance executed upon him. The
Poet is not to add wilful Murder to his ingratitude: he has not
antidote enough for the Poison: his Hell and Furies are not
punishment sufficient for one single crime of that bulk and
aggravation.

> *Em. O thou dull Moor, that Handkerchief thou speakest on*
> *I found by Fortune and did give my Husband;*
> *For often with a solemn earnestness,*
> *More than indeed belong'd to such a trifle,*
> *He beg'd of me to steal it.*

Here we see the meanest woman in the Play takes this
Handkerchief for a *trifle* below her Husband to trouble his head
about it. Yet we find it entered into our Poets head to make a
Tragedy of this *Trifle*.

Then for the *unraveling of the Plot*, as they call it, never was
old deputy Recorder in a Country Town, with his spectacles,
in summoning up the evidence, at such a puzzle, so blunder'd
and be-doultefied, as is our Poet to have a good riddance, And
get the *Catastrophe* off his hands.

What can remain with the Audience to carry home with
them from this sort of Poetry for their use and edification? how
can it work, unless (instead of settling the mind and purging
our passions) to delude our senses, disorder our thoughts,
addle our brain, pervert our affections, hair our imaginations,
corrupt our appetite, and fill our head with vanity, confusion,
Tintamarre, and Jingle-jangle, beyond what all the Parish
Clarks of *London* with their *old Testament* farces and inter-
ludes, in *Richard* the seconds time, cou'd ever pretend to? Our
only hopes for the good of their Souls can be that these people
go to the Playhouse as they do to Church, to sit still, look on
one another, make no reflection, nor mind the Play more than
they would a Sermon.

There is in this Play some burlesk, some humour and ramble of Comical Wit, some shew and some *Mimickry* to divert the spectators; but the tragical part is plainly none other than a Bloody Farce, without salt or savour.

Samuel Johnson

GENERAL REMARKS ON *OTHELLO* (1765)

THE BEAUTIES of this play impress themselves so strongly upon the attention of the reader, that they can draw no aid from critical illustration. The fiery openness of *Othello*, magnanimous, artless, and credulous, boundless in his confidence, ardent in his affection, inflexible in his resolution, and obdurate in his revenge; the cool malignity of *Iago*, silent in his resentment, subtle in his designs, and studious at once of his interest and his vengeance; the soft simplicity of *Desdemona*, confident of merit, and conscious of innocence, her artless perseverance in her suit, and her slowness to suspect that she can be suspected, are such proofs of *Shakespeare*'s skill in human nature, as, I suppose, it is vain to seek in any modern writer. The gradual progress which *Iago* makes in the Moor's conviction, and the circumstances which he employs to inflame him, are so artfully natural, that, though it will perhaps not be said of him as he says of himself, that he is *a man not easily jealous*, yet we cannot but pity him when at last we find him *perplexed in the extreme*.

There is always danger lest wickedness conjoined with abilities should steal upon esteem, though it misses of approbation; but the character of *Iago* is so conducted, that he is from the first scene to the last hated and despised.

Even the inferiour characters of this play would be very conspicuous in any other piece, not only for their justness but their strength. *Cassio* is brave, benevolent, and honest, ruined only by his want of stubbornness to resist an insidious invitation. *Roderigo*'s suspicious credulity, and impatient submission to the cheats which he sees practised upon him, and which by persuasion he suffers to be repeated, exhibit a strong picture of a weak mind betrayed by unlawful desires, to a false friend; and the virtue of *Aemilia* is such as we often find, worn loosely, but not cast off, easy to commit small crimes, but quickened and alarmed at atrocious villanies.

The Scenes from the beginning to the end are busy, varied by happy interchanges, and regularly promoting the progression of the story; and the narrative in the end, though it tells but what is known already, yet is necessary to produce the death of *Othello*.

Had the scene opened in *Cyprus,* and the preceding incidents been occasionally related, there had been little wanting to a drama of the most exact and scrupulous regularity.

SOURCE: Johnson's *Shakespeare* (1765).

S. T. Coleridge

MARGINALIA ON *OTHELLO*

[I iii 292–4.

> *Bra.* Look to her, Moor, if thou hast eyes to see:
> She has deceived her father, and may thee.
> *Oth.* My life upon her faith!]

IN REAL life how do we look back to little speeches, either as presentimental [of], or most contrasted with, an affecting event. Shakespeare, as secure of being read over and over, of becoming a family friend, how he provides this for *his readers*, and leaves it to them.

[I iii 319–20.

> *Iago.* Virtue! a fig! 'tis in ourselves that we are thus or thus.]

Iago's passionless character, all *will* in intellect; therefore a bold partizan here of a truth, but yet of a truth converted into falsehood by absence of all the modifications by the frail nature of man. And the *last sentiment* –

[... our raging motions, our carnal stings, our unbitted lusts; whereof I take this, that you call love, to be a sect or scion] –

There lies the Iagoism of how many! And the repetition, 'Go make money!' – a pride in it, of an anticipated dupe, stronger than the love of lucre.

[I iii 377–8. First Quarto and Stockdale text:

> *Iago.* Go to, farewell, put money enough in your purse:
> Thus do I ever make my fool my purse.]

The triumph! Again, 'put money,' after the effect has been fully produced. The last speech, [Iago's soliloquy,] the motive-hunting of motiveless malignity – how awful! In itself fiendish; while yet he was allowed to bear the divine image, too fiendish for his own steady view. A being next to devil, only *not* quite devil – and this Shakespeare has attempted – executed – without disgust, without scandal!

S. T. Coleridge

REPORT OF A LECTURE AT BRISTOL
(November 1813)

[LECTURE IV]

[*Winter's Tale, Othello*]

AT THE commencement of the fourth lecture last evening, Mr
Coleridge combated the opinion held by some critics, that the
writings of Shakespeare were like a wilderness, in which were
desolate places, most beautiful flowers, and weeds; he argued
that even the titles of his plays were appropriate and shewed
judgment, presenting as it were a bill of fare before the feast.
This was peculiarly so in *The Winter's Tale*, – a wild story,
calculated to interest a circle round a fireside. He maintained
that Shakespeare ought not to be judged of in detail, but on the
whole. A pedant differed from a master in cramping himself
with certain established rules, whereas the master regarded
rules as always controllable by and subservient to the end. The
passion to be delineated in *The Winter's Tale* was *jealousy*.
Shakespeare's description of this, however, was perfectly
philosophical: the mind, in its first harbouring of it, became
mean and despicable, and the first sensation was perfect
shame, arising from the consideration of having possessed an
object unworthily, of degrading a person to a thing. The mind
that once indulges this passion has a predisposition, a vicious
weakness, by which it kindles a fire from every spark, and from
circumstances the most innocent and indifferent finds fuel to
feed the flame. This he exemplified in an able manner from the
conduct and opinion of Leontes, who seized upon occurrences

54

of which he himself was the cause, and when speaking of Hermione, combined his anger with images of the lowest sensuality, and pursued the object with the utmost cruelty. This character Mr Coleridge contrasted with that of Othello, whom Shakespeare had portrayed the very opposite to a jealous man: he was noble, generous, open-hearted; unsuspicious and unsuspecting; and who, even after the exhibition of the handkerchief as evidence of his wife's guilt, bursts out in her praise. Mr C. ridiculed the idea of making Othello a negro. He was a gallant Moor, of royal blood, combining a high sense of Spanish and Italian feeling, and whose noble nature was wrought on, not by a fellow with a countenance predestined for the gallows, as some actors represented Iago, but by an accomplished and artful villain, who was indefatigable in his exertions to poison the mind of the brave and swarthy Moor. It is impossible, with our limits, to follow Mr Coleridge through those nice discriminations by which he elucidated the various characters in this excellent drama. Speaking of the character of the women of Shakespeare, or rather, as Pope stated, the absence of character, Mr Coleridge said this was the highest compliment that could be paid to them: the elements were so commixed, so even was the balance of feeling, that no one protruded in particular, – everything amiable as sisters, mothers, and wives, was included in the thought. To form a just estimation and to enjoy the beauties of Shakespeare, Mr Coleridge's lectures should be *heard* again and again. Perhaps at some future period we may occasionally fill our columns with an analysis of his different lectures similar to what we presented last week of the first; at present we must content ourselves with generals.

SOURCE: *Shakespearean Criticism* (ed. T. M. Raysor; 2nd edition, 1960).

PART TWO
Recent Studies

A. C. Bradley

From *SHAKESPEAREAN TRAGEDY* (1904)*

... OTHELLO is, in one sense of the word, by far the most romantic figure among Shakespeare's heroes; and he is so partly from the strange life of war and adventure which he has lived from childhood. He does not belong to our world, and he seems to enter it we know not whence – almost as if from wonderland. There is something mysterious in his descent from men of royal siege; in his wanderings in vast deserts and among marvellous peoples; in his tales of magic handkerchiefs and prophetic Sibyls; in the sudden vague glimpses we get of numberless battles and sieges in which he has played the hero and has borne a charmed life; even in chance references to his baptism, his being sold to slavery, his sojourn in Aleppo.

And he is not merely a romantic figure; his own nature is romantic. He has not, indeed, the meditative or speculative imagination of Hamlet; but in the strictest sense of the word he is more poetic than Hamlet. Indeed, if one recalls Othello's most famous speeches – those that begin, 'Her father loved me', 'O now for ever', 'Never, Iago', 'Had it pleased Heaven', 'It is the cause', 'Behold, I have a weapon', 'Soft you, a word or two before you go' – and if one places side by side with these speeches an equal number by any other hero, one will not doubt that Othello is the greatest poet of them all. There is the same poetry in his casual phrases – like 'These nine moons wasted', 'Keep up your bright swords, for the dew will rust

* [*Editor's note.*] The fragment here reprinted is not intended to represent Bradley's detailed and subtle essay in anything like its full range, but it should illustrate his attitude and method. The full text is easily available.

them', 'You chaste stars', 'It is a sword of Spain, the ice-
brook's temper', 'It is the very error of the moon' – and in
those brief expressions of intense feeling which ever since have
been taken as the absolute expression, like

> If it were now to die,
> 'Twere now to be most happy; for, I fear,
> My soul hath her content so absolute
> That not another comfort like to this
> Succeeds in unknown fate,

or

> If she be false, O then Heaven mocks itself,
> I'll not believe it;

or

> No, my heart is turned to stone; I strike it, and it hurts my hand,

or

> But yet the pity of it, Iago! O Iago, the pity of it, Iago!

or

> O thou weed,
> Who are so lovely fair and smell'st so sweet
> That the sense aches at thee, would thou hadst ne'er been born.

And this imagination, we feel, has accompanied his whole life.
He has watched with a poet's eye the Arabian trees dropping
their med'cinable gum, and the Indian throwing away his
chance-found pearl; and has gazed in a fascinated dream at the
Pontic sea rushing, never to return, to the Propontic and the
Hellespont; and has felt as no other man ever felt (for he
speaks of it as none other ever did) the poetry of the pride,
pomp, and circumstance of glorious war.

So he comes before us, dark and grand, with a light upon
him from the sun where he was born; but no longer young, and
now grave, self-controlled, steeled by the experience of
countless perils, hardships and vicissitudes, at once simple and
stately in bearing and in speech, a great man naturally modest

but fully conscious of his worth, proud of his services to the state, unawed by dignitaries and unelated by honours, secure, it would seem, against all dangers from without and all rebellion from within. And he comes to have his life crowned with the final glory of love, a love as strange, adventurous and romantic as any passage of his eventful history, filling his heart with tenderness and his imagination with ecstasy. For there is no love, not that of Romeo in his youth, more steeped in imagination than Othello's.

The sources of danger in this character are revealed but too clearly by the story. In the first place, Othello's mind, for all its poetry, is very simple. He is not observant. His nature tends outward. He is quite free from introspection, and is not given to reflection. Emotion excites his imagination, but it confuses and dulls his intellect. On this side he is the very opposite of Hamlet, with whom, however, he shares a great openness and trustfulness of nature. In addition, he has little experience of the corrupt products of civilized life, and is ignorant of European women.

In the second place, for all his dignity and massive calm (and he has greater dignity than any other of Shakespeare's men), he is by nature full of the most vehement passion. Shakespeare emphasizes his self-control, not only by the wonderful pictures of the First Act, but by references to the past. Lodovico, amazed at his violence, exclaims:

> Is this the noble Moor whom our full Senate
> Call all in all sufficient? Is this the nature
> Whom passion could not shake? whose solid virtue
> The shot of accident nor dart of chance
> Could neither graze nor pierce?

Iago, who has here no motive for lying, asks:

> Can he be angry? I have seen the cannon
> When it hath blown his ranks into the air,
> And, like the devil, from his very arm
> Puffed his own brother – and can he be angry?*

---

* For the actor, then, to represent him as violently angry when he cashiers Cassio is an utter mistake.

This, and other aspects of his character, are best exhibited by a single line – one of Shakespeare's miracles – the words by which Othello silences in a moment the night-brawl between his attendants and those of Brabantio:

> Keep up your bright swords, for the dew will rust them.

And the same self-control is strikingly shown where Othello endeavours to elicit some explanation of the fight between Cassio and Montano. Here, however, there occur ominous words, which make us feel how necessary was this self-control, and make us admire it the more:

> Now, by heaven,
> My blood begins my safer guides to rule,
> And passion, having my best judgment collied,
> Assays to lead the way.

We remember these words later, when the sun of reason is 'collied', blackened and blotted out in total eclipse.

Lastly, Othello's nature is all of one piece. His trust, where he trusts, is absolute. Hesitation is almost impossible to him. He is extremely self-reliant, and decides and acts instantaneously. If stirred to indignation, as 'in Aleppo once', he answers with one lightning stroke. Love, if he loves, must be to him the heaven where either he must live or bear no life. If such a passion as jealousy seizes him, it will swell into a well-nigh incontrollable flood. He will press for immediate conviction or immediate relief. Convinced, he will act with the authority of a judge and the swiftness of a man in mortal pain. Undeceived, he will do like execution on himself.

This character is so noble, Othello's feelings and actions follow so inevitably from it and from the forces brought to bear on it, and his sufferings are so heart-rending, that he stirs, I believe, in most readers a passion of mingled love and pity which they feel for no other hero in Shakespeare, and to which not even Mr Swinburne can do more than justice. Yet there are some critics and not a few readers who cherish a grudge against him. They do not merely think that in the later stages of his temptation he showed a certain obtuseness, and that, to speak pedantically, he acted with unjustifiable precipitance and violence; no one, I suppose, denies that. But, even when they admit that he was not of a jealous temper, they consider that he *was* 'easily jealous'; they seem to think that it was inexcusable in him to feel any suspicion of his wife at all; and they blame him for never suspecting Iago or asking him for evidence. I refer to this attitude of mind chiefly in order to draw attention to certain points in the story. It comes partly from mere inattention (for Othello did suspect Iago and did ask him for evidence); partly from a misconstruction of the text which makes Othello appear jealous long before he really is so;* and partly from failure to realize certain essential facts. I will begin with these.

1. Othello, we have seen, was trustful, and thorough in his trust. He put entire confidence in the honesty of Iago, who had not only been his companion in arms, but, as he believed, had just proved his faithfulness in the matter of the marriage. This confidence was misplaced, and we happen to know it; but it was no sign of stupidity in Othello. For his opinion of Iago was the opinion of practically everyone who knew him: and that opinon was that Iago was before all things 'honest', his very faults being those of excess in honesty. This being so, even if Othello had not been trustful and simple, it would have been quite unnatural in him to be unmoved by the warnings of so honest a friend, warnings offered with extreme reluctance and manifestly from a sense of a friend's duty.† *Any* husband would have been troubled by them.

2. Iago does not bring these warnings to a husband who had lived with a wife for months and years and knew her like his sister or his bosom-friend. Nor is there any ground in Othello's character for supposing that, if he had been such a man, he would have felt and acted as he does in the play. But he was

---

* I cannot deal fully with this point in the lecture.

† It is important to observe that, in his attempt to arrive at the facts about Cassio's drunken misdemeanour, Othello had just had an example of Iago's unwillingness to tell the whole truth where it must injure a friend. No wonder he feels in the Temptation-scene that 'this honest creature doubtless Sees and knows more, much more, than he unfolds'.

newly married; in the circumstances he cannot have known much of Desdemona before his marriage; and further he was conscious of being under the spell of a feeling which can give glory to the truth but can also give it to a dream.

3. This consciousness in any imaginative man is enough, in such circumstances, to destroy his confidence in his powers of perception. In Othello's case, after a long and most artful preparation, there now comes, to reinforce its effect, the suggestions that he is not an Italian, nor even a European; that he it totally ignorant of the thoughts and the customary morality of Venetian women*; that he had himself seen in Desdemona's deception of her father how perfect an actress she could be. As he listens in horror, for a moment at least the past is revealed to him in a new and dreadful light, and the ground seems to sink under his feet. These suggestions are followed by a tentative but hideous and humiliating insinuation of what his honest and much-experienced friend fears may be the true explanation of Desdemona's rejection of acceptable suitors, and of her strange, and naturally temporary, preference for a black man. Here Iago goes too far. He sees something in Othello's face that frightens him, and he breaks off. Nor does this idea take any hold of Othello's mind. But it is not surprising that his utter powerlessness to repel it on the ground of knowledge of his wife, or even of that instinctive interpretation of character which is possible between persons of the same race,† should complete his misery, so that he feels he can bear no more, and abruptly dismisses his friend (III iii 238).

Now I repeat that *any* man situated as Othello was would

---

* To represent that Venetian women do not regard adultery so seriously as Othello does, and again that Othello would be wise to accept the situation like an Italian husband, is one of Iago's most artful and most maddening devices.

† If the reader has even chanced to see an African violently excited, he may have been startled to observe how completely at a loss he was to interpret those bodily expressions of passion which in a fellow-countryman he understands at once, and in a European foreigner with somewhat less certainty. The effect of difference in blood in increasing Othello's bewilderment regarding his wife is not sufficiently realized. The same effect has to be remembered in regard to Desdemona's mistakes in dealing with Othello in his anger.

have been disturbed by Iago's communications, and I add that many men would have been made wildly jealous. But up to this point, where Iago is dismissed, Othello, I must maintain, does not show jealousy. His confidence is shaken, he is confused and deeply troubled, he feels even horror; but he is not yet jealous in the proper sense of that word. In his soliloquy (III iii 258 ff.) the beginning of this passion may be traced; but it is only after an interval of solitude, when he has had time to dwell on the idea presented to him, and especially after statements of fact, not mere general grounds of suspicion, are offered, that the passion lays hold of him. Even then, however, and indeed to the very end, he is quite unlike the essentially jealous man, quite unlike Leontes. No doubt the thought of another man's possessing the woman he loves is intolerable to him; no doubt the sense of insult and the impulse of revenge are at times most violent; and these are the feelings of jealousy proper. But these are not the chief or the deepest source of Othello's suffering. It is the wreck of his faith and his love. It is the feeling,

> If she be false, oh then Heaven mocks itself;

the feeling,

> O Iago, the pity of it, Iago!

the feeling,

> But there where I have garner'd up my heart,
> Where either I must live, or bear no life;
> The fountain from the which my current runs,
> Or else dries up – to be discarded thence. . . .

You will find nothing like this in Leontes.

Up to this point, it appears to me, there is not a syllable to be said against Othello. But the play is a tragedy, and from this point we may abandon the ungrateful and undramatic task of awarding praise and blame. When Othello, after a brief interval, re-enters (III iii 330), we see at once that the poison has been at work, and 'burns like the mines of sulphur'.

> Look where he comes! Not poppy, nor mandragora,
> Nor all the drowsy syrups of the world,
> Shall ever medicine thee to that sweet sleep
> Which thou owedst yesterday.

He is 'on the rack', in an agony so unbearable that he cannot endure the sight of Iago. Anticipating the probability that Iago has spared him the whole truth, he feels that in that case his life is over and his 'occupation gone' with all its glories. But he has not abandoned hope. The bare possibility that his friend is deliberately deceiving him – though such a deception would be a thing so monstrously wicked that he can hardly conceive it credible – is a kind of hope. He furiously demands proof, ocular proof. And when he is compelled to see that he is demanding an impossibility he still demands evidence. He forces it from the unwilling witness, and hears the maddening tale of Cassio's dream. It is enough. And if it were not enough, has he not sometimes seen a handkerchief spotted with strawberries in his wife's hand? Yes, it was his first gift to her.

> I know not that; but such a handkerchief –
> I am sure it was your wife's – did I to-day
> See Cassio wipe his beard with.

'If it be that,' he answers – but what need to test the fact? The 'madness of revenge' is in his blood, and hesitation is a thing he never knew. He passes judgment, and controls himself only to make his sentence a solemn vow.

The Othello of the Fourth Act is Othello in his fall. His fall is never complete, but he is much changed. Towards the close of the Temptation-scene he becomes at times most terrible, but his grandeur remains almost undiminished. Even in the following scene (III iv), where he goes to test Desdemona in the matter of the handkerchief, and receives a fatal confirmation of her guilt, our sympathy with him is hardly touched by any feeling of humiliation. But in the Fourth Act 'Chaos has come'. A slight interval of time may be admitted here. It is but slight; for it was necessary for Iago to hurry on, and terribly dangerous to leave a chance for a meeting of Cassio with

Othello; and his insight into Othello's nature taught him that his plan was to deliver blow on blow, and never to allow his victim to recover from the confusion of the first shock. Still there is a slight interval; and when Othello reappears we see at a glance that he is a changed man. He is physically exhausted, and his mind is dazed. He sees everything blurred through a mist of blood and tears. He has actually forgotten the incident of the handkerchief and has to be reminded of it. When Iago, perceiving that he can now risk almost any lie, tells him that Cassio has confessed his guilt, Othello, the hero who has seemed to us only second to Coriolanus in physical power, trembles all over; he mutters disjointed words; a blackness suddenly intervenes between his eyes and the world; he takes it for the shuddering testimony of nature to the horror he has just heard,* and he falls senseless to the ground. When he recovers it is to watch Cassio, as he imagines, laughing over his shame. It is an imposition so gross, and should have been one so perilous, that Iago would never have ventured it before. But he is safe now. The sight only adds to the confusion of intellect the madness of rage; and a ravenous thirst for revenge, contending with motions of infinite longing and regret, conquers them. The delay till night-fall is torture to him. His self-control has wholly deserted him, and he strikes his wife in the presence of the Venetian envoy. He is so lost to all sense of reality that he never asks himself what will follow the deaths of Cassio and his wife. An ineradicable instinct of justice, rather than any last quiver of hope, leads him to question Emilia; but nothing

---

* Cf. *Winter's Tale,* I ii 137ff.:

> Can thy dam? – may't be? –
> Affection! thy intention stabs the centre:
> Thou dost make possible things not so held,
> Communicatest with dreams; – how can this be?
> With what's unreal thou coactive art,
> And fellow'st nothing: then 'tis very credent
> Thou may'st cojoin with something; and thou dost,
> And that beyond commission, and I find it,
> And that to the infection of my brains
> And hardening of my brows.

could convince him now, and there follows the dreadful scene
of accusation; and then, to allow us the relief of burning hatred
and burning tears, this interview of Desdemona with Iago, and
that last talk of hers with Emilia, and her last song.

But before the end there is again a change. The supposed
death of Cassio (V i) satiates the thirst for vengeance. The
Othello who enters the bed-chamber with the words,

> It is the cause, it is the cause, my soul,

is not the man of the Fourth Act. The deed he is bound to do is
no murder, but a sacrifice. He is to save Desdemona from
herself, not in hate but in honour; in honour, and also in love.
His anger has passed; a boundless sorrow has taken its place;
and

> this sorrow's heavenly:
> It strikes where it doth love.

Even when, at the sight of her apparent obduracy, and at the
hearing of words which by a crowning fatality can only recon-
vince him of her guilt, these feelings give way to others, it is to
righteous indignation they give way, not to rage; and, terribly
painful as this scene is, there is almost nothing here to dimin-
ish the admiration and love which heighten pity. And pity
itself vanishes, and love and admiration alone remain, in the
majestic dignity and sovereign ascendancy of the close. Chaos
has come and gone; and the Othello of the Council-chamber
and the quay of Cyprus has returned, or a greater and nobler
Othello still. As he speaks those final words in which all the
glory and agony of his life – long ago in India and Arabia and
Aleppo, and afterwards in Venice, and now in Cyprus – seem
to pass before us, like the pictures that flash before the eyes of a
drowning man, a triumphant scorn for the fetters of the flesh
and the littleness of all the lives that must survive him sweeps
our grief away, and when he dies upon a kiss the most painful
of all tragedies leaves us for the moment free from pain, and
exulting in the power of 'love and man's unconquerable mind'.

T. S. Eliot

From 'SHAKESPEARE AND THE STOICISM OF SENECA' (1927)

I WANT to be quite definite in my notion of the possible influence of Seneca on Shakespeare. I think it is quite likely that Shakespeare read some of Seneca's tragedies at school. I think it quite unlikely that Shakespeare knew anything of that extraordinarily dull and uninteresting body of Seneca's prose, which was translated by Lodge and printed in 1612. So far as Shakespeare was influenced by Seneca, it was by his memories of school conning and through the influence of the Senecan tragedy of the day, through Kyd and Peele, but chiefly Kyd. That Shakespeare deliberately took 'a view of life' from Seneca there seems to be no evidence whatever.

Nevertheless, there is, in some of the great tragedies of Shakespeare, a new attitude. It is not the attitude of Seneca, but is derived from Seneca; it is slightly different from anything that can be found in French tragedy in Corneille or in Racine; it is modern, and it culminates, if there is ever any culmination, in the attitude of Nietzsche, I cannot say that it is Shakespeare's philosophy'. Yet many people have lived by it; though it may only have been Shakespeare's instinctive recognition of something of theatrical utility. It is the attitude of self-dramatization assumed by some of Shakespeare's heroes at moments of tragic intensity. It is not peculiar to Shakespeare; it is conspicuous in Chapman: Bussy, Clermont and Biron, all die in this way. Marston – one of the most interesting and least explored of all the Elizabethans – uses it; and Marston and Chapman were particularly Senecan. But Shakespeare, of course, does it very much better than any of the others, and makes it somehow more integral with the human nature of his characters. It is less verbal, more real. I have always felt that I have never read a more terrible exposure of human weakness – of universal human weakness – than the last great speech of Othello. (I am ignorant whether anyone else has ever adopted this view, and it may appear subjective and fantastic in the extreme.) It is usually taken on its face value, as expressing the greatness in defeat of a noble but erring nature.

> *Soft you; a word or two before you go.*
> *I have done the state some service, and they know't.*
> *No more of that. I pray you, in your letters,*
> *When you shall these unlucky deeds relate,*
> *Speak of me as I am; nothing extenuate,*
> *Nor set down aught in malice: then must you speak*
> *Of one that loved not wisely but too well;*
> *Of one not easily jealous, but, being wrought,*
> *Perplex'd in the extreme; of one whose hand,*
> *Like the base Indian, threw a pearl away*
> *Richer than all his tribe; of one whose subdued eyes,*
> *Albeit unused to the melting mood,*
> *Drop tears as fast as the Arabian trees*
> *Their medicinal gum. Set you down this;*
> *And say, besides, that in Aleppo once,*
> *Where a malignant and a turban'd Turk*
> *Beat a Venetian and traduced the state,*
> *I took by the throat the circumcised dog,*
> *And smote him, thus.*

What Othello seems to me to be doing in making this speech is *cheering himself up*. He is endeavouring to escape reality, he has ceased to think about Desdemona, and is thinking about himself. Humility is the most difficult of all virtues to achieve; nothing dies harder than the desire to think well of oneself. Othello succeeds in turning himself into a pathetic figure, by adopting an *aesthetic* rather than a moral attitude, dramatizing himself against his environment. He takes in the spectator, but the human motive is primarily to take in himself. I do not believe that any writer has ever exposed this *bovarysme*, the human will to see things as they are not, more clearly than Shakespeare.

If you compare the deaths of several of Shakespeare's heroes – I do not say *all*, for there are very few generalizations that can be applied to the whole of Shakespeare's work – but notably Othello, Coriolanus and Antony – with the deaths of heroes of dramatists such as Marston and Chapman, consciously under Senecan influence, you will find a strong similarity – except only that Shakespeare does it both more poetically and more lifelike.

SOURCE: *Selected Essays* (1932).

G. Wilson Knight

THE *OTHELLO* MUSIC (1930)

IN *Othello* we are faced with the vividly particular rather than
the vague and universal. The play as a whole has a distinct
formal beauty: within it we are ever confronted with beautiful
and solid forms. The persons tend to appear as warmly
human, concrete. They are neither vaguely universalized, as in
King Lear or *Macbeth*, nor deliberately mechanized and vital-
ized by the poet's philosophic plan as in *Measure for Measure*
and *Timon of Athens*, wherein the significance of the dramatic
person is dependent almost wholly on our understanding of the
allegorical or symbolical meaning. It is true that Iago is here a
mysterious, inhuman creature of unlimited cynicism: but the
very presence of the concrete creations around, in differentiat-
ing him sharply from the rest, limits and defines him. *Othello* is
a story of intrigue rather than a visionary statement. If, however, we tend to regard Othello, Desdemona, and Iago as
suggestive symbols rather than human beings, we may, from a
level view of their interaction, find a clear relation existing
between *Othello* and other plays of the hate-theme. Such an
analysis will be here only in part satisfactory. It exposes certain underlying ideas, abstracts them from the original: it is
less able to interpret the whole positive beauty of the play.
With this important reservation, I shall push the interpretative
method as far as possible.

Othello is dominated by its protagonist. Its supremely
beautiful effects of style are all expressions of Othello's personal passion. Thus, in first analysing Othello's poetry, we
shall lay the basis for an understanding of the play's symbolism: this matter of style is, indeed, crucial, and I shall now

indicate those qualities which clearly distinguish it from other
Shakespearian poetry. It holds a rich music all its own, and
possesses a unique solidity and precision of picturesque phrase
or image, a peculiar chastity and serenity of thought. It is, as a
rule, barren of direct metaphysical content. Its thought does
not mesh with the reader's: rather it is always outside us, aloof.
This aloofness is the resultant of an inward aloofness of image
from image, word from word. The dominant quality is separation, not, as is more usual in Shakespeare, cohesion. Consider
these exquisite poetic movements:

> O heavy hour!
> Methinks it should be now a huge eclipse
> Of sun and moon, and that the affrighted globe
> Should yawn at alteration.
>
> (v ii 97)

Or,

> It is the very error of the moon;
> She comes more near the earth than she was wont,
> And makes men mad.
>
> (v ii 107)

These are solid gems of poetry which lose little by divorce from
their context: wherein they differ from the finest passages of
King Lear or *Macbeth*, which are as wild flowers not to be
uptorn from their rooted soil if they are to live. In these two
quotations we should note how the human drama is thrown
into sudden contrast and vivid unexpected relation with the
tremendous concrete machinery of the universe, which is
thought of in terms of individual heavenly bodies: 'sun' and
'moon'. The same effect is apparent in:

> Nay, had she been true,
> If Heaven would make me such another world
> Of one entire and perfect chrysolite,
> I'd not have sold her for it.
>
> (v ii 141)

Notice the single word 'chrysolite' with its outstanding and
remote beauty: this is typical of *Othello*.

The effect in such passages is primarily one of contrast. The vastness of the night sky, and its moving planets, or the earth itself – here conceived objectively as a solid, round, visualized object – these things, though thrown momentarily into sensible relation with the passions of man, yet remain vast, distant, separate, seen but not apprehended; something against which the dramatic movement may be silhouetted, but with which it cannot be merged. This poetic use of heavenly bodies serves to elevate the theme, to raise issues infinite and unknowable. Those bodies are not, however, implicit symbols of man's spirit, as in *King Lear*: they remain distinct, isolated phenomena, sublimely decorative to the end. In *Macbeth* and *King Lear* man commands the elements and the stars: they are part of him. Compare the above quotations from *Othello* with this from *King Lear*:

> You nimble lightnings, dart your blinding flames
> Into her scornful eyes! Infect her beauty,
> You fen-suck'd fogs, drawn by the powerful sun,
> To fall and blast her pride.
>
> (II iv 167)

This is typical: natural images are given a human value. They are insignificant, visually: their value is only that which they bring to the human passion which cries out to them. Their aesthetic grandeur, in and for themselves, is not relevant to the *King Lear* universe. So, too, Macbeth cries

> Stars, hide your fires;
> Let not light see my black and deep desires.
>
> (I iv 50)

And Lady Macbeth:

> Come, thick night,
> And pall thee in the dunnest smoke of Hell,
> That my keen knife see not the wound it makes,
> Nor Heaven peep through the blanket of the dark,
> To cry 'Hold, hold!'
>
> (I v 51)

Here, and in the *King Lear* extract, there is no clear visual effect as in *Othello*: tremendous images and suggestions are evoked only to be blurred as images by the more powerful passion which calls them into being. Images in *Macbeth* are thus continually vague, mastered by passion; apprehended, but not seen. In *Othello*'s poetry they are concrete, detached; seen but not apprehended. We meet the same effect in:

> Like to the Pontic sea,
> Whose icy current and compulsive course
> Ne'er feels retiring ebb, but keeps due on
> To the Propontic and the Hellespont,
> Even so my bloody thoughts, with violent pace,
> Shall ne'er look back, ne'er ebb to humble love,
> Till that a capable and wide revenge
> Swallow them up. Now, by yond marble heaven,
> In the due reverence of a sacred vow
> I here engage my words.
>
> (III iii 454)

This is, indeed, a typical speech. The long comparison, explicitly made, where in *King Lear* or *Macbeth* a series of swiftly evolving metaphors would be more characteristic, is another example of the separateness, obtaining throughout *Othello*. There is no fusing of word with word, rather a careful juxtaposition of one word or image with another. And there are again the grand single words, 'Propontic', 'Hellespont', with their sharp, clear, consonant sounds, constituting defined aural solids typical of the *Othello* music: indeed, fine single words, especially proper names, are a characteristic of this play – Anthropophagi, Ottomites, Arabian trees, 'the base Indian', the Egyptian, Palestine, Mauretania, the Sagittary, Olympus, Mandragora, Othello, Desdemona. This is a rough assortment, not all used by Othello, but it points the Othello quality of rich, often expressly consonantal, outstanding words. Now Othello's prayer, with its 'marble heaven', is most typical and illustrative. One watches the figure of Othello silhouetted against a flat, solid, moveless sky: there is a plastic, static suggestion about the image. Compare it with a similar *King Lear* prayer:

> O heavens,
> If you do love old men, if your sweet sway

> Allow obedience, if yourselves are old,
> Make it your cause; send down and take my part!
>
> (II iv 192)

Here we do not watch Lear: 'We are Lear'. There is no visual effect, no rigid subject–object relation between Lear and the 'heavens', nor any contrast, but an absolute unspatial unity of spirit. The heavens blend with Lear's prayer, each is part of the other. There is an intimate interdependence, not a mere juxtaposition. Lear thus identifies himself in kind with the heavens to which he addresses himself directly: Othello speaks of 'yond marble heaven', in the third person, and swears by it, does not pray to it. It is conceived as outside his interests.

This detached style, most excellent in point of clarity and stateliness, tends also to lose something in respect of power. At moments of great tension, the *Othello* style fails of a supreme effect. Capable of fine things quite unmatched in their particular quality in any other play, it nevertheless sinks sometimes to a studied artificiality, nerveless and without force. For example, Othello thinks of himself as:

> . . . one whose subdued eyes,
> Albeit unused to the melting mood,
> Drop tears as fast as the Arabian trees
> Their medicinal gum.
>
> (v ii 347)

Beside this we might place Macduff's

> O I could play the woman with mine eyes
> And braggart with my tongue! But, gentle heavens,
> Cut short all intermission. . . .
>
> (IV iii 229)

. . . The *Othello* style is diffuse, leisurely, like a meandering river; the *Macbeth* style compressed, concentrated, and explosive; often jerky, leaping like a mountain torrent. . . . The *Othello* style does not compass the overpowering effects of *Macbeth* or *King Lear*: nor does it, as a rule, aim at them. At the most agonizing moments of Othello's story, however, there is apparent weakness: we find an exaggerated, false rhetoric.

There is a speech in *Othello* that begins in the typical re-strained manner, but degenerates finally to what might almost be called bombast. It starts:

> Where should Othello go?
> Now, how dost thou look now? O ill-starr'd wench!
> Pale as thy smock! When we shall meet at compt,
> This look of thine will hurl my soul from Heaven,
> And fiends will snatch at it. Cold, cold, my girl!
> Even like thy chastity.
>
> (v ii 270)

Here we have the perfection of the *Othello* style. Concrete, visual, detached. Compare it with Lear's, 'Thou art a soul in bliss . . .', where the effect, though perhaps more powerful and immediate, is yet vague, intangible, spiritualized. Now this speech, started in a style that can in its own way challenge that of *King Lear*, rapidly degenerates as Othello's mind is repre-sented as collapsing under the extreme of anguish:

> O cursed, cursed slave! Whip me, ye devils,
> From the possession of this heavenly sight!
> Blow me about in winds! roast me in sulphur!
> Wash me in steep-down gulfs of liquid fire!
> O Desdemona! Desdemona! dead!
> Oh! Oh! Oh!
>
> (v ii 276)

There is a sudden reversal of poetic beauty: these lines lack cogency because they exaggerate rather than concentrate the emotion. Place beside these violent eschatological images the passage from *King Lear*:

> And my poor fool is hang'd! No, no, no life!
> Why should a dog, a horse, a rat have life,
> And thou no breath at all? Thou'lt come no more,
> Never, never, never, never, never!
> Pray you, undo this button: thank you, sir.
> Do you see this? Look on her, look, her lips,
> Look there, look there!
>
> (v iii 307)

Notice by what rough, homely images the passion is transmit-ted – which are as truly an integral part of the naturalism of

King Lear as the mosaic and polished phrase, and the abstruse and picturesque allusion are, in its best passages, characteristic of Othello's speech. Thus the extreme, slightly exaggerated beauty of Othello's language is not maintained. This is even more true elsewhere. Othello, who usually luxuriates in deliberate and magnificent rhetoric, raves, falls in a trance:

Lie with her! lie on her! We say lie on her, when they belie her. Lie with her! that's fulsome. Handkerchief – confessions – handkerchief! To confess, and be hanged for his labour; first, to be hanged, and then to confess – I tremble at it. Nature would not invest herself in such shadowing passion without some instruction. It is not words that shake me thus. Pish! Noses, ears, and lips. – Is't possible? – Confess – handkerchief! – O devil!

(IV i 35)

Whereas Lear's madness never lacks artistic meaning, whereas its most extravagant and grotesque effects are presented with imaginative cogency, Othello can speak words like these. This is the Iago-spirit, the Iago, medicine, at work, like an acid eating into bright metal. This is the primary fact of Othello and therefore of the play: something of solid beauty is undermined, wedged open so that it exposes an extreme ugliness.

When Othello is represented as enduring loss of control he is, as Macbeth and Lear never are, ugly, idiotic; but when he has full control he attains an architectural stateliness of quarried speech, a silver rhetoric of a kind unique in Shakespeare:

It is the cause, it is the cause, my soul –
Let me not name it to you, you chaste stars! –
It is the cause. Yet I'll not shed her blood;
Nor scar that whiter skin of hers than snow,
And smooth as monumental alabaster.
Yet she must die, else she'll betray more men.
Put out the light, and then put out the light.
If I quench thee, thou flaming minister,
I can again thy former light restore,
Should I repent me: but once put out thy light,
Thou cunning'st pattern of excelling nature,
I know not where is that Promethean heat

That can thy light relume. When I have pluck'd the rose,
I cannot give it vital growth again,
It needs must wither: I'll smell it on the tree.

                                               (v ii 1)

This is the noble *Othello* music: highly-coloured, rich in sound
and phrase, stately. Each word solidifies as it takes its place in
the pattern. This speech well illustrates the *Othello* style:
the visual or tactile suggestion – 'whiter skin of hers than
snow', 'smooth as monumental alabaster', the slightly over-
decorative phrase, 'flaming minister'; the momentary juxtaposition of humanity and the vast spaces of the night, the
'chaste stars'; the concrete imagery of 'thou cunning'st pattern
of excelling nature', and the lengthy comparison of life with
light; the presence of simple forward-flowing clarity of dignified statement and of simile in place of the super-logical
welding of thought with molten thought as in the more compressed, agile, and concentrated poetry of *Macbeth* and *King
Lear*; and the fine outstanding single word, 'Promethean'. In
these respects Othello's speech is nearer the style of the after-
math of Elizabethan literature, the settle lava of that fiery
eruption, which gave us the solid image of Marvell and the
'marmoreal phrase' of Browne: it is the most Miltonic thing in
Shakespeare.

This peculiarity of style directs our interpretation in two
ways. First, the tremendous reversal from extreme, almost
over-decorative, beauty, to extreme ugliness – both of a kind
unusual in Shakespeare – will be seen to reflect a primary
truth about the play. That I will demonstrate later in my
essay. Second, the concreteness and separation of image, word,
or phrase, contrasting with the close-knit language elsewhere,
suggests a proper approach to *Othello* which is not proper to
Macbeth or *King Lear*. Separation is the rule throughout *Othello*.
Whereas in *Macbeth* and *King Lear* we have one dominant
atmosphere, built of a myriad subtleties of thought and
phraseology entwining throughout, subduing our minds wholly
to their respective visions, whereas each has a single quality,
expresses as a whole a single statement, *Othello* is built rather

of outstanding differences. In *Othello* all is silhouetted, defined, concrete. Instead of reading a unique, pervading, atmospheric suggestion – generally our key to interpretation of what happens within that atmosphere – we must here read the meaning of separate persons. The persons here are truly separate. Lear, Cordelia, Edmund all grow out of the *Lear* universe, all are levelled by its characteristic atmosphere, all blend with it and with each other, so that they are less closely and vividly defined. They lack solidity. Othello, Desdemona, Iago, however, are clearly and vividly separate. All here – but Iago – are solid, concrete. Contrast is raised to its highest pitch. Othello is statuesque, Desdemona most concretely human and individual, Iago, if not human or in any usual sense 'realistic', is quite unique. Within analysis of these three persons and their interaction lies the meaning of *Othello*. In *Macbeth* or *King Lear* we interpret primarily a singleness of vision. Here, confronted with a significant diversity, we must have regard to the essential relation existing between the three main personal conceptions. Interpretation must be based not on unity but differentiation. Therefore I shall pursue an examination of this triple symbolism; which analysis will finally resolve the difficulty of Othello's speech, wavering as it does between what at first sight appear an almost artificial beauty and an equally inartistic ugliness.

Othello radiates a world of romantic, heroic, and picturesque adventure. All about him is highly coloured. He is a Moor; he is noble and generally respected; he is proud in the riches of his achievement. Now his prowess as a soldier is emphasized. His arms have spent 'their dearest action in the tented field' (I iii 85). . . .

But we also meet a curious discrepancy. Othello tells us:

> Rude am I in my speech,
> And little bless'd with the soft phrase of peace.
>
> (I iii 81)

Yet the dominant quality in this play is the exquisitely moulded language, the noble cadence and chiselled phrase, of

Othello's poetry. Othello's speech, therefore, reflects not a soldier's language, but the quality of soldiership in all its glamour of romantic adventure; it holds an imaginative realism. It has a certain exotic beauty, is a storied and romantic treasure-house of rich, colourful experiences. . . .

Swords are vivid, spiritualized things to Othello. There is his famous line:

> Keep up your bright swords, for the dew will rust them.
>
> (I ii 59)

And in the last scene, he says:

> I have another weapon in this chamber;
> It is a sword of Spain, the ice-brook's temper.
>
> (v ii 251)

In his address at the end, he speaks of himself as

> one whose hand,
> Like the base Indian, threw a pearl away
> Richer than all his tribe.
>
> (v ii 345)

His tears flow as the gum from 'Arabian trees' (v ii 349); he recounts how in Aleppo he smote 'a malignant and a turban'd Turk' (v ii 352) for insulting Venice. Finally there is his noble apostrophe to his lost 'occupation':

> Farewell the plumed troop and the big wars,
> That make ambition virtue! O, farewell!
> Farewell the neighing steed and the shrill trump,
> The spirit-stirring drum, the ear-piercing fife,
> The royal banner and all quality,
> Pride, pomp, and circumstance of glorious war!
> And, O you mortal engines, whose rude throats
> The immortal Jove's dread clamours counterfeit,
> Farewell! Othello's occupation's gone.
>
> (III iii 350)

Again, we have the addition of phrase to separate phrase, rather than the interdependence, the evolution of thought from thought, the clinging mesh of close-bound suggestions of other plays. This noble eulogy of war is intrinsic to the conception.

War is in Othello's blood. When Desdemona accepts him, she knows she must not be 'a moth of peace' (I iii 258). Othello is a compound of highly coloured, romantic adventure – he is himself 'coloured' – and war; together with a great pride and a great faith in those realities. His very life is dependent on a fundamental belief in the validity and nobility of human action – with, perhaps, a strong tendency towards his own achievements in particular. Now war, in Shakespeare, is usually a positive spiritual value, like love. There is reference to the soldiership of the protagonist in all the plays analysed in my present treatment. Soldiership is almost the condition of nobility, and so the Shakespearian hero is usually a soldier. Therefore Othello, with reference to the Shakespearian universe, becomes automatically a symbol of faith in human values of love, of war, of romance in a wide and sweeping sense. He is, as it were, conscious of all he stands for: from the first to the last he loves his own romantic history. He is, like Troilus, dedicated to these values, has faith and pride in both. Like Troilus he is conceived as extraordinarily direct, simple, 'credulous' (IV i 46). Othello, as he appears in the action of the play, may be considered the high-priest of human endeavour, robed in the vestments of romance, whom we watch serving in the temple of war at the altar of love's divinity.

Desdemona is his divinity. She is, at the same time, warmly human. There is a certain domestic femininity about her. She is 'a maiden never bold' (I iii 94). We hear that 'the house affairs' (had Cordelia any?) drew her often from Othello's narrative (I iii 147). But she asks to hear the whole history:

> I did consent,
> And often did beguile her of her tears,
> When I did speak of some distressful stroke
> That my youth suffered. My story being done,
> She gave me for my pains a world of sighs:
> She swore, in faith, 'twas strange, 'twas passing strange,
> 'Twas pitiful, 'twas wondrous pitiful:
> She wish'd she had not heard it, yet she wish'd
> That heaven had made her such a man.
>
> (I iii 155)

The same domesticity and gentleness is apparent throughout.
She talks of 'to-night at supper' (III iii 57) or 'to-morrow
dinner' (III iii 58); she is typically feminine in her attempt to
help Cassio, and her pity for him. This is how she describes her
suit to Othello:

> Why, this is not a boon;
> 'Tis as I should entreat you wear your gloves,
> Or feed on nourishing dishes, or keep you warm,
> Or sue to you to do a peculiar profit
> To your own person . . .
>
> (III iii 76)

– a speech reflecting a world of sex-contrast. She would bind
Othello's head with her handkerchief – that handkerchief
which is to become a terrific symbol of Othello's jealousy. The
Othello world is eminently domestic, and Desdemona expressly
feminine. We hear of her needlework (IV i 197), her fan, gloves,
mask (IV ii 8). In the exquisite willow-song scene, we see her
with her maid, Emilia. Emilia gives her 'her nightly wearing'
(IV iii 16). Emilia says she has laid on her bed the 'wedding
sheets' (IV ii 104) Desdemona asked for. Then there is the
willow-song, brokenly sung whilst Emilia 'unpins' (IV iii 34)
Desdemona's dress:

> My mother had a maid called Barbara:
> She was in love, and he she loved proved mad
> And did forsake her. . . .
>
> (IV iii 26)

The extreme beauty and pathos of this scene are largely dependent on the domesticity of it. *Othello* is eminently a domestic
tragedy. But this element in the play is yet to be related to
another more universal element. Othello is concretely human,
so is Desdemona. Othello is very much the typical middle-
aged bachelor entering matrimony late in life, but he is also, to
transpose a phrase of Iago's, a symbol of human – especially
masculine – 'purpose, courage, and valour' (IV ii 218), and, in
a final judgement, is seen to represent the idea of human faith
and value in a very wide sense. Now Desdemona, also very

human, with an individual domestic feminine charm and simplicity, is yet also a symbol of woman in general daring the
unknown seas of marriage with the mystery of man. Beyond
this, in the far flight of a transcendental interpretation, it is
clear that she becomes a symbol of man's ideal, the supreme
value of love. At the limit of the series of wider and wider
suggestions which appear from imaginative contemplation of a
poetic symbol she is to be equated with the divine principle. In
one scene of *Othello*, and one only, direct poetic symbolism
breaks across the vividly human, domestic world of this play.*
As everything in *Othello* is separated, defined, so the plot itself
is in two distinct geographical divisions: Venice and Cyprus.
Desdemona leaves the safety and calm of her home for the
stormy voyage to Cyprus and the tempest of the following
tragedy. Iago's plot begins to work in the second part. The
storm scene, between the two parts, is important.

Storms are continually symbols of tragedy in Shakespeare.
This scene contains some most vivid imaginative effects,
among them passages of fine storm-poetry of the usual kind:

> For do but stand upon the foaming shore,
> The chidden billow seems to pelt the clouds;
> The wind-shak'd surge, with high and monstrous mane,
> Seems to cast water on the burning bear,
> And quench the guards of the ever-fixed pole:
> I never did like molestation view,
> On the enchafed flood.
>
> (II ii 11)

This storm-poetry is here closely associated with the human
element. And in this scene where direct storm-symbolism
occurs it is noteworthy that the figures of Desdemona and
Othello are both strongly idealized:

> *Cassio.* Tempests themselves, high seas and howling winds,
> The gutter'd rocks and congregated sands –
> Traitors ensteep'd to clog the guiltless keel –

---

* But note too the significance of the magic handkerchief *as both a symbol of
domestic sanctity and the play's one link with the supernatural* (1947).

As having sense of beauty, do omit
Their mortal natures, letting go safely by
The divine Desdemona.
Montano.   What is she?
Cassio. She that I spake of, our great captain's captain,
    Left in the conduct of the bold Iago,
    Whose footing here anticipates our thoughts
    A se'nnight's speed. Great Jove, Othello guard,
    And swell his sail with thine own powerful breath,
    That he may bless this bay with his tall ship,
    Make love's quick pants in Desdemona's arms,
    Give renewed fire to our extinct spirits,
    And bring all Cyprus comfort!
                Enter Desdemona, &c.
                            O, behold,
    The riches of the ship is come on shore!
    Ye men of Cyprus, let her have your knees.
    Hail to thee, lady! and the grace of Heaven,
    Before, behind thee, and on every hand,
    Enwheel thee round!

                                    (II i 68)

Desdemona is thus endued with a certain transcendent quality
of beauty and grace. She 'paragons description and wild fame'
says Cassio: she is

            One that excels the quirks of blazoning pens,
            And in the essential vesture of creation
            Does tire the ingener.

                                    (II i 63)

And Othello enters the port of Cyprus as a hero coming to
'bring comfort', to 'give renewed fire' to men. The entry of
Desdemona and that of Othello are both heralded by discharge of guns: which both merges finely with the tempest-
symbolism and the violent stress and excitement of the scene
as a whole, and heightens our sense of the warrior nobility of
the protagonist and his wife, subdued as she is 'to the very
quality' of her lord (I iii 253). Meeting Desdemona, he speaks:

Othello. O my fair warrior!
Desdemona.   My dear Othello!
Othello. It gives me wonder great as my content
    To see you here before me. O my soul's joy!

> If after every tempest come such calms,
> May the winds blow till they have waken'd death!
> And let the labouring bark climb hills of seas
> Olympus-high and duck again as low
> As Hell's from Heaven! If it were now to die,
> 'Twere now to be most happy; for, I fear,
> My soul hath her content so absolute
> That not another comfort like to this
> Succeeds in unknown fate.
>
> (II i 185)

This is the harmonious marriage of true and noble minds. Othello, Desdemona, and their love are here apparent, in this scene of storm and reverberating discharge of cannon, as things of noble and conquering strength: they radiate romantic valour. Othello is essential man in all his prowess and protective strength; Desdemona essential woman, gentle, loving, brave in trust of her warrior husband. The war is over. The storm of sea or bruit of cannonade are powerless to hurt them: yet there is another storm brewing in the venomed mind of Iago. Instead of merging with and accompanying tragedy the storm here is thus contrasted with the following tragic events: as usual in *Othello*, contrast and separation take the place of fusion and unity. This scene is thus a microcosm of the play, reflecting its action. Colours which are elsewhere softly toned are here splashed vividly on the play's canvas. Here especially Othello appears a prince of heroes. Desdemona is lit by a divine feminine radiance: both are transfigured. They are shown as coming safe to land, by Heaven's 'grace', triumphant, braving war and tempestuous seas, guns thundering their welcome. The reference of all of this, on the plane of high poetic symbolism, to the play as a whole is evident.

Against these two Iago pits his intellect. In this scene too Iago declares himself with especial clarity:

> O gentle lady, do not put me to't;
> For I am nothing, if not critical.
>
> (II i 118)

His conversation with Desdemona reveals his philosophy. Presented under the cloak of fun, it exposes nevertheless his attitude to life: that of the cynic. Roderigo is his natural companion: the fool is a convenient implement, and at the same time continual food for his philosophy. Othello and Desdemona are radiant, beautiful: Iago opposes them, critical intellectual. Like cold steel his cynic skill will run through the warm body of their love. Asked to praise Desdemona, he draws a picture of womanly goodness in a vein of mockery; and concludes:

> *Iago.* She was a wight if ever such wight were –
> *Desdemona.* To do what?
> *Iago.* To suckle fools and chronicle small beer.
>
> (II i 158)

Here is his reason for hating Othello's and Desdemona's love: he hates their beauty, to him a meaningless, stupid thing. That is Iago. Cynicism is his philosophy, his very life, his 'motive' in working Othello's ruin. The play turns on this theme: the cynical intellect pitted against a lovable humanity transfigured by qualities of heroism and grace. As Desdemona and Othello embrace he says:

> O you are well tuned now!
> But I'll set down the pegs that make this music,
> As honest as I am.
>
> (II i 202)

'Music' is apt: we remember Othello's rich harmony of words. Against the *Othello* music Iago concentrates all the forces of cynic villainy.

Iago's cynicism is recurrent:

> Virtue! a fig! 'tis in ourselves that we are thus or thus. . . .
>
> (II iii 323)

Love to him is

> . . . merely a lust of the blood and a permission of the will.
>
> (I iii 339)

He believes Othello's and Desdemona's happiness will be short-lived, since he puts no faith in the validity of love. Early in the play he tells Roderigo:

It cannot be that Desdemona should long continue her love to the
Moor . . . nor he his to her. . . . These Moors are changeable in their
wills . . . the food that to him now is as luscious as locusts, shall be to
him shortly as bitter as coloquintida. She must change for youth:
when she is sated with his body, she will find the error of her choice:
she must have change, she must.

(I iii 347)

This is probably Iago's sincere belief, his usual attitude to
love: he is not necessarily deceiving Roderigo. After this, when
he is alone, we hear that he suspects Othello with his own
wife: nor are we surprised. And, finally, his own cynical
beliefs suggest to him a way of spiting Othello. He thinks of
Cassio:

> After some time, to abuse Othello's ear
> That he is too familiar with his wife.

(I iii 401)

The order is important: Iago first states his disbelief in Othello's
and Desdemona's continued love, and next thinks of a way of
precipitating its end. That is, he puts his cynicism into action.
The same rhythmic sequence occurs later. Iago witnesses
Cassio's meeting with Desdemona at Cyprus, and comments
as follows:

He takes her by the palm: ay, well said, whisper: with as little a web
as this will I ensnare as great a fly as Cassio. Ay, smile upon her, do; I
will gyve thee in thine own courtship. . . .

(II i 168)

Iago believes Cassio loves Desdemona. He has another cynical
conversation with Roderigo as to Desdemona's chances of
finding satisfaction with Othello, and the probability of her
love for Cassio (II i 223–79). A kiss, to Iago, cannot be 'courtesy': it is

Lechery, by this hand; an index and obscure prologue to the history of
lust and foul thoughts.

(II i 265)

Iago is sincere enough and means what he says. Cynicism is
the key to his mind and actions. After Roderigo's departure, he

again refers to his suspicions of Othello – and Cassio too –
with his own wife. He asserts definitely – and here there is no
Roderigo to impress – his belief in Cassio's guilt:

> That Cassio loves her, I do well believe it;
> That she loves him, 'tis apt and of great credit.
>
> (II i 298)

In this soliloquy he gets his plans clearer: again, they are
suggested by what he believes to be truth. I do not suggest that
Iago lacks conscious villainy: far from it. Besides, in another
passage he shows that he is aware of Desdemona's innocence
(IV i 48). But it is important that we observe how his attitude
to life casts the form and figure of his meditated revenge. His
plan arises out of the cynical depths of his nature. When, at the
end, he says, 'I told him what I thought' (V ii 174), he is
speaking at least a half-truth. He hates the romance of Othello
and the loveliness of Desdemona because he is by nature the
enemy of these things. Cassio, he says,

> hath a daily beauty in his life
> That makes mine ugly.
>
> (V i 19)

This is his 'motive' throughout: other suggestions are surface
deep only. He is cynicism loathing beauty, refusing to allow its
existence. Hence the venom of his plot: the plot is Iago – both
are ultimate, causeless, self-begotten. Iago is cynicism incarnate
and projected into action.

Iago is thus utterly devilish: there is no weakness in his
casing armour of unrepentant villainy. He is a kind of Mephistopheles, closely equivalent to Goethe's devil, the two possessing
the same qualities of mockery and easy cynicism. Thus he is
called a 'hellish villain' by Lodovico (V ii 367), a 'demi-devil'
by Othello (V ii 300). Othello says:

> I look down towards his feet; but that's a fable.
> If that thou be'est a devil, I cannot kill thee.
>
> (V ii 285)

Iago himself recognizes a kinship:

> Hell and night
> Must bring this monstrous birth to the world's sight.
>
> (I iii 409)

And,

> Divinity of Hell!
> When devils will the blackest sins put on,
> They do suggest at first with heavenly shows
> As I do now.
>
> (II iii 359)

He knows that his 'poison' (III iii 326) will 'burn like the mines of sulphur' (III iii 330) in Othello. Thus Iago is, to Othello, the antithesis of Desdemona: the relation is that of the spirit of denial to the divine principle. Desdemona 'plays the god' (II iii 356) with Othello: if she is false, 'Heaven mocks itself' (III iii 278). During the action, as Iago's plot succeeds, her essential divinity changes, for Othello, to a thing hideous and devilish – that is to its antithesis:

> Her name that was as fresh
> As Dian's visage, is now begrimed and black
> As mine own face.
>
> (III iii 387)

She is now 'devil' (IV i 252, 255) or 'the fair devil' (III iii 479); her hand, 'a sweating devil' (III iv 43); the 'devils themselves' will fear to seize her for her heavenly looks (IV ii 35). Thus Iago, himself a kind of devil, insidiously eats his way into this world of romance, chivalry, nobility. The word 'devil' occurs frequently in the latter acts: devils are alive here, ugly little demons of black disgrace. They swarm over the mental horizon of the play, occurring frequently. Iago is directly or indirectly their author and originator. 'Devil', 'Hell', 'damnation' – these words are recurrent, and continually juxtaposed to thoughts of 'Heaven', prayer, angels. We are clearly set amid 'Heaven and men and devils' (V ii 219). Such terms are related here primarily to sexual impurity. In *Othello*, pure love is the supreme good; impurity damnation. This pervading religious tonal significance relating to infidelity explains lines such as:

> Turn thy complexion there,
> Patience, thou young and rose-lipped cherubin –
> Ay, there, look grim as Hell!
>
> (IV ii 61)

Othello addresses Emilia:

> You, mistress,
> That have the office opposite to Saint Peter,
> And keep the gate of Hell!
>
> (IV ii 89)

Here faithful love is to be identified with the divine, the 'heavenly'; unfaithful love, or the mistrust which imagines it, or the cynic that gives birth to that imagination – all these are to be identified with the devil. The hero is set between the forces of Divinity and Hell. The forces of Hell win and pure love lies slain. Therefore Othello cries to 'devils' to whip him from that 'heavenly' sight (V ii 276). He knows himself to have been entrapped by hell-forces. The Iago–Devil association is of importance.

It will be remembered that *Othello* is a play of concrete forms. This world is a world of visual images, colour, and romance. It will also be clear that the mesh of devil-references I have just suggested show a mental horizon black, formless, colourless. They contrast with the solid, chiselled, enamelled *Othello* style of elsewhere. This devil-world is insubstantial, vague, negative. Now on the plane of personification we see that Othello and Desdemona are concrete, moulded of flesh and blood, warm. Iago contrasts with them meta-physically as well as morally: he is unlimited, formless villainy. He is the spirit of denial, wholly negative. He never has visual reality. He is further blurred by the fact of his being something quite different from what he appears to the others. Is he to look like a bluff soldier, or Mephistopheles? He is a different kind of being from Othello and Desdemona: he belongs to a different world. They, by their very existence, assert the positive beauty of

created forms – hence Othello's perfected style of speech, his
strong human appeal, his faith in creation's values of love and
war. This world of created forms, this sculptured and yet
pulsing beauty, the Iago-spirit undermines, poisons, disintegrates. Iago is a demon of cynicism, colourless, formless, in
a world of colours, shapes, and poetry's music. Of all these he
would create chaos. Othello's words are apt:

> Excellent wretch! Perdition catch my soul
> But I do love thee! And when I love thee not,
> Chaos is come again.
>
> (III iii 90)

Chaos indeed. Iago works at the foundations of human values.
Cassio is a soldier: he ruins him as a soldier, makes him drunk.
So he ruins both Othello's love and warrior-heart. He makes
him absurd, ugly. Toward the end of the play there is hideous
suggestion. We hear of 'cords, knives, poison' (III iii 389), of
lovers 'as prime as goats, as hot as monkeys' (III iii 404); we
meet Bianca, the whore, told by Cassio to 'throw her vile
guesses in the Devil's teeth' (III iv 183); there are Othello's
incoherent mutterings, 'Pish! Noses, ears and lips!' (IV i 43), he
will 'chop' Desdemona 'into messes' (IV i 210); she reminds
him of 'foul toads' (IV ii 60). Watching Cassio, he descends to
this:

> O! I see that nose of yours, but not the dog I shall throw it to.
>
> (IV i 144)

Othello strikes Desdemona, behaves like a raging beast. 'Fire
and brimstone!' (IV i 246) he cries, and again, 'Goats and
monkeys!' (IV i 274). 'Heaven stops the nose' at Desdemona's
impurity (IV ii 76). Othello in truth behaves like 'a beggar in
his drink' (IV ii 120). In all these phrases I would emphasize
not the sense and dramatic relevance alone, but the suggestion
– the accumulative effect of ugliness, hellishness, idiocy, negation. It is a formless, colourless, essence, insidiously undermining a world of concrete, visual, richly-toned forms. That
is the Iago-spirit embattled against the domesticity, the
romance, the idealized humanity of the *Othello* world.

Here, too, we find the reason for the extreme contrast of Othello's styles: one exotically beautiful, the other blatantly absurd, ugly. There is often no dignity in Othello's rage. There is not meant to be. Iago would make discord of the *Othello* music. Thus at his first conquest he filches something of Othello's style and uses it himself:

> Not poppy, nor mandragora,
> Nor all the drowsy syrups of the world,
> Shall ever medicine thee to that sweet sleep
> Which thou owed'st yesterday.
>
> (III iii 331)

To him Othello's pride in his life-story and Desdemona's admiration were ever stupid:

Mark me with what violence she first loved the Moor, but for bragging and telling her fantastical lies: and will she love him still for prating?

> (II i 225)

Iago, 'nothing if not critical', speaks some truth of Othello's style – it is 'fantastical'. As I have shown, it is somewhat over-decorative, highly-coloured. The dramatic value of this style now appears. In fact, a proper understanding of Othello's style reveals Iago's 'motive' so often questioned. There is something sentimental in Othello's language, in Othello. Iago is pure cynicism. That Iago should scheme – in this dramatic symbolism forged in terms of interacting persons – to undermine Othello's faith in himself, his wife, and his 'occupation', is inevitable. Logically, the cynic must oppose the sentimentalist: dramatically, he works his ruin by deceit and deception. That Othello often just misses tragic dignity is the price of his slightly strained emotionalism. Othello loves emotion for its own sake, luxuriates in it, like Richard II. As ugly and idiot ravings, disjointed and with no passionate dignity even, succeed Othello's swell and flood of poetry, Iago's triumph seems complete. The honoured warrior, rich in strength and experience, noble in act and repute, lies in a trance, nerveless, paralysed by the Iago-conception:

Work on, my medicine, work.

(IV i 45)

But Iago's victory is not absolute. During the last scene,
Othello is a nobly tragic figure. His ravings are not final: he
rises beyond them. He slays Desdemona finally not so much in
rage, as for 'the cause' (V ii 1). He slays her in love. Though
Desdemona fails him, his love, homeless, 'perplexed in the
extreme' (V ii 345), endures. He will kill her and 'love her after'
(V ii 19). In that last scene, too, he utters the grandest of his
poetry. The Iago-spirit never finally envelops him, masters
him, disintegrates his soul. Those gem-like miniatures of poetic
movement quoted at the start of my essay are among Othello's
last words. His vast love has, it is true, failed in a domestic
world. But now symbols of the wide beauty of the universe
enrich his thoughts: the 'chaste stars', and 'sun and moon', the
'affrighted globe', the world 'of one entire and perfect chrysolite' that may not buy a Desdemona's love. At the end we know
that Othello's fault if simplicity alone. He is, indeed, 'a gull, a
dolt' (Vii 161); he loves 'not wisely but too well' (V ii 343). His
simple faith in himself endures: and at the end, he takes just
pride in recalling his honourable service.

In this essay I have attempted to expose the underlying
thought of the play. Interpretation here is not easy, nor wholly
satisfactory. As all within *Othello* – save the Iago-theme – is
separated, differentiated, solidified, so the play itself seems at
first to be divorced from wider issues, a lone thing of meaningless beauty in the Shakespearian universe, solitary, separate,
unyielding and chaste as the moon. It is unapproachable,
yields itself to no easy mating with our minds. Its thought does
not readily mesh with our thought. We can visualize it, admire
its concrete felicities of phrase and image, the mosaic of its
language, the sculptural outline of its effects, the precision and
chastity of its form. But one cannot be lost in it, subdued to it,
enveloped by it, as one is drenched and refreshed by the
elemental cataracts of *King Lear*; one cannot be intoxicated by
it as by the rich wine of *Antony and Cleopatra*. *Othello* is
essentially outside us, beautiful with a lustrous, planetary

beauty. Yet the Iago-conception is of a different kind from the rest of the play. This conception alone, if no other reason existed, would point the necessity of an intellectual interpretation. So we see the Iago-spirit gnawing at the root of all the *Othello* values, the *Othello* beauties; he eats into the core and heart of this romantic world, worms his way into its solidity, rotting it, poisoning it. Once this is clear, the whole play begins to have meaning. On the plane of dramatic humanity, we see a story of the cynic intriguing to ruin the soldier and his love. On the plane of poetic conception, in matters of technique, style, personification – there we see a spirit of negation, colourless, and undefined, attempting to make chaos of a world of stately, architectural, and exquisitely coloured forms. The two styles of Othello's speech illustrate this. Thus the different technique of the Othello and Iago conceptions is intrinsic with the plot of the play: in them we have the spirit of negation set against the spirit of creation. That is why Iago is undefined, devisualized, inhuman, in a play of consummate skill in concrete imagery and vivid human delineation. He is a colourless and ugly thing in a world of colour and harmony. His failure lies in this: in the final scene, at the moment of his complete triumph, Emilia dies for her mistress to the words of Desdemona's willow-song, and the *Othello* music itself sounds with a nobler cadence, a richer flood of harmonies, a more selfless and universalized flight of the imagination than before. The beauties of the *Othello* world are not finally disintegrated: they make 'a swanlike end, fading in music'.

SOURCE: *The Wheel of Fire* (1930).

ADDITIONAL NOTE (1947)

Any valuable discussions of Othello's physical appearance and general status as a 'noble Moor' must take full account of Morocco's self-description in *The Merchant of Venice*. Imaginatively, the two conceptions are almost identical, the one being a first sketch of the other.

William Empson

HONEST IN *OTHELLO* (1951)

I

THE FIFTY-TWO uses of *honest* and *honesty* in *Othello* are a very queer business; there is no other play in which Shakespeare worries a word like that. *King Lear* uses *fool* nearly as often but does not treat it as a puzzle, only as a source of profound metaphors. In *Othello* divergent uses of the key word are found for all the main characters; even the attenuated clown plays on it; the unchaste Bianca, for instance, snatches a moment to claim that she is more honest than Emilia the thief of the handkerchief; and with all the variety of use the ironies on the word mount up steadily to the end. Such is the general power of the writing that this is not obtrusive, but if all but the phrases involving *honest* were in the style of Ibsen the effect would be a symbolical charade. Everybody calls Iago honest once or twice, but with Othello it becomes an obsession; at the crucial moment just before Emilia exposes Iago he keeps howling the word out. The general effect has been fully recognized by critics, but it looks as if there is something to be found about the word itself.

What Shakespeare hated in the word, I believe, was a peculiar use, at once hearty and individualist, which was then common among raffish low people but did not become upper-class till the Restoration; here as in Iago's heroic couplets the play has a curious effect of prophecy. But to put it like this is no doubt to oversimplify; the Restoration use, easy to feel though hard to define, seems really different from its earlier parallels, and in any case does not apply well to Iago. I want here to approach the play without taking for granted the previous analysis. But I hope it has become obvious that the word was in the middle of a rather complicated process of change, and that what emerged from it was a sort of jovial cult of independence. At some stage of the development (whether by the date of *Othello* or not) the word came to have in it a covert assertion that the man who accepts the natural desires, who does not live by principle, will be fit for such warm uses of *honest* as imply 'generous' and 'faithful to friends', and to believe this is to disbelieve the Fall of Man. Thus the word, apart from being complicated, also came to raise large issues, and it is not I think a wild fancy to suppose that Shakespeare could feel the way it was going.

Four columns of *honest* in the Shakespeare Concordance show that he never once allows the word a simple hearty use between equals. Some low characters get near it but they are made to throw in contempt. 'An honest fellow enough, and one that loves quails' is said by Thersites in contempt for Ajax; 'honest good fellows' is said by the Nurse in Romeo, but of minstrels that she is turning away; 'as honest a true fellow as any in Bohemia' is from Prince Cloten and to a shepherd; 'I am with thee here and the goats, as the most capricious poet, honest Ovid, was mong the Goths' gets its joke from making the clown patronize Ovid. The nearest case is from Desdemona:

EMIL.:   *I warrant it grieves my husband*
         As if the case were his.
DES.:   Oh, that's an honest fellow.

But Emilia is butting into the talk with Cassio, and Desdemona, in this careless reply to silence her, has a feeling that Iago though reliable and faithful is her social inferior. This indeed is a sufficient reason why Iago talks with irony about the admitted fact that he is 'honest'; the patronizing use carried an obscure social insult as well as a hint of stupidity. Critics have discussed what the social status of Iago and Emilia would actually be, and have succeeded in making clear that the posts of ancient and gentlewoman-in-waiting might be held by people of very varying status; the audience must use its own judgement. The hints seem to place Iago and his wife definitely enough well below Desdemona but well above Ancient Pistol, say. Now at the same date as the refusal by Shakespeare to employ a flat hearty use of the word, there are uses by Dekker (for example) which only differ from the Restoration ones by coming from people of lower rank or bad reputation. One need not say that Shakespeare always had a conscious policy about the word (more likely the flat hearty use bored him; it was a blank space where one might have had a bit of word play) but his uses of it in *Othello*, when his imagination began to work on the loathsome possibilities of this familiar bit of nonsense, are consistent with his normal practice.

Most people would agree with what Bradley, for example, implied, that the way everybody calls Iago honest amounts to a criticism of the word itself; that is, Shakespeare means 'a bluff forthright manner, and amusing talk, which get a man called honest, may go with extreme dishonesty'. Or indeed that this is treated as normal, and the satire is on our nature not on language. But they would probably maintain that Iago is not honest and does not think himself so, and only calls himself so as a lie or an irony. It seems to me, if you leave the matter there, that there is much to be said for what the de-spised Rymer decided, when the implications of the hearty use of *honest* had become simpler and more clear-cut. He said that the play is ridiculous, because that sort of villain (silly–clever, full of secret schemes, miscalculating about people) does not get mistaken for that sort of honest man. This if true is of course a plain fault, whatever you think about 'character-analysis'. It is no use taking short cuts in these things, and I should fancy that what Rymer said had a large truth when he said it, and also that Iago was a plausible enough figure in his own time. The only main road into this baffling subject is to find how the characters actually use the term and thereby think about themselves.

I must not gloss over the fact that Iago once uses the word to say that he proposes to tell Othello lies:

> *The Moor is of a free and open nature,*
> *And thinks men honest that but seem to be so.*

This is at the end of the first Act. And indeed, the first use of the word in the play seems also to mean that Iago does not think himself honest. In his introductory scene with Roderigo, he says of the subservient type of men 'whip me such honest knaves'; they are opposed to the independent men like himself – 'these fellows have some soul'. Later there is a trivial use of the word by Brabantio, but the next important ones do not come till near the end of the act. Then Othello twice calls Iago honest; Iago immediately (to insist on the irony) has a second meeting for plots with Roderigo, and then in soliloquy tells the audience he will cheat Roderigo too. Next he brings out the two lines just quoted; he is enumerating the conditions of his problem, and the dramatic purpose, one may say, is to make certain that nobody in the audience has missed the broad point. The act then closes with 'I have it' and the triumphant claim that he has invented the plot. Even here, I think, there is room for an ironical tone in Iago's use of *honest*; he can imply that Othello's notion of honesty is crude as well as his judgements about which people exemplify it. For that matter, Iago may simply be speaking about Cassio, not about himself. He has just said that Cassio is framed to make women false, and he certainly regards the virtues of Cassio as part of his superficial and over-rewarded charm of manner. But I think that, even so, Iago has himself somewhere in view; to claim that he did not would be overstraining my argument. The introductory phrase 'honest knaves' is of course a direct irony (made clear by contradiction); it can only mean that Iago has a different idea of honesty from the one that these knaves have. To be sure, you may be meant to think that he is lying by implication, but even so, this is the lie that he must be supposed to tell. However, I do not see that the uses at either end of the act put forward definite alternative meanings for the word; they lay the foundations by making it prominent. It is then, so to speak, 'in play' and is used with increasing frequency. The first act has five uses; the second eleven; the third twenty-three; and the last two only six and seven. One might argue that the character of Iago is established in the first act before the verbal ironies are applied to it, since 'honest knaves' is only a sort of blank cheque; but even so we learn a good deal more about him later.

Both Iago and Othello oppose honesty to mere truthtelling:

OTH.:   *I know, Iago,*
         Thy honesty and love doth mince this matter,
         Making it light to Cassio. . . .
IAGO: *It were not for your quiet, nor your good,*
         Nor for my manhood, honesty, or wisdom
         To let you know my thoughts.

No doubt the noun tends to be more old-fashioned than the adjective, but anyway the old 'honourable' sense is as broad and vague as the new slang one; it was easy enough to be puzzled by the word. Iago means partly 'faithful to friends', which would go with the Restoration use, but partly I think 'chaste', the version normally used of women; what he has to say is improper. Certainly one cannot simply treat his version of *honest* as the Restoration one – indeed, the part of the snarling critic involves a rather Puritanical view, at any rate towards other people. It is the two notions of being ready to blow the gaff on other people and frank to yourself about your own desires that seem to me crucial about Iago; they grow on their own, independently of the hearty feeling that would normally humanize them; though he can be a good companion as well.

One need not look for a clear sense when he toys with the word about Cassio; the question is how it came to be so mystifying. But I think a queer kind of honesty is maintained in Iago through all the puzzles he contrives; his emotions are always expressed directly, and it is only because they are clearly genuine ('These stops of thine', Othello tells him, 'are close relations, working from the heart') that he can mislead Othello as to their cause.

OTH.:   *Is he not honest?* (Faithful, etc.)
IAGO: *Honest, my lord?* (Not stealing, etc. Shocked)
OTH.:   *Ay, honest,* ('Why repeat? The word is clear enough.')
IAGO: *My lord, for aught I know.* . . . ('In some sense.')

IAGO: *For Michael Cassio*
        I dare be sworn I think that he is honest.
OTH.:   *I think so too.*
IAGO: *Men should be what they seem,*
        Or, those that be not, would they might seem none.
OTH.:   *Certain, men should be what they seem.*
IAGO: *Why then, I think that Cassio's an honest man.*

Othello has just said that Cassio 'went between them very oft', so Iago now learns that Cassio lied to him in front of Braban- tio's house when he pretended to know nothing about the marriage. Iago feels he has been snubbed,* as too coarse to be trusted in such a manner, and he takes immediate advantage of his discomposure. The point of his riddles is to get 'not hypocritical' – 'frank about his own nature' accepted as the relevant sense; Iago will readily call him honest on that basis and Othello cannot be reassured. 'Chaste' (the sense normally used of women) Cassio is not, but he is 'not a hypocrite' about Bianca. Iago indeed, despises him for letting her make a fool of him in public; for that and for other reasons (Cassio is young and without experience) Iago can put a contemptuous tone into the word; the feeling is genuine, but not the sense it may imply. This gives room for a hint that Cassio has been 'frank' to Iago in private about more things than may honestly be told. I fancy too, that the idea of 'not being men' gives an extra twist. Iago does not think Cassio manly nor that it is specially manly to be chaste; this allows him to agree that Cassio may be honest in the female sense about Desdemona and still keep a tone which seems to deny it – if he is, after so much encour- agement, he must be 'effeminate' (there is a strong idea of 'manly' in *honest*, and an irony on that gives its opposite). Anyway, Iago can hide what reservations he makes but show

---

* Cassio does not call Iago *honest* till he can use the word warmly (II iii 108); till then he calls him 'good Iago' (II i 97; II iii 34) – apparently a less obtrusive form of the same trick of patronage. Possibly as they have been rivals for his present job he feels it more civil to keep his distance. However the social con- tempt which he holds in check is hinted jovially to Desdemona (II i 165) and comes out plainly when he is drunk; Iago returns the 'good' to him and is firmly snubbed for it as not a 'man of quality' (II iii 108).

that he makes reservations; this suggests an embarrassed defence – 'Taking a broad view, with the world as it is, and Cassio my friend, I can decently call him honest.' This forces home the Restoration idea – 'an honest dog of a fellow, straightforward about women', and completes the suspicion. It is a bad piece of writing unless you are keyed up for the shifts of the word.

The play with the feminine version is doubtful here, but he certainly does it the other way round about Desdemona, where it had more point; in the best case it is for his own amusement when alone.

> *And what's he then that says I play the villain?*
> *When this advice is free I give and honest,*
> *Probal to thinking, and indeed the course*
> *To win the Moor again? For 'tis most easy*
> *The inclining Desdemona to subdue*
> *In any honest suit. She's framed as fruitful*
> *As the free elements.*

Easy, inclining, fruitful, free all push the word the same way, from 'chaste' to 'flat, frank and natural'; all turn the ironical admission of her virtue into a positive insult against her. The delight in juggling with the word here is close to the Machiavellian interest in plots for their own sake, which Iago could not resist and allowed to destroy him. But a good deal of the 'motive-hunting' of the soliloquies must, I think, be seen as part of Iago's 'honesty'; he is quite open to his own motives or preferences and interested to find out what they are.

The clear cases where Iago thinks himself honest are at a good distance from the Restoration use; they bring him into line with the series of sharp unromantic critics like Jacques and Hamlet:

> *For I am nothing if not critical*

he tells Desdemona to amuse her; his faults, he tells Othello, are due to an excess of this truthful virtue –

> *I confess, it is my nature's plague*
> *To spy into abuses, and oft my jealousy*
> *Shapes faults that are not.*

There seems no doubt that he believes this and thinks it creditable, whatever policy made him say it here; indeed we know it is true from the soliloquies. Now this kind of man is really very unlike the Restoration 'honest fellow', and for myself I find it hard to combine them in one feeling about the word. But in a great deal of Iago's talk to Roderigo – 'drown thyself! drown cats and blind puppies ... why, thou silly gentleman, I will never love thee after' – he is a wise uncle, obviously honest in the cheerful sense, and for some time this is our main impression of him.* It is still strong during the business of making Cassio drunk; there is no reason why he should praise the English for their powers of drinking except to make sure that the groundlings are still on his side.

Perhaps the main connection between the two sorts of honest men is not being indulgent towards romantic love:

> OTH.: *I cannot speak enough of this content,*
> *It stops me here; it is too much of joy.*
> *And this, and this, the greatest discords be*
> *That e'er our hearts shall make. (Kissing her.)*
> IAGO: *Oh you are well tun'd now;*
> *But I'll set down the peggs that make this Musick,*
> *As honest as I am.*

The grammar may read 'because I am so honest' as well as 'though I am so honest' and the irony may deny any resultant sense. He is ironical about the suggestions in the patronizing use, which he thinks are applied to him – 'low-class, and stupid, but good-natured'. But he feels himself really 'honest' as the kind of man who can see through nonsense; Othello's affair is a passing lust which has become a nuisance, and Iago can get it out of the way.

It may well be objected that this is far too mild a picture of

---

* It is a very bold and strange irony to make Othello repeat the phrase 'love thee after' just before he kills Desdemona.

Iago's plot, and indeed he himself is clearly impressed by its wickedness; at the end of the first act he calls it a 'monstrous birth' and invokes Hell to assist it. But after this handsome theatrical effect the second act begins placidly, in a long scene which includes the 'As honest as I am' passage, and at the end of this scene we find that Iago still imagines he will only

> Make the Moor thank me, love me, and reward me
> For making him egregiously an ass

– to be sure, the next lines say he will practise on Othello 'even to madness', but even this can be fitted into the picture of the clown who makes 'fools' of other people; it certainly does not envisage the holocaust of the end of the play. Thinking in terms of character, it is clear that Iago has not yet decided how far he will go.

The suggestion of 'stupid' in a patronizing use of *honest* (still clear in 'honest Thompson, my gardener', a Victorian if not a present-day use) brings it near to *fool*; there is a chance for these two rich words to overlap. There is an aspect of Iago in which he is the Restoration 'honest fellow', who is good company because he blows the gaff; but much the clearest example of it is in the beginning of the second act, when he is making sport for his betters. While Desdemona is waiting for Othello's ship, which may have been lost in the tempest, he puts on an elaborate piece of clowning to distract her; and she takes his real opinion of love and women for a piece of hearty and good-natured fun. Iago's kind of honesty, he feels, is not valued as it should be; there is much in Iago of the Clown in Revolt, and the inevitable clown is almost washed out in this play to give him a free field. It is not, I think, dangerously far-fetched to take almost all Shakespeare's uses of *fool* as metaphors from the clown, whose symbolism certainly rode his imagination and was explained to the audience in most of his early plays. Now Iago's defence when Othello at last turns on him, among the rich ironies of its claim to honesty, brings in both *Fool* and the Vice used in *Hamlet* as an old name for the clown.

IAGO: *O wretched fool,*
          *That lov'st to make thine Honesty, a Vice!**
          Oh monstrous world! Take note, take note (O World)
          To be direct and honest is not safe
          I thank you for this profit, and from hence
          I'll love no Friend, sith Love breeds such offence.
OTH.:   *Nay stay; thou should'st be honest.*
IAGO: *I should be wise; for Honesty's a Fool,*
          And loses that it works for.
OTH.:   *By the world,*
          I think my wife be honest, and think she is not.

What comes out here is Iago's unwillingness to be the Fool he
thinks he is taken for; but it is dramatic irony as well, and that
comes back to his notion of *honest*; he is fooled by the way his
plans run away with him; he fails in knowledge of others and
perhaps even of his own desires.

Othello swears *by the world* because what Iago has said
about being honest in the world, suggesting what worldly
people think, is what has made him doubtful; yet the senses of
honest are quite different – chastity and truth-telling. Desdemona is called a supersubtle Venetian, and he may suspect she
would agree with what Iago treats as worldly wisdom; whereas
it was her simplicity that made her helpless; though again, the
fatal step was her lie about the handkerchief: *Lov'st* in the
second line (Folios) seems to me better than *liv'st* (Quarto), as
making the frightened Iago bring in his main claim at once;
the comma after *Honesty* perhaps makes the sense 'love with
the effect of making' rather than 'delights in making'; in any
case *love* appears a few lines down. *Breeds* could suggest sexual
love, as if Iago's contempt for that has spread to his notions of
friendship; Othello's marriage is what has spoilt their relations
(Cassio 'came a-wooing with' Othello, as a social figure, and
then got the lieutenantship). In the same way Othello's two
uses of *honest* here jump from 'loving towards friends, which
breeds honour' to (of women) 'chaste'. It is important I think
that the feminine sense, which a later time felt to be quite
distinct, is so deeply confused here with the other ones.

* 'And make thyself a motley to the view': Sonnet CX.

It is not safe to be *direct* either way, to be *honest* in Othello's sense or Iago's. The sanctimonious metaphor *profit* might carry satire from Iago on Puritans or show Iago to be like them. Iago is still telling a good deal of truth; the reasons he gives have always made him despise those who are faithful to their masters, if not to their friends. It is clear that he would think himself a bad friend to his real friends. He believes there is a gaff to blow about the ideal love affair, though his evidence has had to be forced. Of course he is using *honest* less in his own way than to impose on Othello, yet there is a real element of self-pity in his complaint. It is no white-washing of Iago – you may hate him the more for it – but he feels he is now in danger because he has gone the 'direct' way to work, exposed false pretensions, and tried to be 'frank' to himself about the whole situation. I do not think this is an oversubtle treatment of his words; behind his fear he is gloating over his cleverness, and seems to delight in the audience provided by the stage.

In the nightmare scene where Othello clings to the word to justify himself he comes near accepting Iago's use of it.

> EMIL.: *My husband!*
> OTH.:   *Ay, 'twas he that told me first:*
>   *An honest man he is, and hates the slime*
>   *That sticks on filthy deeds. . . .*
> EMIL.: *My husband say that she was false?*
> OTH.:   *He, woman;*
>   *I say thy husband: dost understand the word?*
>   *My friend, thy husband, honest, honest Iago.*

From the sound of the last line it seems as bitter and concentrated as the previous question; to the audience it is. Yet Othello means no irony against Iago, and it is hard to invent a reason for his repetition of *honest*. He may feel it painful that the coarse Iago, not Desdemona or Cassio, should be the only honest creature, or Iago's honesty may suggest the truth he told; or indeed you may call it a trick on the audience, to wind up the irony to its highest before Iago is exposed. Yet Iago would agree that one reason why he was honest was that he hated the slime. The same slime would be produced, by

Desdemona as well as by Othello one would hope, if the act of love were of the most rigidly faithful character; the disgust in the metaphor is disgust at all sexuality. Iago playing 'honest' as prude is the rat who stands up for the ideal; as soon as Othello agrees he is finely cheated; Iago is left with his pleasures and Othello's happiness is destroyed. Iago has always despised his pleasures, always treated sex without fuss, like the lavatory; it is by this that he manages to combine the 'honest dog' tone with honesty as Puritanism. The twist of the irony here is that Othello now feels humbled before such clarity. It is a purity he has failed to attain, and he accepts it as a form of honour. The hearty use and the horror of it are united in this appalling line.

Soon after there is a final use of *fool*, by Emilia, which sums up the clown aspect of Iago, but I ought to recognize that it may refer to Othello as well:

EMIL.:	*He begged of me to steal it.*
IAGO.:	*Villainous whore!*
EMIL.:	*She give it Cassio! no, alas; I found it,*
	And I did give't my husband.
IAGO.:	*Filth, thou liest!*
EMIL.:	*By heaven, I do not, I do not, gentlemen.*
	O murderous coxcomb, what should such a fool
	Do with so good a wife?
	(Iago stabs Emilia and escapes.)

On the face of it she praises herself to rebut his insults, which are given because she is not a 'good wife' in the sense of loyal to his interests. But her previous speech takes for granted that 'she' means Desdemona, and we go straight on to Emilia's death-scene, which is entirely selfless and praises Desdemona only. I think she is meant to turn and upbraid Othello, so that she praises Desdemona in this sentence: it would be a convenience in acting, as it explains why she does not notice Iago's sword. *Coxcomb* in any case insists on the full meaning of 'fool', which would make a startling insult for Othello; the idea becomes not that he was stupid to be deceived (a reasonable complaint) but that he was vain of his clownish authority, that is, self-important about his position as a husband and his suspicions, murderous merely because he wanted to show what he could do, like a child. She is the mouthpiece of all the feelings in us which are simply angry with Othello, but this judgement of him is not meant to keep its prominence for long. Indeed as her death-scene goes on the interpretation which the producer should reject is I think meant to come back into our minds; the real murderous coxcomb, the clown who did kill merely out of vanity, was Iago. The cynic had always hated to be treated as a harmless joker, and what finally roused him into stabbing her was perhaps that he thought she had called him a clown. The Lion and the Fox are thus united in the word, but as so many things happen in the play by a mis-understanding. It is perhaps an unnecessarily elaborate inter-pretation (the reference to Iago is much the more important one) but I think it is needed for our feelings about Emilia that she should not deliberately give herself the praise which we none the less come to feel she deserves.

Some other words which combine the ideas of truth-telling and generosity are affected by the same process as *honest*, though without becoming so important. Desdemona while giggling at the jokes of Iago in the second Act says, 'Is he not a most profane and liberal counsellor?', and Othello echoes this *liberal* when he catches from Iago the trick of sneering at the generosity of Desdemona.

> OTH.:   *... here's a young and sweating devil here*
> *That commonly rebels. Tis a good hand,*
> *A* frank *one.*
> DES.:   *You may indeed say so,*
> *For twas that hand that gave away my heart.*
> OTH.:   *A* liberal *hand ...*
> EMILIA: *No, I will speak as* liberal *as the air*
> *Let heaven and men, and devils, let them all*
> *All, all, cry shame against me, yet I'll speak ...*
> *So* speaking as I think, *I die, I die.*

Indeed the whole power of Emilia's death-scene is that she ties up a variety of sacrificial virtues into a bundle labelled 'mere

coarse frankness'. *Honest* itself seems to have rather minor
connections with truth-telling, but the play as a whole is far
from indifferent to that virtue, and Emilia has to steal the
limelight from Iago in the eyes of those who preferred a
character who could blow the gaff.

The only later use of *honest* comes when Othello's sword is
taken from him by the State officer; a mark of disgrace, a
symbol of cuckoldry; two possible negations of honour and
honesty.

> OTH.:   *I am not valiant neither,*
> *But every puny whisper gets my sword.*
> *But why should honour outlive honesty?*
> *Let it go all.*

The straightforward meaning, I take it (though commentators
have disagreed a good deal), is something like 'I have lost my
civilian reputation, because the killing of my wife has turned
out unjust; why then should I care about my military reputation, which depends on keeping my sword?' But the poetic or
dramatic effect clearly means a great deal more. The question
indeed so sums up the play that it involves nearly all of both
words; it seems finally to shatter the concept of honesty whose
connecting links the play has patiently removed. There are
thirteen other uses of *honour* (and *honourable*); four of them by
Othello about himself and five by others about Othello.* The

---

* The remaining four can all I think be connected with Othello. His wife's
honour concerns him directly – the comparison of it to the handkerchief even
implies that he has given it to her (IV i 14); Cassio, we hear, is to have an
honourable position – because he is to take Othello's place (IV iii 240); the
state officer is 'your honour' because he represents the source of that position.
The only difficult case is

> *Three lads of Cyprus – noble swelling spirits*
> *That hold their honours in a wary distance . . .*
> *Have I this night flustered with flowing cups*
>
> (II iii 53)

It will be hard for Cassio not to get drunk with them because they are 'tough';
their boastful virility is likely to make them dangerous customers unless they

effect has been to make Othello the personification of honour; if honour does not survive some test of the idea nor could Othello. And to him *honest* is 'honourable', from which it was derived; a test of one is a test of the other. Outlive Desdemona's chastity, which he now admits, outlive Desdemona herself, the personification of chastity (lying again, as he insisted, with her last breath), outlive decent behaviour in, public respect for, self-respect in, Othello – all these are honour, not honesty; there is no question whether Othello outlives them. But they are not tests of an idea; what has been tested is a special sense of *honest*. Iago has been the personification of honesty, not merely to Othello but to his world; why should honour, the father of the word, live on and talk about itself; honesty, that obscure bundle of assumptions, the play has destroyed. I can see no other way to explain the force of the question here.

There is very little for anybody to add to A. C. Bradley's magnificent analysis, but one can maintain that Shakespeare, and the audience he had, and the audience he wanted, saw the thing in rather different proportions. Many of the audience were old soldiers disbanded without pension; they would dislike Cassio as the new type of officer, the boy who can displace men of experience merely because he knows enough mathematics to work the new guns. The tragedy plays into their hands by making Cassio a young fool who can't keep his mistress from causing scandals and can't drink. I don't know why Shakespeare wanted to tell us that Iago was exactly twenty-eight, but anyway he is experienced and Cassio seems about six years younger. Iago gets a long start at the beginning of the play, where he is enchantingly amusing and may be in the right. I am not trying to deny that by the end of the first

---

are handled on their own footing. I think they act as a faint parody of Othello's Honour, which is a much idealized version of the same kind of thing. And on the other hand Iago does not use the word at all when he is making contradictory speeches in favour of 'good name' and against 'reputation', because that would make it less specific.

Act he is obviously the villain, and that by the end of the play
we are meant to feel the mystery of his life as Othello did:

> *Will you, I pray, demand that semi-devil*
> *Why he hath thus ensnared my soul and body?*

Shakespeare can now speak his mind about Iago through the
convention of the final speech by the highest in rank:

> *O Spartan dog,*
> *More fell than anguish, hunger, or the sea!*

Verbal analysis is not going to weaken the main shape of the
thing. But even in this last resounding condemnation the dog
is not simple. Dogs come in six times. Roderigo when dying
also calls his murderer Iago a dog, and Othello does it con-
ditionally, if Iago prove false. Roderigo says that he himself 'is
not like a hound that hunts but one that fills up the cry' – Iago
is the dog that hunts, we are to reflect.* Iago says that Cassio
when drunk will be 'as full of quarrel and offence as my young
mistress's dog'; now Iago himself clearly knows what it feels
like to be ready to take offence, and one might think that this
phrase helps to define the sort of dog he is, the spoiled favourite of
his betters. He has also a trivial reference to dogs when encouraging Cassio and saying that Othello only pretends to be
angry with him 'as one would beat his offenceless dog, to
affright an imperious lion'. It seems rather dragged in, as if
Iago was to mention dogs as much as possible. The typical
Shakespearean dog-men are Apemantus and Thersites (called
'dog' by Homer), malign underdogs, snarling critics, who yet
are satisfactory as clowns and carry something of the claim of
the disappointed idealist; on the other hand, if there is an
obscure prophecy in the treatment of *honest*, surely the 'honest
dog' of the Restoration may cast something of his shadow
before. Wyndham Lewis' interesting treatment of Iago as 'fox'
(in *The Lion and the Fox*) leaves out both these dogs, though

---

* Mr Granville-Barker indeed said that Iago was 'like a hound on the trail,
sensitive and alert, nose to the ground, searching and sampling, appetite and
instinct combining to guide him past error after error to his quarry'.

the dog is more relevant than the fox on his analogy of tragedy
to bull-baiting; indeed the clash of the two dogs goes to the
root of Iago. But the dog symbolism is a mere incident, like
that of *fool*; the thought is carried on *honest*, and I throw in the
others only not to over-simplify the thing. Nor are they used to
keep Iago from being a straightforward villain; the point is
that more force was needed to make Shakespeare's audience
hate Iago than to make them accept the obviously intolerable
Macbeth as a tragic hero.

There seems a linguistic difference between what Shakespeare meant by Iago and what the nineteenth-century critics
saw in him. They took him as an abstract term 'Evil'; he is a
critique on an unconscious pun. This is seen more clearly in
their own personifications of their abstract word; e.g. *The Turn
of the Screw* and *Dr Jekyll and Mr Hyde*. Henry James got a
great triumph over some critic who said that his villains were
sexual perverts (if the story meant anything they could hardly
be anything else). He said: 'Ah, you have kept letting yourself
have fancies about Evil; I kept it right out of my mind.' That
indeed is what the story is about. Stevenson rightly made clear
that *Dr Jekyll* is about hypocrisy. You can only consider Evil as
all things that destroy the good life; this has no unity; for
instance, Hyde could not be both the miser and the spendthrift
and whichever he was would destroy Jekyll without further
accident. Evil here is merely the daydream of a respectable
man, and only left vague so that respectable readers may
equate it unshocked to their own daydreams. Iago may not be
a 'personality', but he is better than these; he is the product of
a more actual interest in a word.

II

It struck me on reading this over that it is not likely to convince a supporter of Bradley, since it bows to the master as if
taking his results for granted and then appears to include him
among the nineteenth-century critics who are denounced; also,

what is more important, it does not answer the central question that Bradley put – 'Why does Iago plot at all?' I shall try
now to summarize Bradley's position and explain the points at
which I disagree from it.

We are shown, says Bradley, that Iago is clear-sighted, and
he appears to have been prudent till the play begins; he must
have realized that his plot was extremely dangerous to himself
(in the event it was fatal); and yet we feel that he is not
actuated by any passion of hatred or ambition – in fact, so far
as he pretends that he is, he seems to be wondering what his
motives for action can be, almost as Hamlet (in the immediately
previous play by Shakespeare) wonders what his motives can
be for inaction.* Some recent critics have objected to this sort
of analysis, but I think it is clearly wrong to talk as if coherence
of character is not needed in poetic drama, only coherence of
metaphor and so on. The fair point to make against Bradley's
approach (as is now generally agreed) is that the character of
Iago must have been intended to seem coherent to the first-
night audience; therefore the solution cannot be reached by
learned deductions from hints in the text about his previous
biography, for instance; if the character is puzzling nowadays,
the answer must be a matter of recalling the assumptions of the
audience and the way the character was put across. Of course
it is also possible that Shakespeare was cheating, and that the
audience would not care as long as they got their melodrama.
Indeed there are lines in Iago's soliloquies which seem to be
using the older convention, by which the villain merely
announced his villainy in terms such as the good people would
have used about him. But I should maintain that the character
was an eminently interesting one to the first-night audience
(they did not take the villain for granted) and that even the
crudities could be absorbed into a realistic view of him. Such
at any rate is the question at issue.

Bradley's answer is in brief that Iago is tempted by vanity

---

* One might indeed claim that Iago is a satire on the holy thought of
Polonius – 'To thine own self be true . . . thou canst not then be false to any
man.'

and love of plotting. Iago says he likes 'to plume up his will/In double knavery', to heighten his sense of power by plots, and Bradley rightly points out that this reassurance to the sense of power is a common reason for apparently meaningless petty cruelties. Iago particularly wants to do it at this time, because he has been slighted by Cassio's appointment and is in irritating difficulties with Roderigo, so that 'his thwarted sense of superiority demands satisfaction'. But he knows at the back of his mind that his plot is dangerous to the point of folly, and that is why he keeps inventing excuses for himself. Bradley opposes what seems to have been a common Victorian view that Iago had a 'general disinterested love of evil', and says that if he had a 'motiveless malignity' (Coleridge) it was only in the more narrow but more psychologically plausible way that Bradley has defined.

All this I think is true, and satisfies the condition about the first-night audience. The thwarted sense of superiority in Iago is thrust upon them in the first scene, and they are expected to feel a good deal of sympathy for it; at the end of the first Act they are to appreciate the triumph with which he conceives the plot. However the question 'why does he do it?' would hardly present itself as a problem; obviously the play required a villain; the only question likely to arise is 'why does everybody take the villain for a good man?' Bradley of course recognizes this question but he deals with it in terms of an ethical theory supposed to be held only by Iago, whereas you clearly need to consider how it was understood by the audience; and the effect of this twist is to take Bradley some way back towards the idea that Iago embodies Pure Evil.

He says that Iago has 'a spite against goodness in men as a thing not only stupid but, both in its nature and by its success, contrary to Iago's nature and irritating to his pride'. Not only that, but 'His creed – for he is no sceptic, he has a definite creed – is that absolute egoism is the only rational and proper attitude, and that conscience or honour or any kind of regard for others is an absurdity'. Bradley therefore finds it contradictory and somewhat pathetic when Iago shouts 'villainous whore' at his wife, or implies that since Cassio would like to be an adulterer it is not so bad to say he is one (III i 311). This, he says, shows that Iago has a 'secret subjection to morality', an 'inability to live up to his creed'; also the soliloquies betray a desire to convince himself, so that his natural egoism is not perfect. Perfection is attained, however, in the way he hides his ethical theory from other people; when we consider his past life, says Bradley, 'the inference, which is accompanied by a thrill of admiration, (is) that Iago's power of dissimulation and of self-control must have been prodigious'. Since a thrill about his past life is not properly part of the play, this amounts to an admission that the stage character is not consistent. In effect, Bradley is agreeing with Rymer here.

It seems clear that Iago was not meant as a secret theoretician of this sort, and that the audience would not be misled into thinking him one. His opinions, so far as he has got them clear, are shared by many people around him, and he boasts about them freely. To be sure, he could not afford to do this if they were not very confused, but even the confusion is shared by his neighbours. When Iago expounds his egotism to Roderigo, in the first scene of the play, he is not so much admitting a weak criminal to his secrets as making his usual claim to Sturdy Independence in a rather coarser form. He is not subservient to the interests of the men in power who employ him, he says; he can stand up for himself, as they do. No doubt an Elizabethan employer, no less than Professor Bradley, would think this a shocking sentiment; but it does not involve Pure Egotism, and I do not even see that it involves Machiavelli. It has the air of a spontaneous line of sentiment among the lower classes, whereas Machiavelli was interested in the deceptions necessary for a ruler. Certainly it does not imply that the Independent man will betray his friends (as apart from his employer), because if it did he would not boast about it to them. This of course is the answer to the critics who have said that Roderigo could not have gone on handing all his money to a self-confessed knave. And, in the same way, when it turns out that Iago does mean to betray Roderigo, he has

only to tell the audience that this fool is not one of his real
friends; indeed he goes on to claim that it would be *wrong* to
treat him as one. I do not mean to deny there is a paradox
about the whole cult of the Independent Man (it is somehow
felt that his selfishness makes him more valuable as a (friend);
but the paradox was already floating in the minds of the
audience. No doubt Shakespeare thought that the conception
was a false one, and gave a resounding demonstration of it, but
one need not suppose that he did this by inventing a unique
psychology for Iago, or even by making Iago unusually conscious of the problem at issue.

Indeed, when Iago is a conscious hypocrite, I should have
thought that he was laughably unconvincing:

> *Though in the trade of war I have slain men,*
> *Yet I do hold it very stuff of the conscience*
> *To do no contrived murder: I lack iniquity*
> *Sometimes to do me service; nine or ten times*
> *I thought to have yerked him here under the ribs.*

' 'Tis better as it is', answers Othello rather shortly; they are
his first words in the play. Iago's attempt to show fine feelings
has only made him sound like a ruffian in Marlowe. But this is
not at all likely to shake Othello's faith in him; the idea is that,
if you are in the way of needing a reliable bodyguard, you must
put up with something rough. It is true that the soliloquies
make him seem a more intellectual type; and when he says, as
a reason for murdering Cassio, 'He has a daily beauty in his
life, Which makes me ugly', one can hardly deny that Shakespeare is making a crude use of the soliloquy convention. But
even this line, though false, is only so in a marginal way. We
feel that Iago would not have used those words, but Shakespeare is already committed to the convention of making him
talk poetry. The trouble is that the phrase seems to refer to the
moral beauty of Cassio, on which Bradley expresses some
delicate thoughts, and indeed this line is probably what made
Bradley believe that Iago has both a clear recognition of good-

ness and a positive spite against it.* But it is plausible enough
(as a 'second level' interpretation of the crude convention) to
say that Iago only means that Cassio has smarter clothes and
more upper-class manners which give him an unfair advantage
over Iago (for one thing, that is why Iago fears Cassio with his
nightcap). The resentment of the lower classes towards the
graces of the upper really has been known to take ugly forms,
and Shakespeare with his new coat of arms was ready to go out
of his way to reprove it. The phrase comes late in the play
(early in the fifth Act) where Iago can in any case be treated
simply as the villain; it is assumed that the feeling of the
audience has been swung firmly against him. Mr Granville-
Baker said that it is a 'strange involuntary phrase' which Iago
'quickly obliterates under more matter-of-fact language', and
marks the point where 'even his nerve is strained', so that he is
beginning to bungle a situation which has got more complicated than he meant (he has obviously got to kill Cassio
anyhow). This seems to me an excellent tip for a modern actor
but not necessarily part of the first idea.

As to the puzzle about why he is not suspected, he boasts of
that too, in a prominent place, at the end of a soliloquy and a
scene (II i).

> *Knavery's plain face is never seen, till us'd.*

Shakespeare here outfaces the difficulty by a challenge to the
audience: 'You would have been fooled too, though you may
think you wouldn't'. And the reason seems clear enough from
the preceding soliloquy, though it is not what Iago meant to
say. His accumulating resentments at his inferior position have
become explosive, so that he imagines slights from every direc-

---

* Mr Wilson Knight, in 'The *Othello* Music', also regards the 'daily beauty'
speech as the essence of the matter; in the same way, he says, Iago hates the
romance of Othello and the purity of Desdemona, and 'this is his "motive"
throughout; other suggestions are surface deep only'. No doubt he is drawn as
a cynic, but I do not think the audience would take cynicism as such to be
something purely devilish and consciously devoted to destroying goodness or
beauty in any form; because the cynic had a claim to be a Puritan.

tion; but people cannot expect this because it seems to them natural that his position should be inferior. And yet (says the line) his knavery has always had a 'plain face' – his jeering wit and his sturdy independence had always been his stock-in-trade.

I have gone into the matter at perhaps tedious length without using the word *honest* at all, because there seems a suggestion of trickery or triviality about saying that the character is only made plausible by puns on one word. Perhaps this is a risky manoeuvre, because the more I succeeded in it the harder it would become to claim that the puns on *honest* were essential to the play. But it is clear I think that all the elements of the character are represented in the range of meanings of *honest*, and (what is more important) that the confusion of moral theory in the audience, which would make them begin by approving of Iago (though perhaps only in the mixed form of the 'ironical cheer'), was symbolized or echoed in a high degree by the confusion of the word. When opinion had become more settled or conventionalized, and the word had itself followed this movement by becoming simpler, there were of course two grounds for finding a puzzle in the character; but, of the two, I should say that failure to appreciate the complexity of the word was the more important ground, because after all the complexity of moral judgement had not become so difficult – what people had lost was the verbal pointer directing them to it. I think indeed that the Victorians were not ready enough to approve the good qualities of being 'ready to blow the gaff' and 'frank to yourself about your own desires'; and it is not likely that any analysis of one word would have altered their opinions. And I must admit (as a final effort to get the verbalist approach into its right proportion) that my opinions about the play date from seeing an actual performance of it, with a particularly good Iago, and that I did not at the time think about the word *honest* at all. The verbal analysis came when I looked at the text to see what support it gave to these impressions. But I do not feel this to be any reason for doubting that the puns on *honesty* really do support them.

SOURCE: *The Structure of Complex Words* (1951).

F. R. Leavis

DIABOLIC INTELLECT AND THE NOBLE HERO (1952)

Othello, it will be very generally granted, is of all Shakespeare's great tragedies the simplest: the theme is limited and sharply defined, and the play, everyone agrees, is a brilliantly successful piece of workmanship. The effect is one of a noble, 'classical' clarity – of firm, clear outlines, unblurred and undistracted by cloudy recessions, metaphysical aura, or richly symbolical ambiguities.[1] There would, it seems, be something like a consensus in this sense. And yet it is of *Othello* that one can say bluntly, as if no other of the great tragedies, that it suffers in current appreciation an essential and denaturing falsification.

The generally recognized peculiarity of *Othello* among the tragedies may be indicated by saying that it lends itself as no other of them does to the approach classically associated with Bradley's name: even *Othello* (it will be necessary to insist) is poetic drama, a dramatic poem, and not a psychological novel written in dramatic form and draped in poetry, but relevant discussion of its tragic significance will nevertheless be mainly a matter of character-analysis. It would, that is, have lent itself uniquely well to Bradley's approach if Bradley had made his approach consistently and with moderate intelligence. Actually, however, the section on *Othello* in *Shakespearean Tragedy* is more extravagant in misdirected scrupulosity than any of the others; it is, with a concentration of Bradley's comical solemnity, completely wrong-headed – grossly and palpably false to the evidence it offers to weigh. Grossly and palpably? – yet Bradley's *Othello* is substantially that of common acceptance. And here is the reason for dealing with it, even though not only Bradley but, in its turn, disrespect for Bradley (one gathers) has gone out of fashion (as a matter of fact he is still a very potent and mischievous influence).

According to the version of *Othello* elaborated by Bradley the tragedy is the undoing of the noble Moor by the devilish cunning of Iago. Othello we are to see as a nearly faultless hero whose strength and virtue are turned against him. Othello and Desdemona, so far as their fate depended on their characters and untampered-with mutual relations, had every ground for expecting the happiness that romantic courtship had promised. It was external evil, the malice of the demi-devil, that turned a happy story of romantic love – of romantic lovers who were qualified to live happily ever after, so to speak – into a tragedy. This – it is the traditional version of *Othello* and has, moreover, the support of Coleridge – is to sentimentalize Shakespeare's tragedy and to displace its centre.

Here is Bradley:

> Turning from the hero and the heroine to the third principal character we observe (what has often been pointed out) that the action and catastrophe of *Othello* depend largely on intrigue. We must not say more than this. We must not call the play a tragedy of intrigue as distinguished from a tragedy of character.
>
> (p. 179)

And we must not suppose that Bradley sees what is in front of him. The character he is thinking of isn't Othello's. 'Iago's plot', he goes on.

> Iago's plot is Iago's character in action.

In fact the play (we need hardly stop short of saying) is Iago's character in action. Bradley adds, it is true, that Iago's plot 'is built on his knowledge of Othello's character, and could not otherwise have succeeded'. But Iago's knowledge of Othello's character amounts pretty much to Bradley's knowledge of it (except, of course, that Iago cannot realize Othello's nobility quite to the full): Othello is purely noble, strong, generous, and trusting, and as tragic hero is, however formidable and destructive in his agonies, merely a victim – the victim of

's devilish 'intellectual superiority' (which is 'so great that
watch its advance fascinated and appalled'). It is all in
der, then, that Iago should get one of the two lectures that
Bradley gives to the play, Othello sharing the other with
Desdemona. And it is all in the tradition; from Coleridge
down, Iago – his motivation or his motivelessness – has
commonly been, in commentaries on the play, the main focus
of attention.

The plain fact that has to be asserted in the face of this
sustained and sanctioned perversity is that in Shakespeare's
tragedy of *Othello* Othello is the chief personage – the chief
personage in such a sense that the tragedy may fairly be said to
be Othello's character in action. Iago is subordinate and merely
ancillary. He is not much more than a necessary piece of
dramatic mechanism – that at any rate is a fit reply to the view
of Othello as necessary material and provocation for a display
of Iago's fiendish intellectual superiority. Iago, of course, is
sufficiently convincing as a person; he could not perform his
dramatic function otherwise. But something has gone wrong
when we make him interesting in this kind of way:

His fate – which is himself – has completely mastered him: so that, in
the later scenes, where the improbability of the entire success of a
design built on so many different falsehoods forces itself on the reader,
Iago appears for moments not as a consummate schemer, but as a
man absolutely infatuated and delivered over to certain destruction.

We ought not, in reading those scenes, to be paying so much
attention to the intrinsic personal qualities of Iago as to attribute to him tragic interest of that kind.

This last proposition, though its justice is perhaps not self-
evident, must remain for the time being a matter of assertion.
Other things come first. Othello has in any case the prior claim
on our attention, and it seems tactically best to start with
something as easy to deal with as the view – Bradley's and
Coleridge's[2] – and of course, Othello's before them – that
Othello was 'not easily jealous'. Easy to deal with because
there, to point to, is the text, plain and unequivocal. And yet

the text was there for Coleridge, and Bradley accompanies his
argument with constant particular reference to it. It is as
extraordinary a history of triumphant sentimental perversity
as literary history can show. Bradley himself saves us the need
of insisting on this diagnosis by carrying indulgence of his
preconception, his determined sentimental preconception, to
such heroic lengths:

Now I repeat that *any* man situated as Othello was would have been
disturbed by Iago's communications, and I add that many men
would have been made wildly jealous. But up to this point, where
Iago is dismissed [III iii 238], Othello, I must maintain, does not show
jealousy. His confidence is shaken, he is confused and deeply troubled,
he feels even horror; but he is not yet jealous in the proper sense of
that word.

The 'proper sense of that word' is perhaps illustrated by these
lines (not quoted by Bradley) in which, Bradley grants, 'the
beginning of that passion may be traced':

> Haply, for I am black
> And have not those soft parts of conversation
> That chamberers have, or for I am declined
> Into the vale of years – yet that's not much –
> She's gone; I am abused, and my relief
> Must be to loathe her. O curse of marriage,
> That we can call these delicate creatures ours,
> And not their appetites! I had rather be a toad,
> And live upon the vapour of a dungeon,
> Than keep a corner in the thing I love
> For others' uses.

Any reader not protected by a very obstinate preconception
would take this, not for a new development of feeling, but for
the fully explicit expression of something he had already, pages
back, registered as an essential element in Othello's behaviour
– something the evoking of which was essential to Iago's
success. In any case, jealous or not jealous 'in the proper sense
of that word', Othello has from the beginning responded to
Iago's communications' in the way Iago desired and with a

promptness that couldn't be improved upon, and has dismissed Iago with these words:

> Farewell, farewell:
> If more thou dost perceive, let me know more;
> Set on thy wife to observe,

to observe Desdemona, concerning whom Iago has just said:

> Ay, there's the point: as – to be bold with you –
> Not to affect many proposed matches
> Of her own clime, complexion and degree,
> Whereto we see in all things nature tends –
> Foh! one may smell in such a will most rank,
> Foul disproportion, thoughts unnatural.
> But pardon me: I do not in position
> Distinctly speak of her, though I may fear
> Her will, recoiling to her better judgment,
> May fall to match you with her country forms,
> And happily repent.

To say that it's not jealousy here is hardly (one would have
thought) to bring Othello off clean; but Bradley's conclusion is
not (as might have seemed inevitable) that there may be other
faults than jealousy that are at least damaging to a man in the
character of husband and married lover. He is quite explicit:

> Up to this point, it seems to me, there is not a syllable to be said
> against Othello.
>
> (p. 194)

With such resolute fidelity does Bradley wear these blinkers
that he can say,

> His trust, where he trusts, is absolute,

without realizing the force of the corollary: Othello's trust,
then, can never have been in Desdemona. It is the vindication
of Othello's perfect nobility that Bradley is preoccupied with,
and we are to see the immediate surrender to Iago as part of
that nobility. But to make absolute trust in Iago – trust at
Desdemona's expense – a manifestation of perfect nobility is
(even if we ignore what it makes of Desdemona) to make Iago

a very remarkable person indeed. And that, Bradley, tradition aiding and abetting, proceeds to do.

However, to anyone not wearing these blinkers it is plain that no subtilization and exaltation of the Iago-devil (with consequent subordination of Othello) can save the noble hero of Bradley's devotion. And it is plain that what we should see in Iago's prompt success is not so much Iago's diabolic intellect as Othello's readiness to respond. Iago's power, in fact, in the temptation-scene is that he represents something that is in Othello – in Othello the husband of Desdemona: the essential traitor is within the gates. For if Shakespeare's Othello too is simple-minded, he is nevertheless more complex than Bradley's. Bradley's Othello is, rather, Othello's; it being an essential datum regarding the Shakespearean Othello that he has an ideal conception of himself.

The tragedy is inherent in the Othello–Desdemona relation, and Iago is a mechanism necessary for precipitating tragedy in a dramatic action. Explaining how it should be that Othello, who is so noble and trustful ('Othello, we have seen, was trustful, and thorough in his trust'), can so immediately doubt his wife, Bradley says:

> But he was newly married; in the circumstances he cannot have known much of Desdemona before his marriage.
>
> (p. 192)

Again we read:

> But it is not surprising that his utter powerlessness to repel it [Iago's insinuation] on the ground of knowledge of his wife . . . should complete his misery. . . .
>
> (p. 193)

Bradley, that is, in his comically innocent way, takes it as part of the datum that Othello really knows nothing about his wife. Ah, but he was in love with her. And so poetically. 'For', says Bradley, 'there is no love, not that of Romeo in his youth, more steeped in imagination than Othello's.' Othello, however, we are obliged to remark (Bradley doesn't make the point in this connection) is not in his youth; he is represented as middle-aged – as having attained at any rate to maturity in that sense. There might seem to be dangers in such a situation, quite apart from any intervention by an Iago. But then, we are told Othello is 'of a great openness and trustfulness of nature'. It would be putting it more to the point to say that he has great consciousness of worth and confidence of respect.

The worth is really and solidly there; he is truly impressive, a noble product of the life of action – of

> The big wars
> That make ambition virtue.

'That make ambition virtue' – this phrase of his is a key one: his virtues are, in general, of that kind; they have, characteristically, something of the quality suggested. Othello, in his magnanimous way, is egotistic. He really is, beyond any question, the nobly massive man of action, the captain of men, he sees himself as being, but he does very much see himself:

> Keep up your bright swords, for the dew will rust them.

In short, a habit of self-approving self-dramatization is an essential element in Othello's make-up, and remains so at the very end.

It is, at the best, the impressive manifestation of a noble egotism. But, in the new marital situation, this egotism isn't going to be the less dangerous for its nobility. This self-centredness doesn't mean self-knowledge: that is a virtue which Othello, as soldier of fortune, hasn't had much need of. He has been well provided by nature to meet all the trials a life of action has exposed him to. The trials facing him now that he has married this Venetian girl with whom he's 'in love' so imaginatively (we're told) as to outdo Romeo and who is so many years younger than himself (his colour, whether or not 'colour-feeling' existed among the Elizabethans, we are certainly to take as emphasizing the disparity of the match) – the trials facing him now are of a different order.

And here we have the significance of the storm, which puts so great a distance between Venice and Cyprus, between the old life and the new, and makes the change seem so complete and so momentous. The storm is rendered in that characteristic heroic mode of the play which Professor Wilson Knight[3] calls the '*Othello* music':

> For do but stand upon the foaming shore,
> The chidden billows seem to chide the clouds;
> The wind-shaked surge, with high and monstrous mane,
> Seems to cast water on the burning bear,
> And quench the guards of the ever-fixed pole:
> I never did like molestation view
> On the enchafed flood.
>
> (II i)

This mode (Professor Wilson Knight, in his own way, describes it well) gives the effect of a comparatively simple magnificence; the characteristic verse of *Othello* is firm, regular in outline, buoyant and sonorous. It is in an important sense Othello's own verse, the 'large-mouthed utterance' of the noble man of action. Bradley's way of putting it is that Othello, though he 'has not, indeed, the meditative or speculative imagination of Hamlet', is 'in the strictest sense of the word' 'more poetic than Hamlet' (p. 188). We need not ask Bradley what the 'strictest sense of the word' is, or stop to dispute with him whether or not Othello is 'the greatest poet' of all Shakespeare's heroes. If characters in poetic drama speak poetry we ought to be able to notice the fact without concluding that they are poets. In *Othello*, which is poetic drama, Shakespeare works by poetic means: it is through the characteristic noble verse described above that, very largely, we get our sense of the noble Othello. If the impression made by Othello's own utterance is often poetical as well as poetic, that is Shakespeare's way, not of representing him as a poet, but of conveying the romantic glamour that, for Othello himself and others, invests Othello and what he stands for.

'For Othello himself' – it might be said that to express Othello's sense of himself and make us share it is the essential function of this verse, the '*Othello* music'. But, of course, there are distinctions to be noted. The description of the storm quoted above, though it belongs to the general heroic mode of the play, cannot be said to exhibit the element of self-dramatization that is characteristic of Othello's own utterances. On the other hand, the self-dramatizing trick commands subtle modulations and various stops. It is not always as assertive as in

> Behold, I have a weapon
>
> (v ii 257)

or the closing speech. In these speeches, not only is it explicit, it clearly involves, we may note, an attitude *towards* the emotion expressed – an attitude of a kind we are familiar with in the analysis of sentimentality.

The storm, within the idealizing mode, is at the other extreme from sentimentality; it serves to bring out the reality of the heroic Othello and what he represents. For his heroic quality, realized in this verse (here the utterance of others), is a real thing, though it is not, as Othello takes it to be, the whole of the reality. Another way of making the point would be to say that the distinctive style under discussion, the style that lends itself to Othello's self-dramatization and conveys in general the tone and ideal import of this, goes, in its confident and magnificent buoyancy, essentially with the outer storm that both the lovers, in their voyage to Cyprus, triumphantly outride.

With that kind of external stress the noble Othello is well qualified to deal (if he went down – and we know he won't – he would go down magnificently). But it is not that kind of stress he has to fear in the new life beginning at Cyprus. The stresses of the spiritual climate are concentrated by Iago (with his deflating, un-beglamouring, brutally realistic mode of speech) into something immediately apprehensible in drama and comparable with the storm. In this testing, Othello's inner timbers begin to part at once, the stuff of which he is made begins at once to deteriorate and show itself unfit. There is even a symbolic foundering when, breaking into incoherent ejaculations, he 'falls in a trance' (IV i 35).

As for the justice of this view that Othello yields with extraordinary promptness to suggestion, with such promptness as to make it plain that the mind that undoes him is not Iago's but his own, it does not seem to need arguing. If it has to be argued, the only difficulty is the difficulty, for written criticism, of going in detailed commentary through an extended text. The text is plain enough. Iago's sustained attack begins at about line 90 in Act III, scene iii, immediately upon Desdemona's exit and Othello's exclamation:

> Excellent wretch! Perdition catch my soul,
> But I do love thee! and when I love thee not,
> Chaos is come again.

In seventy lines Othello is brought to such a state that Iago can, without getting any reply but

> O misery,

say

> O, beware, my lord, of jealousy,

and use the word 'cuckold'. In ninety lines Othello is saying

> Why did I marry?

The explanation of this quick work is given plainly enough here:

> *Iago*: I would not have your free and noble nature
>   Out of self-bounty be abused; look to't:
>   I know our country disposition well;
>   In Venice they do let heaven see the pranks
>   They dare not show their husbands; their best conscience
>   Is not to leave't undone, but keep't unknown.
> *Othello*: Dost thou say so?
> *Iago*: She did deceive her father, marrying you;
>   And when she seem'd to shake and fear your looks,
>   She loved them most.
> *Othello*: And so she did.

There in the first two lines is, explicitly appealed to by Iago,* Othello's ideal conception of himself: it would be a pity if he let

---

* Who has described Othello (I i 12) as 'loving his own pride and purposes'.

it be his undoing (as it actually was – the full irony Iago can hardly be credited with intending). And there in the last line we have the noble and magnanimous Othello, romantic hero and married lover, accepting as evidence against his wife the fact that, at the willing sacrifice of everything else, she had made with him a marriage of romantic love. Iago, like Bradley, points out that Othello didn't really know Desdemona, and Othello acquiesces in considering her as a type – a type outside his experience – the Venetian wife. It is plain, then, that his love is composed very largely of ignorance of self as well as ignorance of her: however nobly he may feel about it, it isn't altogether what he, and Bradley with him, thinks it is. It may be love, but it can be only in an oddly qualified sense love of her: it must be much more a matter of self-centred and self-regarding satisfactions – pride, sensual possessiveness, appetite, love of loving – than he suspects.

This comes out unmistakably when he begins to let himself go; for instance, in the soliloquy that follows Iago's exit:

> She's gone; I am abused, and my relief
> Must be to loathe her. O curse of marriage,
> That we can call these delicate creatures ours,
> And not their appetites! I had rather be a toad,
> And live upon the vapour of a dungeon,
> Than keep a corner in the thing I love
> For others' uses.

Even the actual presence of Desdemona, who enters immediately upon the close of this soliloquy, can avail nothing against the misgivings of angry egotism. Pointing to his forehead he makes an allusion to the cuckold's horns, and when she in her innocence misunderstands him and offers to soothe the pain he rebuffs her. The element of angry sensuality is insistent:

> What sense had I of her stol'n hours of lust?
> . . .
> I had been happy if the general camp,
> Pioneers and all, had tasted her sweet body.

It is significant that, at the climax of the play, when Othello, having exclaimed

> O blood, blood, blood,

kneels to take a formal vow of revenge, he does so in the heroic strain of the '*Othello* music'. To Iago's

> Patience, I say; your mind perhaps may change,

he replies:

> Never, Iago. Like to the Pontic sea,
> Whose icy current and compulsive course
> Ne'er feels retiring ebb, but keeps due on
> To the Propontic and the Hellespont;
> Even so my bloody thoughts, with violent pace,
> Shall ne'er look back, ne'er ebb to humble love,
> Till that a wide and capable revenge
> Swallow them up. Now, by yond marble heaven,
> In the due reverence of a sacred vow
> I here engage my words.

At this climax of the play, as he sets himself irrevocably in his vindictive resolution, he reassumes formally his heroic self-dramatization – reassumes the Othello of 'the big wars that make ambition virtue'. The part of this conscious nobility, this noble egotism, this self-pride that was justified by experience irrelevant to the present trials and stresses, is thus underlined. Othello's self-idealization, his promptness to jealousy and his blindness are shown in their essential relation. The self-idealization is shown as blindness and the nobility as here no longer something real, but the disguise of an obtuse and brutal egotism. Self-pride becomes stupidity, ferocious stupidity, an insane and self-deceiving passion. The habitual 'nobility' is seen to make self-deception invincible, the egotism it expresses being the drive to catastrophe. Othello's noble lack of self-knowledge is shown as humiliating and disastrous.

Bradley, however, his knowledge of Othello coinciding virtually with Othello's, sees nothing but the nobility. At the cost of denaturing Shakespeare's tragedy, he insistently idealizes. The 'feelings of jealousy proper', he says (p. 194), 'are not the chief or deepest source of Othello's suffering. It is the feeling, "If she be false, oh then Heaven mocks itself;" the feeling, "O

Iago, the pity of it, Iago!"' It is Shakespeare's tragedy of
Othello that the man who exclaims this can exclaim three lines
later, when he next speaks (IV i 204):

> I will chop her into messes. Cuckold me!

Again, three lines further on he says:

Get me some poison, Iago; this night. I'll not expostulate with her,
lest her body and beauty unprovide my mind again: this night, Iago.

This surely has some bearing on the nature of 'the pity of it': to
equate Bradley's knowledge of Othello with Othello's own was
perhaps unfair to Othello.

   In any case, this association of strong sensuality with ugly
vindictive jealousy is insistent in Shakespeare's play:

Now he tells how she plucked him to my chamber. O, I see that nose
of yours, but not that dog I shall throw it to.

> (IV i 140)

I would have him nine years a-killing. A fine woman! a fair woman! a
sweet woman!

> (IV i 181)

'O Iago, the pity of it, Iago!': it is plain here that 'fine', 'fair'
and 'sweet' apply, not to Desdemona as a complete person (the
immediate provocation is Iago's remark, 'she gave it him and
he hath given it [the handkerchief] his whore'), but to her
person in abstraction from the character of the owner, whom
Othello hardly, at this point, respects. And the nature of this
regret, this tragically expressed regret, bears an essential relation to the nature of the love with which Othello, however
imaginatively and Romeo-like, loved Desdemona. That romantic idealizing love could be as dubiously grounded in reality as
this is an essential condition of the tragedy. But Bradley's own
idealizing is invincible. He can even say (p. 197):

An ineradicable instinct of justice, rather than any last quiver of hope,
leads him to question Emilia.

That's no doubt how Othello would have put it; but for the
reader – the unidealizing reader – what the questioning of

Emilia (IV ii) shows in brutal, resolute, unrestricted predominance is the antithesis of any instinct of justice.

With obtuseness to the tragic significance of Shakespeare's play goes insensibility to his poetry – to his supreme art as exhibited locally in the verse (it is still not superfluous to insist that the poetic skill is one with the dramatic). This is Bradley's commentary on Act V, scene ii:

> The supposed death of Cassio (V i) satiates the thirst for vengeance. The Othello who enters the bedchamber with the words,
>
> > It is the cause, it is the cause, my soul,
>
> is not the man of the Fourth Act. The deed he is bound to do is no murder, but a sacrifice. He is to save Desdemona from herself, not in hate but in honour; in honour, and also in love. His anger has passed; a boundless sorrow has taken its place; and
>
> > this sorrow's heavenly:
> > It strikes where it doth love.
>
> Even when, at the sight of her apparent obduracy, and at the hearing of words which by a crowning fatality can only reconvince him of her guilt, these feelings give way to others, it is to righteous indignation they give way, not to rage: and, terribly painful as this scene is, there is almost nothing here to diminish the admiration and love which heighten pity.
>
> (p. 197)

That again, no doubt, is how Othello (though as for satiated thirst, he says at line 74,

> Had all his hairs been lives, my great revenge
> Had stomach for them all)

would like to see it. But Bradley, in the speech he quotes from, misses all the shifts of tone by which Shakespeare renders the shifting confusion of Othello's mind. For it is a speech one might have chosen with the express view of illustrating that subtle command of tone which marks Shakespeare's mature art, and which makes the poetry of *Othello* so different in kind from that of *Romeo and Juliet*, and the two dramas consequently incomparable.

It opens with the accent of a contained holy revulsion, the containing power appearing as inexorable, impersonal justice

> It is the cause, it is the cause, my soul!
> Let me not name it to you, you chaste stars!
> It is the cause.

Now comes a shrinking back from the deed:

> Yet I'll not shed her blood,
> Nor scar that whiter skin of hers than snow
> And smooth as monumental alabaster.

Tenderness here quite clearly is that characteristic voluptuousness of Othello's which, since it is unassociated with any real interest in Desdemona as a person, slips so readily into possessive jealousy. Now the accent of impersonal justice is heard again –

> Yet she must die, else she'll betray more men

– but the accent is so clearly unrelated to any effectual motive in Othello that the concern for justice, the self-bracing to noble sacrifice, appears as self-deception. Next come misgivings over the finality of the deed:

> Put out the light, and then put out the light:
> If I quench thee, thou flaming minister,
> I can again thy former light restore,
> Should I repent me: but once put out thy light,
> Thou cunning'st pattern of excelling nature,
> I know not where is that Promethean heat
> That can thy light relume. When I have pluck'd the rose
> I cannot give it vital growth again,
> It must needs wither: I'll smell it on the tree.

Tenderness here is less specifically voluptuous sensuality than it was earlier, but we nevertheless remember:

Get me some poison, Iago; this night. I'll not expostulate with her, lest her body and beauty unprovide my mind again: this night, Iago.

(IV i 208)

And there is in Othello a curious and characteristic effect of self-preoccupation, of preoccupation with his emotions rather than with Desdemona in her own right:

> O balmy breath, that almost dost persuade
> Justice to break her sword! One more, one more:
> Be thus when thou art dead, and I will kill thee,
> And love thee after: one more, and this the last.
> So sweet was ne'er so fatal. I must weep,
> But they are cruel tears: this sorrow's heavenly;
> It strikes where it doth love. She wakes.

When she is awake and so is no longer a mere body, but a person, it is not sorrowful love or noble self-bracing to a sacrifice that she becomes aware of in Othello:

> Alas, why gnaw you so your nether lip?
> Some bloody passion shakes your very frame:
> These are portents.

Moreover, though Othello says

> I would not kill thy unprepared spirit,

actually he refuses her the time to say one prayer.

When he discovers his mistake, his reaction is an intolerably intensified form of the common 'I could kick myself':

> Whip me, ye devils
> From the possession of this heavenly sight!
> Blow me about in winds! roast me in sulphr!
> Wash me in steep-down gulfs of liquid fire!
> O Desdemona! Desdemona! dead!
> Oh! Oh! Oh!

But he remains the same Othello; he has discovered his mistake, but there is no tragic self-discovery. The speech closing with the lines just quoted is that beginning

> Behold, I have a weapon,

one of the finest examples in the play of the self-dramatizing trick. The noble Othello is now seen as tragically pathetic, and he sees himself as pathetic too:

> Man but a rush against Othello's breast,
> And he retires. Where shall Othello go?

He is ruined, but he is the same Othello in whose essential
make-up the tragedy lay: the tragedy doesn't involve the idea
of the hero's learning through suffering. The fact that Othello
tends to sentimentalize should be the reverse of a reason for
our sentimentalizing too.

For even, or rather especially, in that magnificent last
speech of his Othello does tend to sentimentalize,[4] though to
say that and no more would convey a false impression, for the
speech conveys something like the full complexity of Othello's
simple nature, and in the total effect the simplicity is tragic
and grand. The quiet beginning gives us the man of action
with his habit of effortless authority:

> Soft you; a word or two before you go.
> I have done the State some service, and they know't.
> No more of that. I pray you in your letters,
> When you shall these unlucky deeds relate,
> Speak of me as I am; nothing extenuate,
> Nor set down aught in malice. . . .

Othello really is, we cannot doubt, the stoic-captain whose few
words know their full sufficiency: up to this point we cannot
say he dramatizes himself, he simply *is*. But then, in a marvellous way (if we consider Shakespeare's art), the emotion works
itself up until in less than half-a-dozen lines the stoic of few
words is eloquently weeping. With

> Then must you speak
> Of one that loved not wisely but too well,

the epigrammatic terseness of the dispatch, the dictated dispatch, begins to quiver. Then, with a rising emotional swell,
description becomes unmistakably self-dramatization – self-
dramatization as un-self-comprehending as before:

> Of one not easily jealous, but being wrought,
> Perplex'd in the extreme; of one whose hand,
> Like the base Indian, threw a pearl away
> Richer than all his tribe; of one whose subdued eyes,
> Albeit unused to the melting mood,
> Drop tears as fast as the Arabian trees
> Their medicinal gum.

Contemplating the spectacle of himself, Othello is overcome with the pathos of it. But this is not the part to die in: drawing himself proudly up, he speaks his last words as the stern soldier who recalls, and re-enacts, his supreme moment of deliberate courage:

> Set you down this;
> And say besides, that in Aleppo once,
> Where a malignant and a turban'd Turk
> Beat a Venetian and traduced the state,
> I took by the throat the circumcised dog
> And smote him, thus.   (*Stabs himself.*)

It is a super *coup de théâtre*.

As, with that double force, a *coup de théâtre*, it is a peculiarly right ending to the tragedy of Othello. The theme of the tragedy is concentrated in it – concentrated in the final speech and action as it could not have been had Othello 'learnt through suffering'. That he should die acting his ideal part is all in the part: the part is manifested here in its rightness and solidity, and the actor as inseparably the man of action. The final blow is as real as the blow it re-enacts, and the histrionic intent symbolically affirms the reality: Othello dies belonging to the world of action in which his true part lay.

That so many readers – Coleridge, Swinburne, Bradley, for instance – not belonging to that world should have found Othello's part irresistibly attractive, in the sense that they have preferred to see the play through Othello's eyes rather than Shakespeare's, is perhaps not after all surprising. It may be suggested that the cult of T. E. Lawrence has some relevance here. And Othello is not merely a glamorous man of action who dominates all companies, he is (as we have all been) cruelly and tragically wronged – a victim of relentless intrigue, and, while remaining noble and heroic, is allowed to appreciate the pathos of his own fate. He has, in fact, all the advantages of that last speech, where the invitation to identify oneself with him is indeed hardly resistible. Who does not (in some moments) readily see himself as the hero of such a *coup de théâtre?*

The exaltation of Iago, it has already been suggested, is a corollary of this response to Othello. What but supremely subtle villainy could have brought to this kind of ruin the hero whose perfect nobility we admire and love? Bradley concludes that

to compare Iago with the Satan of *Paradise Lost* seems almost absurd, so immensely does Shakespeare's man exceed Milton's fiend in evil.
(p. 206)

However, to be fair to Bradley, we must add that he also finds Iago decidedly less great than Napoleon.[5] Nevertheless, even if Iago hasn't 'intellectual supremacy', we are to credit him with vast 'intellectual superiority': 'in intellect ... and in will ... Iago *is* great' (p. 219). If we ask the believers in Iago's intellect where they find it, they can hardly point to anything immediately present in the text, though it is true that he makes some acute and cynical observations at times. The evidence of his intellect is the success of his plot: if he hadn't had an extraordinary intellect, how could he have succeeded? That is the essential argument. It is an odd kind of literary criticism. 'The skill of Iago was extraordinary,' says Bradley, 'but', he adds, with characteristic scrupulousness, 'so was his good fortune.'

Yes, so was his good fortune – until Shakespeare gave him bad. That it should be possible to argue so solemnly and pertinaciously on the assumption that Iago, his intellect and his good fortune belong, like Napoleon and his, to history, may be taken as showing that Shakespeare succeeded in making him plausible enough for the purposes of the drama. And yet even Bradley betrays certain misgivings. Noting the astonishing (when one thinks of it) contrast between the devilish reality of Iago and the impression he makes on everyone (including his wife)[6] except Roderigo, Bradley comments (p. 217):

What further conclusions can be drawn from it? Obviously, to begin with, the inference, which is accompanied by a thrill of admiration, that Iago's powers of dissimulation and of self-control must have been prodigious. . . .

There we have the process by which the prodigious Iago is

created. But the scrupulous Bradley nevertheless records the passing doubt:

> In fact so prodigious does his self-control appear that a reader might be excused for feeling a doubt of its possibility.

Of course, it is recorded only to be overcome:

> But there are certain observations and further inferences which, apart from a confidence in Shakespeare, would remove this doubt.

Actually, if we are to be saved from these doubts (those of us who are not strengthened by this confidence in Shakespeare), we must refrain from careful observations, comparative notes and scrupulous inferences. Shakespeare's genius carries with it a large facility in imposing conviction locally, and before we ask for more than this we should make sure we know just what is being offered us in the whole. The title tells us where, in this play (it is not, of course, so in all the plays), we are to focus. As for Iago, we know from the beginning that he is a villain; the business of Roderigo tells us that. In the other scenes we have no difficulty in taking him as we are meant to take him; and we don't (at any rate in the reading, and otherwise it's the actor's problem) ask how it is that appearance and reality can have been so successfully divorced. Considered as a comprehensibly villainous person, he represents a not uncommon kind of grudging, cynical malice (and he's given, at least in suggestion, enough in the way of grievance and motive). But in order to perform his function as dramatic machinery he has to put on such an appearance of invincibly cunning devilry as to provide Coleridge and the rest with some excuse for their awe, and to leave others wondering, in critical reflection, whether he isn't a rather clumsy mechanism. Perhaps the most serious point to be pondered is that, if Othello is to retain our sympathy sufficiently, Iago must, as devil, claim for himself an implicit weight of emotional regard that critical reflection finds him unfit to carry.

'Clumsy', however, is not the right word for anything in *Othello*. It is a marvellously sure and adroit piece of workmanship; though closely related to that judgement is the further one that, with all its brilliance and poignancy, it comes below Shakespeare's supreme – his very greatest – works.

SOURCE: *The Common Pursuit* (1952).

NOTES

1. Cf. 'We seem to be aware in it of a certain limitation, a partial suppression of that element in Shakespeare's mind which unites him with the mystical poets and with the great musicians and philosophers' – A. C. Bradley, *Shakespearean Tragedy*, p. 185.

'*Othello* is a story of intrigue rather than a visionary statement' – G. Wilson Knight, *The Wheel of Fire*, p. 107.

2. 'Finally, let me repeat that Othello does not kill Desdemona in jealousy, but in a conviction forced upon him by the almost superhuman art of Iago, such a conviction as any man would and must have entertained who had believed Iago's honesty as Othello did' – Coleridge, *Essays and Lectures on Shakespeare*.

3. See that valuable book, *The Wheel of Fire*.

4. There is, I find, an admirable note on this speech in T. S. Eliot's essay 'Shakespeare and the Stoicism of Seneca'.

5. 'But compare him with one who may perhaps be roughly called a bad man of supreme intellectual power, Napoleon, and you see how mean and negative Iago's mind is, incapable of his military achievements, much more incapable of his political constructions' (p. 236).

6. 'And it is a fact too little noticed that he presented an appearance not very different to his wife. There is no sign either that Emilia's marriage was downright unhappy, or that she suspected the true nature of her husband.'

Nevill Coghill

From *SHAKESPEARE'S PROFESSIONAL SKILLS* (1964)

FROM THE PREFACE:
INTERPRETATION AND THE
'DISCIPLINE OF THE THEATRE'

... I SAY it is extremely difficult and tiring, when reading a play, to hold it in the mind's eye, and in the mind's ear, with any constancy, as it moves from moment to moment. It asks more concentration than most of us have to remember (for instance) while we are reading, what characters are on the stage, in what costumes and attitudes. The less we can do this, the more we are likely to lose important inflections of meaning. In a small scene, such as that between the Old Countess and Helena in the first act of *All's Well that Ends Well*, we may be able to visualize the two figures, both in their mourning black, each with her special grace – the graces of age and nobility and the grace of youth in love – the Countess seated, perhaps, with Helena kneeling at her side, and see their gestures and expressions, hear the tones of their talk as they flow through the dialogue, packing it with live meaning. But with more complex scenes, who can hold all their detail for long in his imagination, as the moods and movements change, while he reads?

It is false to reply that such visual details cannot carry important significances, as we shall soon see. The Elizabethans were certainly alive to some of them; they had whole systems of colour-symbolism in dress for instance, and a lover would, by wearing the colours of his mistress, 'carry on a silent conversation or flirtation with her'; it was an elaborate language, highly expressive. The instinct survives; this afternoon I saw a young man whose hair was dyed and styled to match precisely the dye and style of the hair of his girl-friend; they were walking hand in hand. It gave an effect of meaning that the eye could not miss, but eludes a full expression in words.

But it is generally not from our incapacities to visualize, that our worst distortions of Shakespeare come; it is from the lawlessness of our imaginations that we are in real danger; ingenious fancies, that lack the discipline of theatre, lead us into every kind of licentious speculation, even to wresting anti-Shakespearean meanings from his texts. Those, however, who are seeking Shakespeare's own meanings – an activity that seems legitimate and not entirely hopeless – can teach themselves, at least in some cases, to distinguish between an interpretation that has genuine Shakespearean validity, and one that has it doubtfully, or not at all, by simply seeing if it could work on the stage; if not, it is a private fantasy.

Let us offer a swift example, taken from many years back, though it is still much quoted. In an essay on 'Shakespeare and the Stoicism of Seneca', by Mr T. S. Eliot, first published in 1927, he discusses Othello's last long speech, that begins:

> Soft you; a word or two before you goe:
>
> (v ii 341)

This he considers an example of what he calls *Bovarysme* in the Moor; *Bovarysme* he defines as 'the human will to see things as they are not', a thing exemplified (he thinks) in a high degree in these lines, though generations of readers and playgoers have mistakenly thought the speech to express 'the greatness in defeat of a noble but erring nature'.

But Mr Eliot will not allow this consoling view to be the true burden of Othello's speech, for he takes it as that of a man 'endeavouring to escape from reality': Othello has 'ceased to think about Desdemona' to indulge in self-pity; what he is really doing is '*cheering himself up*' for the frightful mess his folly has made.

What happens to this interpretation when we try it out in a

theatre? What tones of voice, what move or gesture, can an actor use to suggest a Bovarist cheering himself up? Would he not choose precisely those that would seem to be 'expressing the greatness in defeat of a nobler nature'? For a true Bovarist at such a moment would attempt to see himself as doing exactly that. Unless it be argued that there is no such thing in nature as greatness in defeat, and that any attempt to show it must be instantly recognized by all as fraudulent, how is an audience to know whether Othello is cheering himself up for being so gross a fool and failure, or whether he is cheering his audience up by showing once again, and at the last moment, a true flash of that nobility for which they had first honoured him?

The gravamen of the charge against such criticism is not simply that it is foot-loose from the art it is attempting to criticize, but that it implies a shocking technical incompetence, or else a shocking moral irresponsibility, in Shakespeare as a playwright. For if Shakespeare had wished to convey the 'terrible exposure of human weakness' that Mr Eliot sees in Othello's speech, he could very easily have made this simple purpose plain, unless he was a bungler, or quite indifferent to the effect he was creating. For if Mr Eliot is right, the better this speech is spoken and acted, the more it must deceive the audience; and this is, in effect, conceded by Mr Eliot, who says Othello 'takes in the spectator'. It follows then, that what begins as an attack on Othello's character turns out as undermining Shakespeare's craftsmanship. In the pleasures of self-abasement and the denigration of heroism, many have welcomed Mr Eliot's views without noticing where they were leading, all for want of thinking in terms of the medium Shakespeare used.

It is pardonable for a *reader*, under the spell of Othello's speech, to have forgotten, that Iago is still on stage and in full possession of his faculties. His hatred of Othello is undiminished. Had it been Shakespeare's intention to suggest what Mr Eliot supposes, Iago was there to assist him. Shakespeare had endowed him with the capacity to puncture sentiment; we have heard him use it on Roderigo:

Rod.   I cannot beleeue that in her, she's full of most bless'd condition.
Iago.   Bless'd figges-end.

(II i 245–6)

What prevented Shakespeare, if he wished us to think ignobly of Othello's soul, from using Iago to guide our understanding to this crucial point? Iago had only to choose his moment in Othello's speech to ejaculate 'Thicklips!' or 'Buzze buzze!' (since, alas, the more sophisticated '*Bovarist!*' was not then available) to make his point. But the point was not made.

Under the discipline of theatre, then, the whole Bovarist conjecture collapses, like many other critical glosses on Shakespeare that have been offered without considering what can happen on a stage. An art moves in its own medium. Critics, like producers, must feel for the ways in which the plays they discuss were meant to *work*, both as a whole and in points of detail. These ways, or some of them, are the subject of this book.

FROM CHAPTER VI: 'SOLILOQUY'

... In *Othello* there are two soliloquists, Iago and Othello. Iago has eight soliloquies, Othello three. Iago needs this number to reveal, first, the quality of his own tortuous nature and, secondly, the detail of his intentions. Broadly speaking, his first three soliloquies are epiphanies, the last five, signposts.

The three in which he reveals his nature are unique in Shakespeare. Professor Spivak asks: 'Is it not an undeviating practice of the Elizabethan dramaturgy that the soliloquy is an instrument of direct revelation, providing information that the audience need to have and would not otherwise clearly get at all?'[1] The information Iago gives is indeed necessary; but it is information about himself, not about any objective world. When he tells us of Othello that

> it is though abroad, that 'twixt my sheetes
> Ha's done my office; I know not, if't be true –

(Q I iii 381–2)

this is not to be taken as evidence that there was a rumour of this kind going about. If Shakespeare had meant us to believe this, nothing would have been easier for him than to make Roderigo or Montano, or even the Clown, blurt it out. But we never hear the slightest hint of it; it is one of Iago's inventions, and gives us clear information about his state of mind; he is not under hallucination, as Macbeth is in his 'dagger-speech'; he is in the subtler, but very common condition, which almost everyone experiences in some degree, of one who is entertaining a fantasy in order to feed a passion.

Psychologically, Iago is a slighted man, powerfully possessed by hatred against a master who (as he thinks) has kept him down, and by envy for a man he despises who has been promoted over him. All this comes out in the first lines of the play. Such a man will naturally have a fantasy life in which he can hate these enemies the more, that he may revenge himself upon them the more. The fantasy that comes most easily to him is that of crude copulation; it is his theme-song. In the opening scene his language to Brabantio is all stallion, and now his first thought is

> to abuse *Othello's* eares,
> That he is too familiar with his wife.
>
> (F ii iii 389–90)

His next idea is to diet his revenge on Desdemona himself, 'not out of absolute lust', as he says; but in order to spite Othello, whom (of course) he now fancies to have 'leap't into his seat' and debauched Emilia. So strong with him is this vulgar fantasy that he extends it to Cassio as well.

(For I feare *Cassio* with my Night-Cape* too)

> (F ii i 301)

He indulges these imaginings as a sadist will conjure up whole histories of imaginary crimes committed by the victim he is about to chain up and whip, so that he may 'punish' them. He

---

* [*read* night-cap]

may not exactly 'believe' in the imputed guilt, but he pretends to because it gives relish to his performance.

But these elementary things in psychology are not the most important things in Iago's soliloquies. It does not matter very much whether an audience believes that he has really heard the rumours he speaks of, or whether they have fabricated themselves within him to sharpen his pleasure in revenge.

What is more important (as our analysis will show) is that his first three soliloquies are *graded in order of heinousness*, the foulest last. Their function is not to bring him closer to and create sympathy for him in the audience (as in the case of Brutus) but to distance him from them, to create hatred for him. This is what is unique in them, to create hatred for him. This is what is unique in them. The soliloquies of Richard III, a very different kind of villain and self-revealer, actually win his hearers over to him: just as he wins Anne to be his wife over the dead body of her father-in-law, so he wins the audience (over many other dead bodies) by his fellow conspirator wit in soliloquy; but Iago's soliloquies are designed to make him progressively more repellent. They are the hairpin bends by which we descend into the abysses of his nature.

Yet there is a third purpose to be discerned in these speeches. They are there to offer the living image of a man who is the opposite of what he appears to be. He is a walking illustration of the theme with which he opens the play:

I am not what I am.

(F i i 66)

Just as in the depths of the sea there have been charted great rivers (that make a trickle of the Amazon) which flow in a constant direction in perpetual spate, so in Shakespeare's mind may be tracked certain powerful and constant currents of thought, that flow through many plays; and this is one of them. It breaks surface from time to time among many other themes, and especially perhaps at this period in his life as a writer (between *Hamlet* and *Macbeth*). In no one is it more sharply presented than in Iago, in whom there is no twilight in the night-and-day of his behaviour: the moment we are alone with him, or when he is alone with his dupe Roderigo, his night falls: but when he is seen in any other company he is bright with good fellowship and honest concern for others, as I shall show. By the peculiar use of soliloquy allotted to Iago, Shakespeare sought to give definition to this embodiment of an obsessive theme of his: we see and hear alternately what Iago is and seems.

He begins with no clear plan at all. We are shown him trying treacherously to embroil his master with a senator. It is never told us what he hopes to gain by this, except the satisfaction of a revenge on the Moor for Cassio's promotion. But, for this opportunist, spite is satisfaction enough. Seeing, however, that his own fortunes are dependent upon Othello's, it does not appear that to rouse a senator against the Moor will advance his personal position. He tells Roderigo that he has a 'peculiar end' for his behaviour (I i 61), but this is a fantasy too; his plot against Othello does not become clear to him until much later, when it comes in a flash, in all its monstrous logic, in the third of his graded soliloquies. Let us take them in order.

The first is placed at the end of Act I. The care of Desdemona has just been entrusted to him and he is left with Roderigo, whom he immediately instructs in the means of seducing her. Roderigo, gulled by his hopes and lusts, goes out obediently to sell all his land. It is time for Iago to explain himself a little to the audience. Once again he asserts the basic fact:

> I hate the Moore
>
> (F I iii 380)

and gives us a first pointer to the plot that is forming in his mind:

> Let me see now,
> To get his Place, and to plume vp my will
> In double Knauery. How? How? Let's see.
> After some time, to abuse *Othello*'s eares,
> That he is too familiar with his wife . . .
>
> (F I iii 386–90)

and he finishes this aspect of the soliloquy with

> I haue't: it is engendred: Hell, and Night,
> Must bring this monstrous Birth, to the world's light.
>
> (F I iii 397–8)

In his second soliloquy, he brings his plot into slightly sharper focus; he will abuse Cassio to the Moor and make the Moor thank him and reward him for 'making him egregiously an Asse': but still the line of action is a little blurred:

> 'Tis heere: but yet confus'd,
> Knaueries plaine face, is neuer seene, till vs'd.
>
> (F II i 305–6)

The complete, explicit plot is reserved for the third soliloquy:

> For whiles this honest Foole
> Plies *Desdemona* to repair his Fortune,
> And she for him, pleades strongly to the Moore,
> Ile powre this pestilence into his eare:
> That she repeales him, for her bodies Lust.
>
> (F II iii 342–6)

His five other soliloquies are direct signposts about the working of his plots, and their function is to give a practical shape to his thoughts, rather than a psychological. The three soliloquies we have discussed offer us a progressive clarification of his schemes; they also offer a progressive exhibition of the evil in him. Brutus shows us his soul, Iago his brains, a fresh step down at each epiphany. His first motive is factual: he tells Roderigo that he has been passed over for promotion; but his first soliloquy already passes over into the fantasy we have discussed, the inventive mania of a sense of injury, in a man obsessed by sex:

> I hate the Moore,
> And it is thought abroad, that twixt my sheetes
> Ha's done my office: I know not, if't be true –
> Yet I, for mere suspition in that kind,
> Will doe, as if for surety. . . .
>
> (Q I iii 380–4)

In his first soliloquy he descends from professional jealousy to sexual jealousy; in his second the sexual fantasies begin to proliferate and the sharp pleasure of a revenging copulation begins to rouse in him a kind of lust, leading to the neat, exciting cruelty of

> And nothing can, or shall content my Soule
> Till I am eeuen'd with him, wife, for wift.*
>
> (F iii 292–3)

But there is worse to come. It is not enough for him to use Desdemona's body against Othello, he means to use her soul. We hear no more about his wanting to enjoy her; that fantasy gives way to the foulest he can think of, with a diabolical theology of its own, which he calls 'Divinity of Hell'.

> And by how much she striues to do him good,
> She shall vndo her Credite with the Moore.
> So will I turne her vertue into pitch,
> And out of her owne goodnesse make the Net,
> That shall en-mesh them all.
>
> (F ii iii 347–51)

These three speeches, then, go steadily deeper into a repulsive evil, sauced by a sneering contempt for all that may be thought holy and good. 'Contempt', said Coleridge, 'is never attributed in Shakespeare, but to characters deep in villainy, as Edmund, Iago, Antonio, and Sebastian.'[2]

But Shakespeare is just as careful to show Iago fair in public as he is to show him foul in private. It is this that makes him so detestable, so atrocious in his evil. It is the major strategy of the play, not only that every other character should think him 'honest' but that the audience should see why they do so. Two scenes in particular are planned so as to bring this about. The first is the scene of Desdemona's arrival in Cyprus, and the second is that of the drunken brawl that brings disgrace on Cassio.

Desdemona arrives in the midst of a violent storm; it has separated her from Othello. But why did Shakespeare choose

* [*read* wife]

to place them in different ships to begin with, and then invent a storm to part them? Was it to symbolize the inward storm about to break over and separate them till death? Possibly. But there was also a more practical reason. By telling his story in this way he was able to show what a delightful fellow in company Iago was, and how natural it would be to like and trust him.

The audience has so far only seen him as a secret trouble-maker and may well be thinking 'why does Othello have such a man for his Ensign?' The scene in Cyprus gives a part of the answer.

He had been put in charge of Desdemona by Othello before they left Venice (I iii 285) and now, when she arrives with him in the midst of a tempest that has sunk the Turkish fleet, she is in deep anxiety for Othello's safety, which is still in doubt. It is Iago who rises to the occasion and steps forward to cheer and entertain her by the improvization of a set of verses, tossed off on the spur of the moment, and as elegant as anything in *The Rape of the Lock*. It succeeds completely in taking Desdemona's mind off her worries and shows Iago's amusing social gifts, and care of a mistress entrusted to him. This is the reason for the little scene and therefore for the storm and the separation of man and wife. It has the further usefulness of leaving the audience in doubt whether or not the marriage of Othello and Desdemona has been consummated; for this will add sharpness to the second scene that demonstrates the kindly virtues of Iago.

Delightfulness is one thing, but honest-to-God good com-radeship is another, and that is what we are next shown in him. That we may be certain it is sham, we first hear him priming Roderigo to stir up trouble against Cassio:

Cassio knowes you not: Ile not be farre from you. Do you finde some occasion to anger *Cassio* ... he's rash, and very sodaine in Choller: and happely may strike at you, prouoke him that he may; for euen out of that will I cause these of Cyprus to Mutiny. ...

(F III 262–70)

We then see Iago, in all good fellowship, plying Cassio with drink, singing a rollicking song or two, with every appearance of high spirits and honest affection.

Roderigo plays his part; the pre-arranged fight takes place with a perfect spontaneity, nothing could seem more natural; uproar ensues, at the height of which Iago, decent fellow that he is, intervenes to prevent bloodshed:

> (*Iago*) Nay good Lieutenant. Alas Gentlemen:
> Helpe hoa. Lieutenant. Sir *Montano*:
> Helpe Masters. Here's a goodly Watch indeed.
>
> (F II iii 150–2)

and keeps it up until Othello, dragged by the riot from his wedding-bed, enters and demands the reason for it.

Nobody will tell him. At long last, and very reluctantly, Iago begins:

> I had rather haue this tongue cut from my mouth,
> Then it should do offence to *Michaell Cassio*.
> Yet I perswade my selfe, to speake the truth
> Shall nothing wrong him. . . .
>
> (F II iii 213–16)

What could be fairer, more honest, more convincingly friendly, more reliable and soldierly than Iago's behaviour, so far as Othello, Montana and even Cassio can think? And presently, after Othello has gone back to bed, it is Iago who consoles the stricken Cassio and advises him kindly and intelligently for his good. He only has to importune Desdemona to be reinstated, he tells him.

These two incidents – the storm and the brawl – establish Iago's honesty and kindness, and are the Siamese twins of his soliloquies, opposites that cannot be separated; there are other passages that show his manly delicacy, good faith and zeal:

> I do beseech you,
> Though I perchance am vicious in my guesse
> (As I confesse it is my Natures plague
> To spy into Abuses, and of* my iealousie
> Shapes faults that are not) that your wisedome
> From one, that so imperfectly conceits,
> Would take no notice. . .
>
> (F III iii 148–54)

* [*read* oft]

Such delicacy, such self-doubt, such eagerness for the peace of his master's mind, must convince anyone (who had not heard him in soliloquy) of Iago's honesty. In public he is as amiable and virtuous as Dr Jekyll; in soliloquy he shows us Mr Hyde.

Othello has one soliloquy that specially concerns us here; he needs it badly. He has to recreate the sympathy he has forfeited by striking his wife in public and by calling her 'that cunning whore of Venice' to her face. It would have been easy to have started the last scene – the scene of her murder – without a soliloquy. Desdemona need not have been asleep or even in bed, if Shakespeare had chosen to tell his story so. But the need for Othello to right himself with the audience before his murder of her, the need to show that he thought of it not as murder but as justice, was paramount; only by soliloquy could this be achieved.

Once again, as in the case of Brutus, the argument is over before the soliloquy begins; he has decided upon what to do, and what he says is the embroidery on that decision, not the argument that led him to it.

> It is the Cause, it is the Cause (my Soule)
> Let me not name it to you, you chaste Starres,
> It is the Cause.
>
> (F v ii 1–3)

Underlying the soliloquy of Brutus is the axiom that to seek a crown deserves death. Underlying that of Othello is the axiom that to commit adultery deserves death. Many men have held or acted on these axioms, and, in the theatre, we must accept them while we watch these plays; they are matters in which our disbelief must be suspended, for the sake of the other experiences we can derive from seeing them. Othello never questions the axiom that governs his action; his fault is folly, gullibility.

> O Foole, foole, foole!
>
> (v ii 326)

If the seeming-honesty of Iago, which we have discussed, is given full value in performance, Othello may still seem 'an

honourable murderer'. The structure of the last scene is designed to help in this; it is symmetrically planned. It begins
and ends in an attempt at an act of justice, on a kiss; and there
is visual repetition too, for these acts are both placed on the
wedding-death-bed of Desdemona and Othello. What more
can be done by Othello to even out his fault than by paying for
it in the same coin as he had made her pay? This is what the
eye brings home to confirm what the ear hears in the opening
soliloquy:

> Oh Balmy breath, that dost almost perswade
> Iustice to breake her Sword. One more, one more:
> Be thus when thou art dead, and I will kill thee,
> And loue thee after. One more, and that's the last.
>
> > (*He kisses her.* Q)
>
> So sweet, was ne're so fatall.
>
> > (F v ii 16–20)

On the same gesture the play finds its close:

> I kist thee, ere I kill'd thee: No way but this,
> Killing my selfe, to dye vpon a kisse.
>
> > (F v ii 361–2)

NOTES

1. Bernard Spivak, *Shakespeare and the Allegory of Evil* (Columbia, 1953).

2. This quotation comes from a newspaper report of Coleridge's lecture on *The Tempest* (1818).

John Bayley

TRAGEDY AND CONSCIOUSNESS: *OTHELLO*

'YET I have known those which have walked in their sleep which have died holily in their beds.' The Doctor's words in *Macbeth* remind us, like so much else in the play, of what Goneril calls 'the difference between man and man'. Some could have done Macbeth's deeds and not lost a wink of sleep for it. The tragedies of mind bring out the difference graphically and inevitably, and distinguish those who live in the mind. Othello is the most unexpected hero to do so.

When she describes how she fell in love with him, Desdemona says: 'I saw Othello's visage in his mind'. Loving goes on there; thinking is its ally, determining good and bad. The onlooker should see Othello's visage in his mind too. But the mind takes the opposite course here from its journey in *Hamlet* and *Macbeth*. Their predicament liberates consciousness, even from the prison of Denmark, the haunting terrors of Scotland. Their state – 'cabined, cribbed, confined' as it is – is mysteriously one of freedom for the intellectual being. Like Macbeth, Othello reveals too the extremes in the human heart: that the tender lover can also be the inflexible killer. But Othello is not freed by this sense of his own situation: he has been caught in it as if in a snare. And instead of being freed by the hero's consciousness of things, and sharing it with him, we are forced to stand outside Othello's delusion. The play grips us in its own artifice of incomprehension. And for most onlookers, nowadays, the sensation seems to be more exasperating than it is either thrilling or painful.

And it may produce a strong desire to get out. Othello is in one trap, and our knowledge of it puts us in another one. This separation is very different from the freedom of mind we experience through Hamlet's need to kill his uncle and Macbeth's need to kill the king. Othello's need to kill Cassio and Desdemona belongs only to him; not only because we know it to be deluded, but because the nature and extent of the delusion is such that we cannot imagine ourselves becoming involved in it. We cannot justify and verify its necessity by our involvement. We know it is necessary for Hamlet to revenge his father, and for Macbeth to become king by killing the king, and our knowledge is, like theirs, a duty: it makes us a party to both transactions. We are freely involved in them, and in the states of mind associated with them. But mind in Othello has walked into a trap, and the play both invites us in and keeps us out. We are close to Othello and yet alienated from him.

Othello brings us face to face with the problem not elsewhere encountered in the tragedies, or indeed in Shakespeare's works in general: the distinction between tragic and comic. Normally the question doesn't arise. But it does here, because, to paraphrase Horace Walpole's *mot*, the play is tragic if we can feel a part of it, comic if we look at it from the outside. And the distinction, like all such distinctions where *Othello* is concerned, is very absolute and abrupt. Nothing could be more surprising, in a way, than to find a tension between comic and tragic treatment suddenly making itself felt.

And it was sensed early on. Writing at the end of the same century in which *Othello* was first produced Thomas Rymer called the play 'a bloody farce'. Noun and adjective brings the ideas of comedy and tragedy together in their most depreciatory sense, and no more accurately unsympathetic judgement on the play has ever been made. In our own time more genteel, but also more intellectualized versions of Rymer's disfavour have been voiced by T. S. Eliot and F. R. Leavis, who both consider and reject the personality that Othello presents to the outside world, pointing out that he is not so much deceived as a self-deceiver, a man presented by Shakespeare as constitutionally incapable of seeing the truth about himself. So the

detached, ironic view of the creator contrasts with the tragical
and romantic view taken of himself by the created being. No
one but Othello himself believes that he is 'one that loved not
wisely but too well'.

We note that Eliot and Leavis, like Rymer himself, prefer to
see Othello from the outside. However close the play brings
them to him they prefer to keep a moralist's fastidious distance.
Dr Johnson, a moralist but not a fastidious one, took in his
notes on the play a more charitable view: 'Though it will
perhaps not be said of him as he says of himself, that he is a
man *not easily jealous*, yet we cannot but pity him when we find
him *perplexed in the extreme.*' We may feel pity, implies Johnson, but not terror: not that sense of secret communion in a life
and destiny which we have with the protagonist in other
tragedies. Johnson shows his usual kindness and common
sense in reminding us that we feel pity, but pity is as much the
response of an outsider as is the hard derision of Rymer and
the rather disdainful, intellectual interest of the modern poet
and critic. It may occur to us that no one feels sorry either for
Hamlet or for Macbeth.

Leavis's essay is called 'The Sentimentalist's Othello'. And
indeed there is or has been another widespread reaction to the
play which might be called the sentimental one, suggesting not
a saccharine self-indulgence but a feeling and sympathy which
does not attempt to be discriminating. Very likely the women
in the theatre in Rymer's time, as in Shakespeare's, were
touched by Othello, felt romantic about his personality and
utterance, were secretly rather in love with him. One such
would no doubt have been the housewife in Beaumont's play
The Knight of the Burning Pestle, who loves moving and
eloquent speeches. Very likely the men in the theatre were
aware of this in some sense, and, in a half-conscious defensive
reaction, were the more inclined to see the Moor as a great
booby. Leslie Fiedler makes a good general point about this
aspect of the play when he observes that jealousy simultaneously creates a comic situation for men and a tragic one for
women. Historically speaking, half an audience might well

have been disposed to see the play in terms of tragedy and love, the other half in terms of comedy and sex.

A sentimental response to the play is in some sense in league with love, the love to which Desdemona consecrates her soul and fortunes. No doubt in loving Othello with her we are also loving ourselves; but that may be no bad thing, indeed a necessary one, for a kind of self-love – among other things what his reputation means to Cassio – is at the basis of all honour and decency. As with most things in the play, a paradox is involved; unconscious self-love and self-esteem lends itself to ridicule, which may grow to a kind of hatred. This is certainly at the root of Iago's feelings about Othello, whom he sees as 'loving his own pride and purposes'. On the other hand the opposite reaction can take place: Cassio hero-worships Othello for the same reason that Iago hates him. So in a way have some of the critics, like Swinburne, who asserts that 'we love Othello', and that our feelings about him are different from those we entertain for Shakespeare's other heroes. Perhaps it is natural that the Victorians should have felt about him as Cassio did, rather than Iago. A. C. Bradley describes him as 'coming to us, dark and grand, with a light on him from the sun where he was born'.

Clearly to love Othello, in whatever sense, is to feel with him and to feel his nobility, to see him in his mind. Love, which in the depths of the play displaces drama and tragedy, is in the nature of things subject to conflicting reactions, scepticism and incredulity as well as enthusiasm. 'What can she see in him?' The mixed reactions among onlookers record the same process taking place among the characters of the play. Perhaps it is better, for this reason, even to hate Othello rather than to treat him with detached curiosity. His imperfections, unlike those of Hamlet and Macbeth, are closely connected with the emotions of love. And to disown those imperfections, usually by defining them, is to treat him as an alien, a comedy figure to be exorcised by pity, or found psychologically or sociologically 'interesting'.

It may be that both the welcoming and the defensive

reactions to Othello have something in common underground, a tremor of recognition uniting them in spite of difference. Cynicism and sentiment are two sides of the coin of love. Most people are in their minds on terms with both: the sentiment of love revealing amongst other things our own love for ourselves, while the cynicism about it declares our awareness of how we must look to others, and of how their behaviour so often looks to us. To see Othello in his mind is to see where the sentiment of love predominates, love of another and of self combined in the same happy harmony:

> She loved me for the dangers I had passed
> And I loved her that she did pity them.

Desdemona has taught Othello to love himself, and herself in him – the tenderest of offices and also the most commonplace. The gull Roderigo shares one symptom of his love with Othello himself. He says that Desdemona is 'of most blest condition', to which Iago contemptuously retorts 'Blest fig's end! – the wine she drinks is made of grapes'. So it is, but for Iago that is the end of the matter, and he contrives that it shall come to seem for Othello the end of the matter too.

Love and sex are the opposite poles of the play, not coming together, disturbingly unassimilated to one another. The purpose and function of Iago is to replace the sense of one by the sense of the other. Worked on by Iago, Othello comes to express the same view of the matter as he does:

>   O curse of marriage,
> That we can call these delicate creatures ours
> And not their appetites. I had rather be a toad,
> And live upon the vapour of a dungeon,
> Than keep a corner in the thing I love
> For others' uses.

(III iii 272–7)

What is remarkable and disquieting is the intensity and directness of the expression, and the depressing banality of what is expressed. The voice and language of love are talking sex.

These are the commonplaces of the saloon bar, which vulgar-
ize by public expression of them both secret fears and secret
hopes – coveting one's neighbour's wife while fearing for the
virtue of one's own. This is Iago country, where lust is both
predatory and watchful. Naturally Iago himself desires Desdemona, on the same grounds that he suspects her husband may
have cuckolded him.

> Now I do love her too,
> Not out of absolute lust, though peradventure
> I stand accountant for as great a sin,
> But partly led to diet my revenge,
> For that I do suspect the lusty Moor
> Hath leaped into my seat: the thought whereof
> Doth like a poisonous mineral gnaw my inwards;
> And nothing can or shall content my soul
> Till I am evened with him, wife for wife. . . .
>
> (II i 285–93)

Coleridge's famous phrase about these speeches of Iago's –
the motive-hunting of motiveless malignity' – is in fact very
misleading. From prudish motives (Coleridge also detested the
sexual underworld of *Measure for Measure*, though it is of a
very different kind) it seeks to distract us and turn us away
from the sexual underworld of *Othello*. It would be a mistake to
suppose that Iago is merely making things up, creating
groundless fantasies on which to base his deep hatred for the
general and his lieutenant whom he serves. No audience at the
time would have been surprised by his suspicions, or thought
them to be wholly improbable. And, despite his tone, Iago
does not take this kind of thing at all lightly. We could say that
it was *because* he hates Othello that he thinks of him as a sexual
rival and enemy, but this does not alter the fact that such
resentment would be very practical and real. Emilia evidently
found it so. She knows, as all her friends would do, how highly
motivated are all the mischiefs and malignities that swarm in
the sexual underworld. An immediate parallel occurs to her
when she wonders who could have turned Othello against
Desdemona:

> Some such squire he was
> That turned your wit the seamy side without
> And made you to suspect me with the Moor
>
> (IV ii 146–8)

She refers to the place where such speculations are made, the place to which Iago casually introduces Othello, as if confident that both men came there often:

> Utter my thoughts? Why say they are vile and false;
> As where's that palace whereinto foul things
> Sometimes intrude not?
>
> (III iii 140–2)

The underworld has its own kind of seriousness, its own species of gleeful preoccupation: it is a place of comedy, but black and heartless.

How to reconcile love and sex, how to protect the noble and fragile structure of love against the cheerless black comedy of sexual intrigue? Perhaps there is no way, and perhaps indeed the 'tragedy' in *Othello* – unexpected and yet pervasive, as all such things are in these tragedies – is that there is no way. Such a catastrophe and conclusion would not be exalted ones, merely in a sense a kind of flop. That was the view of Rymer, who saw no way of reconciling the two sides of the play, assuming that one had so obviously cancelled out the other. His tone is that of the comic side, witty, but not witty enough to keep the tone sweet: 'Had it been Desdemona's garter the sagacious Moor might have smelled a rat; but the handkerchief is so remote a trifle no booby this side of Mauritania could make any consequence from it.'

In a modern production of *Othello* little attempt is made to elevate and respect the structure of love. Why should we not prefer the humour and the bracing realism of Iago as we watch the increasingly grotesque agony of *Othello*? Iago's acting vitalizes every scene. Dr Johnson saw that his wit and vigour might 'steal upon esteem, though it misses of approbation'. He is the more fascinating to an audience if they are not much involved in the drama of Othello's mind and the love which is cast out from it. A modern audience is probably suggestible to having reason and good sense put on the side of wit and comedy, and to feeling at home with Iago and his view of things.

We could say that what prevents the natural expansion and freedom of mind in *Othello* is the absolute difference between Iago's and Othello's minds. When Othello shows that he is capable of thinking like Iago, and uttering his sort of thoughts, the difference – and from a dramatic point of view quite rightly – does not disappear but takes on an oppressive and night-marish form. Then what of the peculiar status of mind in these three tragedies? The structure of *Othello* has to be loaded, compensated, the balance kept, by making Othello's own mind a place of apparent and natural romance and innocence, lofty but, as it were, specialized. Can we live there as well as in the mental world of Iago? Can we, as onlookers, live naturally in both? Or do we, as in the critical tradition from Rymer to Leavis, implicitly reject both, and thus make our appreciation of the play an essentially negative thing?

In answering that question it helps to consider again Mac-beth's soliloquy when he is nerving himself for the murder of Duncan:

>   . . . his virtues
> Shall plead like angels, trumpet-tongued, against
> The deep damnation of his taking-off;
> And pity, like a naked new-born babe,
> Striding the blast, or heaven's cherubim horsed
> Upon the sightless couriers of the air,
> Shall blow the horrid deed in every eye
> That tears shall drown the wind. . . .
>
>   (I vii 18–25)

Macbeth's preoccupations lead his mind involuntarily into a spacious and terrifying metaphysical area, the area that Rilke called 'the open'. Yet in this area there is a total blending in poetry of the comic and the tragical. Any such distinction in it would not normally occur to us, but if it does we see that the two do meet, in poetry, without the faintest sign of distinction or embarrassment, just as they do, in a different context of poetry, in *Romeo and Juliet* when Romeo wonders if 'unsubstantial death is amorous'. Into Macbeth's mind great portents like angels appear and enter, yet they are quite at home with every incongruity of the distracted consciousness. We take for granted what is in a sense the comic and touching upshot of their visitation, that Macbeth should reveal his wish, not to seek his salvation by renouncing murder, but to bask in his present reputation and the pleasures it will bring:

> We will proceed no further in this business.
> He hath honoured me of late; and I have bought
> Golden opinions from all sorts of people,
> Which would be worn now in their newest gloss,
> Not cast aside so soon.
>
> (I vii 31–5)

The image in his wife's reply is brutally deflating. So, he has woken up from his dream of ambition like a drunkard with a hangover?

> Was the hope drunk
> Wherein you dressed yourself, Hath it slept since?
> And wakes it now to look so green and pale
> At what it did so freely?
>
> (I vii 35–8)

Othello's and Iago's speeches not only lack this freedom in incongruity but hold the onlooker in the grip of their own separate obsessions. This had been needful, from far back, to the essential structure of the play, which is a dramatic version of the cautionary tale by the Italian intellectual and moralist Cinthio. In the tale there is no love and sex polarity, for the ensign Iago is himself in love with Desdemona, and acts out of jealousy and venomously disappointed passion when she refuses his suit. This brings Othello and Iago together, makes them in fact much the same kind of person. It also defines Iago clearly, just as he is defined, though in a different way, in Verdi's opera. The most frightening thing about Shakespeare's Iago is how inexact he is in his own estimation: his pleased definition of himself is merely that he is not what he seems to be.

The strain imposed on the structure of *Othello* comes from the fact that love in it must be kept apart from sex, Othello's love and Desdemona's apart from the world of sexual commonplace, whether good or evil natured. And this goes against the norm of Shakespearean incongruity. We take it for granted in *Hamlet* and *Macbeth*. But in *Othello* it is like the monster in the thought too hideous to be shown and – more important – too potentially risible. The structure requires something that normal Shakespearean psychology cannot permit, for 'foul things' of a sort must indeed intrude into every mind, into the 'palace' of Othello's as well, and not just because they have been put there by Iago. Yet if Othello's consciousness were in any sense able to anticipate Iago's insinuations they would not have the force that the drama requires.

However, the resulting charged and polarized atmosphere is not only superbly dramatic, but also true to life, to life as Othello and Cassio see it. Iago's hatred for them is completely realistic in terms of the commonest human experience, because it approximates to the gut resentment that is felt against others for belonging to a different class, or for being Indian, Jewish, black, cultivated, refined, etc., etc. This blind hatred of distinction is used by the play to underlie the polarity of its own structure. Publicity hates privacy, prose hates poetry, envy hates generosity, sex hates love. Lines and glimpses in the play are constantly directed and pointed towards discrepancy, setting in every sense the high style against the low. This makes the play a more searching study of daily hatreds and dignities than any other of Shakespeare's: and the structure makes it so. But at a cost. We must forgo that sense of absolute freedom in the mental world which we enjoy with Macbeth and Hamlet, and never more so than when their torments and preoccupations seem half-conscious and half-hidden.

Envy can always show up decorum. That is one source of trouble, almost a technical one. But by the same token decorum is always liable to show up itself, and this is only desirable if the work of art wished it to happen or is indifferent to whether it happens or not. What is disconcerting, in the early stages of temptation, is not Othello's liability to jealousy but the way in which hateful incongruities are thrust into the privacy of his consciousness. The play is bound to bring them together, and the result is an absurdity which it cannot quite let out, which must be left lurking below the surface of emotion. Othello is forced to contemplate the fact that his love is not a wholly private affair, something that is solely a part of his own self and his romantic history. And when he has been made to feel that Desdemona has been and is being made love to by another, his exclamation of woe has a startling and plaintive absurdity:

> I had been happy if the general camp,
> Pioneers and all, had tasted her sweet body,
> So I had nothing known.
>
> (III iii 349–51)

The idea is ineluctably comic. Charmingly so in a way, reflecting as it does an incongruous world of sergeant-majors, populating Othello's military past but grotesquely unsuited to the high romantic image of adventure and hazard. Iago's poison forces him to bring such barrack-room ideas together with those of his love. Yet that word 'tasted' is in a touching way his own, here brought painfully into contact with a licentious jest from army life. We may be reminded of it again before the killing of Desdemona:

> When I have plucked thy rose
> I cannot give it vital growth again,
> It needs must wither: I'll smell it on the tree.
>
> (V ii 13–15)

For Othello the barrack-room and his love are wholly incompatible. For Desdemona, as we shall see, this is not so. She is prepared to go to the wars in all senses.

Shakespeare generally does not in the least distinguish between love and sex: *Romeo and Juliet* shows that. Both in comedy and tragedy the two go naturally and properly together, for men and women alike. Claudius and Gertrude, as much as Portia and Bassanio, have their sexual tenderness as well as love for each other taken for granted; even when, as in the latter case, marriage is a combination of fairy story and business arrangement. But in reconstructing and re-imagining the Othello story for his play Shakespeare had to divorce love from sex as a logical result of separating the romantic nobility of Othello from the underworld intrigue of Iago. The only characters for whom love and sex are taken for granted as parts of the same whole are the three women, Bianca, Emilia, and Desdemona herself.

The consequences of this are bound to be striking, and indeed they are at the root of our divided apprehension of the Othello world and the Iago world. The explicit presence of sex as a kind of basic sport, intrigue and power struggle, whereas love is a lofty affair of adventure and romance, gives the play an atmosphere as much Victorian as Elizabethan, and this goes with its popularity in the nineteenth century after Kean's revival. Historically, men do tend to separate love and sex and to regard both as their due, but in different contexts. Where Shakespeare himself is concerned, a sense of the division, and the need to compensate for it with some bridging material, are shown by his emphasis on the pungent common sense of Emilia, and the no less cheerful and sensible temper of Desdemona, which she displays in conversation with the two officers before Othello's arrival in Cyprus.

Impossible of course to say how the division declared itself to the artist; it might seem his imaginative reaction to the idea of two men who are locked in this dramatic relationship. In Cinthio's tale the relation is in every way more ordinary, and has a kind of low-key plausibility. The commander waits in anxious suspense for days for the proofs of his wife's infidelity which his subordinate has promised to obtain. When convinced, he enters with him into an ingenious conspiracy to make the murder look like an accident, caused by a fall of plaster from the ceiling. Between the pair there is none of the gap between the lover and the connoisseur of sex, no sharp division in outlook. Both indeed in their way have had ample opportunity to feel love for the murdered wife, the ensign

because of his infatuation with her, and the general because he
has been for a long time a tender and happy husband. 'Their
affection was . . . mutual.' 'No word passed between them that
was not affectionate and kind.' This makes the crime more
dreadful but also in its way more probable. The confusion and
duplicity, hatred and sorrow, take place not only in the world
of a newspaper story but are narrated in order to point a
moral, or rather several, about the evils of credulity and
gossip, and of marrying outside one's race and community.

Shakespeare's drastic simplification of the bond between
commander and subordinate has the effect of squeezing out the
onlooker, who can take part, as it were, neither in terms of love
as Othello sees it or in terms of sex as Iago does. The pair drag
into their area of high tension the habitual concordances of sex
and love, and split them violently asunder. Othello's response
to Iago's first tentative hints have led the critics, who see him
as a study in the vulnerability of egotism, to claim that he
meets Iago half-way and makes his work easy and its plausibility absolute. There is truth in this in so far as Iago's suggestions are all about sex, for the mention of sex in connection
with the woman he loves is an explosive subject to Othello.
The inability to conceive of one in terms of another, where she
is concerned, and himself in terms of both, is at the root of the
disaster. None the less love and sex, and the barrier between
them, not only squeeze out the onlooker from the play: they
also squeeze out tragedy. But the variety of ways in which that
happens is always and asset to the Shakespearean work of art.

To the onlooker the fact that Othello, in his effortless and
terribly formidable way, does not fetch Iago at the outset a
blow that would knock him from one end of the stage to
another, is one of the great disappointments of the play. Such
an act would be a sort of parodic fulfilment of the onlooker's
desire to take part. It is denied him, and the hero can never
really recover in his estimation. The first two acts, by engross-
ing the spectator so effectively in Othello's life and being, have
prepared him for some such response. The onlooker is similarly

expectant of Hamlet going on being Hamlet, and Macbeth Macbeth, and he was not disappointed. Nothing they do lets down expectation in this way.

It seems in the proper nature of things that Othello's pride should respond with instant finality to his subordinate's insolence. And it is important to note that if the form of the play barely recovers here from the change in the feel of its hero, that change is brought about by the introduction of Othello to the subject of sex. It is a subject that Iago is, as it were, in charge of; and has been since he holloed out to Brabantio, in the tumultuous opening scene, that an old black ram was tupping his white ewe. Just as Othello can never recover from his first capitulation to Iago, so sex in the play never recovers from the fact that Iago is in charge of it, and corrupts Othello by his own kind of insistence on it.

Both in the foreground and background worlds of this play love never quite manages to include sex, even when love speaks with the voice of Desdemona. It is right that sex should be so disturbing an element in the play, but no bounds can be set to the kind of disturbance it causes, the more especially when it is referred to with the gross casualness of Iago: 'To be naked with her friend in bed, an hour or more. . . .' The purpose of that casualness is to madden Othello, but it also lends its own kind of frivolous, uncontrolled element to the play's love/sex polarity. It is curiously shocking – or would be if we were paying attention to the point at that moment – to hear what Desdemona tells Emilia after the melancholy supper at the end of Act IV, when Lodovico has arrived from Venice, and Othello has struck her in public:

> He says he will return incontinent.
> He hath commanded me to go to bed,
> And bade me to dismiss you.
>
> (IV iii 11–13)

In its adjectival form 'incontinent' is only used in Shakespeare in the sense of 'sexual desire', though adverbially it can mean 'at once', 'without further reflection', and is so used by Roderigo.

The case here seems ambiguous, but suggests Desdemona's hope that the abrupt command means Othello intends to come back and resolve his dark mood in making love to her.

Even so the word is disconcerting, the idea to an onlooker not altogether an attractive one. It seems almost to align itself with Iago's casual patronage of the sex instinct, and to hint, in its rapid note of appeal to what is hidden, of sex as an element not resolvable in human loves. But clearly, and gratefully, it is not so to Desdemona. In her plea before the senate she was as explicit as is consonant with feminine dignity that she 'loved the Moor to live with him'.

> If I be left behind
> A moth of peace, and he go to the war,
> The rites for which I love him are bereft me,
> And I a heavy interim shall support
> By his dear absence.
>
> (I iii 255–9)

This is the voice of love and reason, and no less so is Othello's equally dignified and tender statement that he wants her with him, not for sexual satisfaction, 'but to be free and bounteous to her mind' – the mind in which he had seen and loved himself and her.

None the less it is true to say that no other lover in Shakespeare would make such a statement. In his explicit separation here of the motives of sex and love there is not only something indicative of Othello's own nature but an indication of the dualism that haunts the play. It appears in another form when the lovers are united in Cyprus, and seem to sing their passionately loving aria to one another. '*If it were now to die, 'twere now to be most happy.* . . .' '*The heavens forbid but that our loves and comforts should increase.* . . .' For Desdemona, the whole business is natural and growing: for Othello there is a delight in love that cannot contemplate any ordinary consummation.

For Othello love is a private freedom but sex a public knowledge. The pioneers of the army, whom he imagines making free with Desdemona, are an aspect of that public world which becomes such a nightmare to him. After picking up the handkerchief Emilia tells her husband, 'I have a thing for you.' He replies, 'It is a common thing.' The innuendo is spotted by Emilia who exclaims indignantly at it, and Iago instantly ripostes with 'to have a foolish wife'. That sexual badinage will become grim when Othello calls Desdemona 'Thou public commoner', and behaves to her as if he were in a brothel. Iago is sure that the desire for sex unites us all – 'And knowing what I am know what she shall be'. For him a lust for 'these required conveniences' is a matter for the will to give way to or reject; for the will controls 'unbitted lusts, whereof I take this that you call love to be a sect or scion'.

The tone of such platitudes is familiar, and it is more a comment on their nature and use in life rather than a weakness of the play that is has no way for males to talk about sex other than Iago's way. But there are exceptions. The most significant is Cassio, the unknowing cause of all the trouble, whom Iago admits to have 'a daily beauty in his life'. His conduct to Bianca, though not edifying, has at least a kind of tender geniality that distinguishes it from mere sex; and it is Cassio who, at the summit of the play's happiness, can publicly unite by his chivalrous eloquence explicit sex and love together in an epithalamium for the wedded pair:

> Great Jove, Othello guard,
> And swell his sail with thine own powerful breath,
> That he may bless this bay with his tall ship,
> Make love's quick pants in Desdemona's arms,
> Give renewed fire to our extincted spirits,
> And bring all Cyprus comfort.
>
> (II i 77–82)

It is the only moment of the play when love and desire are united as bringers of public joy and celebration, even though it is in the absence of the lovers.

In *Othello* even Shakespearean double entendre acquires a note of incongruity, and this speech of Cassio's is the only one which knits up all heroic and amorous effect by means of it. The suggestiveness of *bay*, *tall ship*, and so forth, mark a mutuality in the style of eroticism. But this is in contrast with

the style of Othello himself. He seems not to grasp the implications of what he says, any more than those of what is taking
place. He seems ignorant of that commonest of Elizabethan
sexual puns which he has uttered in 'If it were now to die,' and
such incomprehension, however tender and dignified, adds
incongruously to the speech as an omen of disquiet. The
touchingly farcical image of 'I had been happy if the general
camp . . .' begins a speech that ends 'Othello's occupation's
gone'. The two senses of that word were notorious – both
Shakespeare and Ben Jonson in their plays affect to deprecate
its cant meaning – and the audience must have been aware of
it; but Othello seems not to be. The effect is to cut off his
knowledge of sex from the range of his emotional feeling; and
this produces a discrepancy not only exploited by Iago and
derided in his wit, but on offer, as it were, to the audience. In
such a context it can seem as if the play, and its author himself,
were siding against Othello.

Of course the general specification of the play as tragedy
corrects this. The point is made clear through Iago:

> The Moor, howbeit that I endure him not,
> Is of a constant, loving, noble nature;
> And I dare think he'll prove to Desdemona
> A most dear husband.
>
> (II i 282–5)

That we know from our own eyes, but they also see how
Othello has been isolated by his absurd situation. How is a
cuckold to be turned into a tragic hero? How, for that matter,
was a Jewish money-lender to be turned into a passionate
Shylock? In comedy the thing seemed to happen by itself and
naturally, but in tragedy it has to be arranged. And the way it
is done is partly, and precariously, a question of timing.

In Cinthio's tale, where the pair have been happily married
for some time, the motive for murderous jealousy and grief has
to be turned back on Othello's Moorishness, a condition so
outlandish in terms of a mixed marriage that no amount of
cohabitation would cure it. Time, in the story, breaks things

up, and produces the catastrophe. The timing of the play has been endlessly discussed, and long before A. C. Bradley, and the intelligent student who suggested a double time-scheme to him, it had been suggested that when the action reaches Cyprus it can be seen as winding itself up either in a matter of hours, or in a matter of weeks or months. More important, perhaps, is the impression the play gives of the events that *preceded* it, and the way it vividly recalls Othello's courtship. Cassio went wooing with Othello and acted as go-between. Perhaps the hint that Desdemona gave about her feelings for Othello could in fact have been suggested by him? For she, as Othello then said with proud simplicity,

> bade me, if I had a friend that loved her,
> I should but teach him how to tell my story
> And that would woo her. Upon this hint I spake.
>
> (I iii 164–6)

What was spoken in happy tranquillity is recalled by Othello in violent agitation. That friend is now the enemy, his man-oeuvres with Desdemona timeless and dateless. Time and emotion melt together, and the first incision that Iago cuts is designed to make them one in memory.

> IAGO. Did Michael Cassio, when you woo'd my lady,
>   Know of your love?
> OTH. He did, from first to last. Why dost thou ask?
>
> (III iii 95–7)

The query suggests a whole new range of possibilities. Was it indeed the *friend* whom Desdemona loved, and was thinking of when she uttered the hint. The compression of time brings back the moment and perhaps something else: for Cassio seemed not to know what had taken place in that pregnant little scene when he met Othello and Iago in the flurry of the nocturnal opening crisis. Suppose Othello had not told him – had not wished to tell him – of the imminence of his elopement with Desdemona. The contradiction between Cassio's apparent ignorance in that tiny exchange, and what we later hear of his service in Othello's wooing, is like the tricks that time itself plays. It becomes a device to make the atmosphere more uncertain for the protagonist, more bewildering.

More bewildering for Othello, but not more confusing for us. There is no confusion involved in the play, and nothing in the matter of time or relation that looks like mere carelessness. Time is like Othello's blackness, a factor constantly present but never decisive, never leant on by the playwright to under-pin his case. The play eludes with ease any attempt to pin it down to a solution: why it happened, what caused it, what weakness in Othello was involved? Even jealousy as such is not the reason. Jealousy is a long-term affair, with its own rules and customs, its own subterranean animosities and grudges. In *The Winter's Tale* they lie beneath the surface, like reefs laid down in the past. Jealousy is a very intimate topic. What we have in *Othello* is something much more open and elemental: the substitution of the simple public concept of sexual appetite for the complex private reality of daily love. That is what Iago contrives to force on Othello.

And it is this nightmare that Othello strangely refers to as 'the cause', in the exhausted, almost drowsy incantation he utters before he kills Desdemona. It is a love incantation, intended to displace the wickedness of sex. A paradox, which Shakespeare might well have been quite conscious of manipu-lating, is that the black man should be invested not with witch-craft and devilry but with the true power of love, as Shylock had been endowed with the voice of humanity. Iago, the trusted officer and true Venetian, becomes on the other hand the spokesman of sex in its crudest, least regenerate form. But of course this is not something the play makes a point of showing, as a play would today. It emerges naturally from the relationship.

> It is the cause, it is the cause, my soul:
> Let me not name it to you, you chaste stars,
> It is the cause.
>
> (v ii 1–3)

It is wholly in keeping with *Othello* that the 'cause' should not be named or defined: it does not have to be for it is all around us in the play. It is sex itself, the absurdity and horror that stands between Othello and the tragic fate he is determined to have. He cannot live in the dungeon, the toad-ridden cistern of sex as presented by Iago. Tragedy can only be consummated by the removal of this monstrous and farcical image of sex, the sating of bodies, the beast with two backs. It is this image which lurks in the background of Othello's speech and makes its tragic sublimity disquietingly parodic, even as Iago parodied, in deadpan style, his master's vehement invocation of the Pontic sea, and its 'icy current and compulsive course'.

Macbeth, going to commit murder, had spoken in the same vein.

> Witchcraft celebrates
> Pale Hecate's offerings; and withered Murther,
> Alarumed by his sentinel, the wolf,
> Whose howl's his watch, thus with his stealthy pace,
> With Tarquin's ravishing strides, towards his design
> Moves like a ghost.
>
> (II i 51–6)

But in *Macbeth* such a speech seems wholy native to its situation. In *Othello* the incongruity between tragedy and comedy has been growing with every new reference of Iago's. It is time for Othello to use tragical violence on that detestably comic vision of sex which Iago has summoned up. And to kill it requires the killing of Desdemona. As the action has progressed sex has usurped love, a frightful comedy has usurped the tragic expectation. Those inanely casual images dropped by Iago ('Or to be naked with her friend in bed / An hour or more, not meaning any harm') have become so vivid to Othello that tragedy must be restored, since love cannot be.

The play's construction, unique in Shakespeare, keeps sex and love, like tragedy and comedy, together yet apart, sensationally revealing each others' natures and characteristics. The same is true of tragedy and comedy themselves, here sharply revealed in image and setting instead of mixing naturally together. The process is unfair to both: tragedy is bound to look a little bit absurd, comedy and sex malicious and mechanical. Polarizing the two viewpoints are Othello and Iago, both isolated: though for much of the time Iago is in fact not so isolated, for he can appeal to the audience and find it on the side, not of his intrigue, but of his outlook and style. The great risk the play runs is the isolation of Othello, 'a fixed figure' to be pointed at by the audience, and perhaps with a secret derision by the finger of the dramatic mechanism itself.

Certainly there is every indication that once the relationship of Othello and Iago had begun to be imagined by Shakespeare it developed too swiftly to be kept under control. The comic/ tragic polarity is itself taken apart in the process, though the verse and style require it as a visible mechanism. *Macbeth* is probably the tragedy that followed, and we can see there too, on a bigger scale even, the character who is at once created for the tragic and yet imagined and perceived in terms of the domestic. Iago's hatred makes him comparable in a limited way. He is the person known at some time in every community – school, regiment, office, household – who hates quietly and deeply, hates others for being what they are. His hatred is often expressed as a derisive geniality that no one takes seriously.

> She was a wight, if ever such a wight were,
> To suckle fools and chronicle small beer.

Everyone receives such cynicism with 'ohs' and laughs at it, as at any other readily identifiable social ploy. But Iago is kidding on the level, like the snob who makes a point and a style of pretending to be snobbish. He really does loathe innocence and goodness and their hum-drum happy preoccupations. Quite a lot of people are like Iago, and conceal it with 'old fond paradoxes to make fools laugh i' th' alehouse'. We are not exactly intimate with this domestic side of Iago, as we are with that of Macbeth, but most people would recognize it, and would recognize its connection with the really terrifying hatred that seethes out of Iago when he finds the perfect way of making that hatred cause havoc, without breaking his cover.

> Hell and night
> Must bring this monstrous birth to the world's light.

It is in an area of complete psychological truth, therefore, that Iago the social type joins up with Iago the villain of tragedy. Empiric observation marries easily with the 'Spartan dog', the black and bloody villain: null and empty in nature as it is, Iago's hatred in action fits naturally into a correspondingly negative rhetoric, just as his lordship of sex and comedy is wholly compatible with his role as villain. Macbeth is a different matter. The difference between our sense of his mind, and his role as a bloody tyrant, is itself the dramatic surprise and success, as emphatic as the difference between his sense of the open promise of time, and his deception by 'the fiend that lies like truth'. Mind in *Macbeth* is both in league and at variance with tragic action, the incongruity involved being a part of its compelling intimacy.

But in *Othello* such an incongruity threatens the whole stability of the structural relation, making tragedy and comedy look equally at a disadvantage. It separates the heroic Othello from the gull who is made 'egregiously an ass' by Iago; and cuts off any intimacy with Othello, his 'visage in his mind', from the pity or distaste felt for him in his rage and pathos. (It is a striking fact that when he says: 'I'll chop her into messes! Cuckold me!' – the sentiment is much more repulsive than any of Macbeth's murderous utterances, which seem assumed and put on.) Mind in *Othello* is divorced from emotion, as sex is from love.

But whatever the stresses and strains produced by these divisions the rewards in art are none the less enormous. Even the risk of alienating the onlooker from the tragic action produces a corresponding gain: that action and behaviour remain in the play perennially controversial, and the focus of sexual and social awareness sharp and clear. In a production today, the implications of this are usually more interesting than the actual intrigue can be, and a lot of weight is usually put on Emilia's role as a figure of common sense and common humanity, correcting the romantic excesses of the lovers. But no figure in these three tragedies has such a symbolically positional status. Besides, Emilia, for all her virtues, has a stupidity and lack of imagination comparable in its own way to that of her husband; while her views on the sex war, from the feminine angle, are as pungent as his. Certainly the role of the women is important, but it is Desdemona alone who, because of her love, can remain unconscious of the tragedy/comedy element, as she does of the polarity between sex and love.

For her Othello is no more 'the noble Moor whom our full senate / Call all in all sufficient', than he is the hollow man of bombast and self-love seen by Iago. Love needs neither to praise nor to deflate. Could Desdemona have heard her husband's last speech before he kills himself she would have understood it, as she understood and loved when he came to visit and told her of his 'travel's history'. She would have understood in it both the soldier and the man who loved her, the man whom Leavis characteristically finds nothing but a spectacle of self-pity ('Contemplating the spectacle of himself, Othello is overcome with the pathos of it'). Loving as she does, she is not herself subject either to that kind of critical definition and diagnosis, the kind that Iago, and even her own father, seek to make about her. Why did she love? To her father it was witchcraft; to Iago, lust. Is she physically attracted to Othello? Naturally she is and equally naturally she isn't: the question is irrelevant because she loves him. In his wife's eye and mind ('But here's my husband') Othello is none of the things spectators have found him, neither heroic nor credulous, no monster and not a god either, but a man capable alike of good and bad. Her unchanging and undiscriminating love restores the balance between the comic and the tragic and sustains the whole precarious structure.

> Unkindness may do much
> And his unkindness may defeat my life,
> But never taint my love.

That emotion irradiates the play. The few glimpses we have of it do not belong to the world of the tragic or comic vision, the world of Iago and Emilia or of 'the plumed troop and the big wars / That make ambition virtue', or even of those 'antres vast and deserts idle Rough quarries, rocks, and hills whose heads touch heaven'. The glimpses we have are of a private world – too private for a play – and one called into being by a recognition, a marriage of true minds.

> This to hear
> Would Desdemona seriously incline:
> But still the house affairs would draw her thence;
> Which ever as she could with haste dispatch,
> She'd come again, and with a greedy ear
> Devour up my discourse: which I observing,
> Took once a pliant hour, and found good means
> To draw from her a prayer of earnest heart
> That I would all my pilgrimage dilate,
> Whereof by parcels she had something heard,
> But not intentively.
>
> (I iii 145–55)

A sign of love: the impulse to catch up on and complete all the instalments; to possess, and systematically, everything in that past. It is the same possession that will bid Othello wear his gloves and feed on nourishing dishes and keep him warm; and attempt to further his interests in the same way, and with the same single-mindedness, by pleading for Cassio. 'Our general's general' Cassio calls Desdemona. She has committed herself to love as to the wars, and she will be killed by it: but that fate is no more tragic than it is comic that she should fuss the great commander about his gloves. For Desdemona love and sex are undistinguished aspects of the private life, the life that the play and its characters cannot touch, that even Othello's madness cannot touch. *Othello* is a tragedy of privacy, a phrase that itself expresses incongruity, for as with most Shakespearean tragedy, success is achieved by a treatment unsuited to the form. And it is the lack of suiting which makes the theme perennial; the tearing down of a privacy is a subject which fits our age, as it might fit any age. It lets in chaos, and lets out love.

Christopher Norris

From *POST-STRUCTURALIST SHAKESPEARE*

LEAVIS'S ESSAY on *Othello* (Leavis 1952) is a typically comba-
tive and charged piece of writing. It sets out not only to
interpret the play but to treat it as a primer for criticism, a test-
case of what responsive reading ought to be when measured
against the vital complexity of Shakespeare's language. It also
carries on a running polemic against A. C. Bradley and his
idea of 'character' as the primary, psychological reality of Shakespearean drama. More specifically, Leavis pours scorn on
Bradley's portrayal of Iago as a villain of near-superhuman
resourceful cunning, and of Othello as his nobly-suffering idealized counterpart. Leavis's arguments are sufficiently well
known to require no detailed summary here. Sufficient to say that
he views Othello as laid open to Iago's insinuating wiles by a fatal
combination of weaknesses in his own temperament. The Bradleian account is a falsification of the play resulting from the naive
assumption that Othello's opinion of himself is also the opinion
that we, as audience or readers, are supposed to entertain. In
fact, Leavis argues, the contrary signs are unmistakeably *there*
in Othello's strain of grandiloquent rhetoric, his indulgence in
manic alternating moods of heroic projection and plangent
self-pity. Othello falls victim to flaws in his own make-up
which are merely obscured by viewing him, like Bradley, as
the noble dupe of a devilishly complex and interesting Iago.

'Like Bradley' has a pointed ambiguity here. Bradley's
account of *Othello* is branded by Leavis as 'naive', 'sentimental' and 'idealizing' – as sharing, in short, precisely that complex of temperamental flaws that Leavis detects in Othello

178

himself. This is in keeping with the logic of Leavis's argument, and gives rise to some neatly turned jokes at Bradley's expense. Thus 'Iago's knowledge of Othello's character amounts pretty much to Bradley's knowledge of it (except, of course, that Iago cannot realise Othello's nobility quite to the full)' (Leavis 1952, p. 137). Or again, with more heavy-handed irony: 'to equate Bradley's knowledge of Othello with Othello's own was perhaps unfair to Othello'. Every detail of the Bradleian account can be held up to ridicule as yet another instance of patent simple-mindedness and sentimentality. The difference of views between Bradley and Leavis becomes oddly intertwined with the drama played out between Othello and Iago. Leavis conceives himself as speaking up for a tough-minded realist assessment of the play inherently at odds with Bradley's 'idealizing' approach. One desirable result, as Leavis sees it, is to undermine the romantic fascination with Iago as a character of baffling complexity and sinister appeal. Leavis's counter-idealist reading is at any rate 'a fit reply to the view of Othello as necessary material and provocation for a display of Iago's fiendish intellectual superiority' (p. 138).

Leavis can therefore claim support for his reading in the fact that this is, after all *Othello's* and not *Iago's* tragedy. Bradley's account has the absurd upshot of reducing the play to 'Iago's character in action'. Nor is he alone in this, since the Bradleian reading – as Leavis ruefully observes – has been current, even prevalent, at least since Coleridge. It thus remains for Leavis, writing in the face of this 'sustained and sanctioned perversity', to cut through the layers of sentimental falsehood and restore the play to its rightful interpretation.

The plain fact that has to be asserted ... is that in Shakespeare's tragedy of *Othello* Othello is the chief personage – the chief personage in such a sense that the tragedy may fairly be said to be Othello's character in action.

(Leavis 1952, p. 138)

Yet there is clearly a sense in which the logic of Leavis's argument tends to undercut this confidently orthodox assertion. His attitude of prosecuting zeal toward Bradley cannot help but carry over into his treatment of Othello, just as – conversely – Othello's romanticized self-image finds an echo and analogue (according to Leavis) in Bradley's reading. And there is, furthermore, a touch of Iago's corrosive or deflationary cynicism in the way that Leavis sets out to confound those twin representatives of virtuous self-ignorance, Othello and Bradley. The latter, 'his knowledge of Othello coinciding virtually with Othello's, sees nothing but doomed nobility and pathos. By a further twist of the same interpretative logic one can see Othello's nobly suffering innocence. If Bradley's blinkered idealism is, as Leavis says, 'invincible', so also is Leavis's ruthlessly debunking approach.

It is not uncommon for critics to become thus involved in curious patterns of compulsive repetition which take rise from their resolutely *partial* understanding of a literary text. Criticism belongs to what Freud called the work of 'secondary revision', a process aimed at achieving some consistency of 'fit' between manifest and latent sense, but also producing all manner of disguise, repression and 'uncanny' repetition of themes. This compulsion is most in evidence where critics deal with an overtly ambiguous narrative like Henry James's *The Turn of the Screw*. The text seems to support two opposite interpretations – the 'psychological' and 'supernatural' – and to offer no consistent means of deciding between them. Recent deconstructionist readings have shown how critics mostly espouse one side or the other, and are thus forced to suppress or unconsciously distort any textual evidence which controverts their reading (see Felman 1977 and Brooke-Rose 1981). If the story turns – as the 'naturalists' would have it – on neurotic delusions suffered by James's governess-narrator, then her symptoms are oddly reproduced in the gaps and obsessional lapses of argument displayed by the critics. Such 'Freudian' readings are crudely reductive in their wholesale, unmediated use of psychoanalytic terminology and method. On the other hand, the 'supernatural' version of James's tale requires that the interpreter pass over some striking indications of neurosis and paranoid delusion on the part of the governess. In both cases there is an inbuilt bias of approach which unconsciously produces its own tell-tale symptoms of thematic displacement and reworking.

Post-structuralism is perhaps best characterized by its willingness to acknowledge this predicament, rather than set itself up as a 'meta-language' ideally exempt from the puzzles and perplexities of literary texts. The structuralist enterprise aimed at precisely this ideal: that criticism should aspire to a 'science' of the text which would finally uncover its invariant 'grammars' of structure and style. This approach laid down a firm disciplinary line between literature and the systematic discourse of knowledge which sought to comprehend it. But such ambitions soon gave way as critics like Roland Barthes came to recognize the inadequacy of formalistic methods and the way in which textual signification exceeds all merely heuristic limits. Barthes's *S/Z* (1970) marked a turning point in this passage from structuralist to post-structuralist thinking. At the same time Jacques Derrida was developing his powerful deconstructive critique of traditional epistemic categories, including that conservative notion of 'structure' which he found implicit in Saussure, Lévi-Strauss and others (see especially Derrida 1978). Textuality was recognized as breaking all the bounds of a conceptual regime which had striven to hold it in check. And this betokened a corresponding shift in the relations between literature, criticism and textual theory. As the latter relinquished its claim to sovereign knowledge, so it took on something of the complex, contradictory character normally attributed to 'literary' language.

Shoshana Felman (1977) reveals the extraordinary lengths to which this process can be carried in her reading of various critics on *The Turn of the Screw*. Interpretation can only repeat, in compulsive fashion, the acts of misreading exemplified by various, more or less deluded characters *within the tale*. Any attempt to provide an omniscient critical reading is always foredoomed to this chronic partiality of viewpoint. As Felman puts it:

In seeking to 'explain' and *master* literature, in refusing, that is, to become a *dupe* of literature . . . the psychoanalytic reading, ironically enough, turns out to be a reading which *represses the unconscious*, which represses, paradoxically, the unconscious which it purports to be 'explaining'.

(Felman 1977, p. 193)

This applies as much to self-styled 'theoretical' criticism as to essays of a more traditional interpretative cast. Such distinctions break down against the 'uncanny' transference which carries across from the narrative to its various symptomatic partial readings. The tale is *contagious* in the sense that it creates a frustrated desire for coherence, one which can never be satisfied except by certain self-defeating acts of textual repression.

Leavis's essay on *Othello* bears all the marks of this obscure compulsion at work. It is to Iago that Leavis attributes a 'deflating, unbeglamouring, brutally realistic mode of speech' (Leavis 1952, p. 144). But the same description could equally be applied to Leavis's essay, working as it does to 'deflate' and 'unbeglamour' the nobility of character mistakenly imputed to Othello. At times this curious transference of roles comes close to the surface in Leavis's prose:

Iago's power, in fact, in the temptation-scene is that he represents something that is in Othello . . . the essential traitor is within the gates. For if Shakespeare's Othello too is simple-minded, he is nevertheless more complex than Bradley's. Bradley's Othello, is, rather, Othello's; it being an essential datum regarding the Shakespearean Othello that he has an ideal conception of himself.

(Leavis 1952, pp. 140–1)

What makes Othello more rewardingly 'complex' than Bradley can show is the fact that his character (as Leavis reads it) partakes somewhat of Iago's destructive nature. And by the same odd logic it is Leavis's account of *Othello* which raises the play to a level of dramatic complexity undreamt of in Bradley's naive philosophy. The undoing of simple-minded virtue takes place not so much 'in' the play – since Othello is already thus tainted – but in the contest of readings between a tough-minded Leavis and a feebly romanticizing Bradley. As with James's tale, so here: interpretation is drawn into a scene of displaced re-enactment where critics have no choice but to occupy positions already taken up by characters within the play.

This lends an added resonance to Leavis's metaphor of the 'traitor within the gates'. A certain curious logic of host-and-parasite is insistently at work in Leavis's essay. It operates by a series of thematic reversals, substituting 'maturity' for 'inno-cence' ('Bradley, that is, in his comically innocent way'), 'real-ism' for 'idealism' and – ultimately – 'Leavis' for 'Bradley'. In each case the second (dominant) term has a Iago-like ambiva-lence, exposing simple-minded virtue to the trials of an un-deceiving, rock-bottom worldly knowledge. Leavis attacks the sentimental reading which prefers to see the play 'through Othello's eyes rather than Shakespeare's'. His own account is designed to correct this romantic bias by focusing attention on those qualities of Othello's *language* – in particular, his rhetoric of nobly-suffering pathos – which supposedly should lead us to a proper 'Shakespearean' reading. In fact it is quite obvious that Leavis is simply substituting one interpretation for another, his own drastically 'deflating' account for Bradley's idealizing ver-sion. The claim that his approach enables us to see Othello 'through Shakespeare's eyes' is merely an enabling fiction, though one that few critics seem prepared to forego. Othello's great flaw – like Bradley's after him – consists very largely in a failure to grasp the Leavisite criteria of poetic health and vitality.

Leavis makes the point plainly enough in objecting to Bradley's description of Othello as 'the greatest poet' among Shakespeare's tragic heroes. For Leavis, this provides just one more example of Bradley's inveterate romanticism, his habit of seeing Othello through Othello's own self-deluding eyes.

If the impression made by Othello's own utterance is often poetical as well as poetic, that is Shakespeare's way, not of representing him as a poet, but of conveying the romantic glamour that, for Othello himself and others, invests Othello and what he stands for.

(Leavis 1952, p. 143)

Those 'others' include Bradley but not, of course, Leavis – or indeed Iago, who makes some very effective points of his own about Othello's 'romantic glamour'. All the same it is hard to see that Leavis's case rests on anything more than his pre-disposed view of what constitutes 'the Shakespearean use of language'. And that view rests in turn, as I have argued, on a complex of deeply ideological assumptions about language, thought and sensibility. Poetry is conceived as expressing the truth of a vital and properly self-critical response to the re-alities of lived experience. 'Intelligence', 'maturity' and 'life' are the fixed co-ordinates around which Leavis constructs his highly selective 'tradition' of English poetry. It is a view of literary history which locates its main high-point in the early seventeenth century (Shakespeare and Donne), and which judges later poets – especially the Romantics – against that mythical ideal of a 'unified sensibility' belonging to a long-lost 'organic' culture. If Milton and Shelley, among others, are tried by this standard and found sadly wanting, so also is Shakespeare's Othello.

Leavis set out his main criteria in a number of early *Scrutiny* pieces (reprinted in Leavis 1975). Among other critical touchstones (like 'thought' and 'judgement'), he offered close readings of several short poems intended to emphasize the difference between 'emotion' and 'sentimentality'. The hall-mark of sentimental poetry, Leavis argued, was its surrender to a mood of plangent, self-regarding pathos unchecked by any sense of 'mature' critical restraint. Such is the standard that Leavis applies to Othello's characteristic strain. It involves, Leavis writes, 'an attitude *towards* the emotion expressed – an attitude of a kind we are familiar with in the analysis of sentimentality' (Leavis 1952, p. 143). Which of course presupposes that Othello's rhetoric is *placed*, or shown up for what it is, by the implicit contrast with Shakespeare's most vital ('creative-exploratory') style. Leavis would have it that this contrast is self-evident, at least to any reader 'not protected (like Bradley) by a very obstinate preconception'. Romantic misconceptions should be easy to rebut 'because there, to point to, is the text, plain and unequivocal'. This would make it odd, to say the least, that critics have differed so widely over the play's interpretation, and that Leavis should feel summoned to redeem such a history of multiplied error and delusion. But this is to ignore the more likely explanation: that Leavis has invented his own *Othello* in pursuit of an imaginary coherence required by certain pressing ideological imperatives.

These motives are evident in the curious shifts of argument-ation which Leavis adopts in the course of his essay. The central appeal is to a normative idea of human 'character' and 'experience', closely related to the virtues of 'mature', self-critical intelligence which Leavis finds at work in all great poetry. Shakespeare's genius has to consist in this consummate union of truth-to-experience and language raised to its highest creative power. Othello, says Leavis, 'is (as we have all been) cruelly and tragically wronged', so that 'the invitation to identify oneself with him is indeed hardly resistible' (Leavis 1952, p. 153). There is irony here at Bradley's expense, but also a measure of acceptance, necessary if Othello is to retain any remnant of genuine 'tragic' dignity. For it is the nature of Shakespeare's genius, as Leavis goes on to argue, that it 'carries with it a large facility in imposing conviction locally'. Othello's self-deceiving rhetoric must be taken to possess at least a certain moving force if the play is to achieve its effect. 'He is (as we have all been) cruelly and tragically wronged' – the essay founders on this quite undecidable mixture of Iago-like irony and generalized 'human' pathos. Such are the conflicts engendered by a reading which stakes its authority on presupposed absolute values of language, morality and truth. At the close, Leavis writes, 'he is still the same Othello in whose essential make-up the tragedy lay'. It is on this notion of 'essential' human nature – both as norm and as measure of 'tragic' deviation – that Leavis's essay splinters into so many diverse and conflicting claims.

Anthony Brennan

IAGO, THE STRATEGIST OF SEPARATION

IN TRAGEDY the audience is often given knowledge that is denied to the characters. Because the audience is not subject to clouded judgement by participation in the action, it has the freedom to understand why catastrophe must occur and must watch helplessly while the characters use their freedom and proceed in ignorance to make assurance of death double sure. This burden of special knowledge with which the playwright invests his audience can be exploited in a great variety of ways. The tension experienced by the audience can be tuned to an almost unbearable level when the audience feels that the characters are ensnared in a trick of plot which simple information could dispel. Many of Shakespeare's tragedies, however, do not aim to produce a sense of helpless frustration in the audience at its inability to interfere in the course of events.

In *King Lear* we watch Lear stumbling helplessly towards madness but because he has spent a lifetime wreathed in his own illusions about the nature of his power the audience does not feel that it has any special knowledge which would help him out. Most of the things we might think of saying are being spoken to him by the Fool. As an audience we are likely rather to hang back as Lear, in his harrowing quest, constructs an arctic philosophy of the world and endeavours to impose his mad vision on everyone. Only in the writ issued for Cordelia's death are we tested by our helplessness to interfere in events, our inability to prevent the extinction of that last spark of hope in a darkening world. We do not feel inclined, in watching

Macbeth, to call out a warning to the hero that the Weird Sisters are paltering with him in a double sense. Macbeth is not the ignorant, helpless victim of external forces. We move step by step with him into his dark knowledge of the equivocal nature of evil actions as he finds that the pursuit of power and the endeavour to maintain it empties the world of all meaning and comfort. In *Hamlet* we are not made privy to special information which could help the hero. It is true that Hamlet walks unaware into the triple treachery of the fencing match but he has, by that time, reached a level of stoical acceptance of his fate which the audience has been induced to share. We know that revenge cannot be accomplished save at the cost of his life. I am not suggesting that the audience *can* interfere in the action of the play, only that under certain circumstances the playwright can make the audience fervently wish that it could. When we spend much of our time thinking 'if only they knew', itching to pass on simple information which could save their lives, then the playwright achieves his success by bringing the danger his characters are in tantalizingly close and yet manipulating the necessary separation which must be maintained between the audience and the drama.

In *Othello* Shakespeare made radical alterations in his source-story to produce an experience of almost unbearable tension which has no parallel in world drama. There is a convention in English pantomime which generously provides the audience with a release denied by Shakespeare in *Othello*. Early on in a pantomime the hero usually talks to the audience warning of the dangers he anticipates from the villains. He asks for the audience's help in looking out for traps that are set for him in his absence and gives a password which must be shouted out to warn him of trouble. The audience thereafter screams out the word whenever the hero is about to stumble into unexpected snares. By feigning temporary deafness the hero can tune up the audience's involvement to a delirium of lusty bellowing in a co-operative triumph over evil. *Othello* achieves its effect by reversing this process so that the audience is relentlessly victimized.

The structure of *Othello* develops in a series of improvised, undeclared playlets in which Iago organizes roles for his victims. The degree of control he maintains over the characters allows him to induce a psychological alienation and separation between some of them. This produces a physical separation which is registered by the finely judged proportions in the character interactions. Iago is helped over all the weak points in his plot by his victims themselves. Even the mere random contingency of events for a while allows all the accidents to knit up the design where it could unravel and expose Iago's villainy. We may smile indulgently at the many recorded instances of unsophisticated audiences shouting out warnings to Othello about the handkerchief, or invading the stage to belabour the unbearable villain Iago. We have to acknowledge, however, that the play's success depends on arousing our impulsive wish to stop the action and that the more, as civilized playgoers, we stifle that impulse the more the play achieves its ascendancy over us. It is not simply that we lack the release valve provided in pantomime but rather that we are confronted again and again by our helplessness. We have no access to a hero who needs our help, rather we have access to the villain sharing his plans and explaining to us why the characters must fall into the roles he has shaped for them.

What makes Iago unbearable is his ability to combine two roles very familiar to an Elizabethan audience. He is very much like the intermediary, commentator friends, those blunt, honest figures who try to make the tragic heroes see the true nature of their situations – Enobarbus, Kent, Lear's Fool, Menenius Agrippa, Apemantus, Mercutio. He is a soldier, a rough diamond who is foul-mouthed, cynical, and has a low opinion of women. Because he admits to his limitations he is trusted. The role of blunt soldier and honest friend conceal a descendant of the Vice-figure, a man who is an amoral rag-bag of confused motivations invested with a cynicism so profound that he must pervert or destroy any sign of virtue. Shakespeare wrote of other tragic heroes who reject the judgement of their blunt advisers because their very natures make them incapable of cautious restraint. They must embrace their fates even at the cost of the destruction fearfully prophesied for them. Othello, however, accepts the version of reality thrust upon him by his 'honest' friend in the belief that he is saving himself from miserable embroilment in a corrupt world. Thus in most of the tragedies it is the commentating figure who, in the limitations in his understanding, enables us to come to terms with the full complexity of the fate with which the tragic hero is coping. In *Othello* it is the hero who is separated off from the full complexity of the circumstances in the world in which he exists. The very deliberate organization of the play to produce an unbearable tension around Iago as a strategist of separation can be seen in the radical changes Shakespeare makes in the source-story. Cinthio's novella contains, on the face of it, very little promise of dramatic tension. Shakespeare made many alterations of detail especially in tightening up the time-scheme of the sequence of events, in changing the military rank of the originals of Othello and Cassio, and in developing a significant political framework in which his Moor could be featured. He invents a romantic courtship between Othello and Desdemona and the objections of Brabantio to his daughter's secret alliance. He does not make any radical changes in the characters on which Desdemona and Cassio are based. Shakespeare's most significant changes in developing his scenic structures are in the dramatic methods he finds of unfolding Iago's dominating agency in the story.

Cinthio's ensign is quite a conventional villain and there is little indication in the narrative that he has any detailed interaction with any character other than the Moor in securing his aim. His motivation is explained quite clearly as a desire for Desdemona. He tries in devious ways to make her aware of his passion but she takes no notice. He imagines the corporal receives more of her favour than himself and his plot develops out of jealousy and his need for revenge. Shakespeare touches many times on an array of possible motives but they are only threads in the complex web of Iago's evil nature. Cinthio's purpose is to a large degree didactic and he has no interest in ambiguities which would cloud the issues. Shakespeare compels our attention by making us pursue a mystery which we cannot ultimately solve. Cinthio tells us that his ensign is a cunning villain, but his Janus-headed personality, his ability to be convincing in the role of honest, trusty friend, is exhibited only in relations with the Moor. The first specific example of his ability to take others in by role playing comes near the end of the novella in his attempted murder of the corporal. After he has cut off the corporal's leg the ensign runs away so as not to be discovered at the scene of the crime. He mingles with those who find the wounded corporal and grieves as if the injury were to his own brother. That is the only crisis in which Cinthio's ensign has to be fast on his feet in juggling roles. Out of that one example Shakespeare develops an accomplished performer who manipulates his various masks in virtually every scene of the play. In fact before we are 200 lines into the play, in the variety of personae Iago presents to Roderigo, Brabantio and Othello, his quick-changing acting skills are more fully developed than in any circumstance Cinthio creates for his ensign. In the novella the ensign develops a plot which works directly on the Moor and involves scarcely any interaction with other characters. The ensign's wife knows of her husband's villainy but plays no part in his stratagems and, through fear of him, never reveals her knowledge. Desdemona has only one interaction with the ensign when he steals her handkerchief and one brief talk with the corporal. Shakespeare chose to make Iago's 'honesty' a central focus of the play. This allows him to develop scenic structures around the ensign's hair-raising, juggling act of conducting interactions with a variety of victims who turn to him for advice and who, between them, innocently perform the tragedy that his monstrous imagination improvises.

Shakespeare wastes no time in declaring Iago's dedication to the creation of illusion. He follows Othello to serve his turn upon him, 'trimmed in forms and visages of duty' (I i 50), and while he keeps his heart attending on himself he throws 'shows of service' on his lord (I i 52). As soon as he has completed his explanation of his theatrical nature to Roderigo (I i 61–5) he proceeds immediately to a demonstration of his skills as stage manager and prompter. Roderigo, unaware of his role as ventriloquist's dummy, is encouraged to arouse Brabantio and plague him with flies. Desdemona's father, pricked down by Iago for the role of bigoted *senex iratus*, plays his part flawlessly. Ignorant that he is in an undeclared play he does, nevertheless, correctly identify the role being played by the prompter shouting from the shadows. His assertion 'Thou art a villain' (I i 117) has both of its Elizabethan senses – the low-born man of ignoble ideas and the man disposed to criminal actions. Though his role is defined so early Iago ensures that his name is not attached to it. We will be within 140 lines of the end of the play before the man Iago destroys will be able to look at the friend he has trusted and see him for what he is – 'Precious villain!' (V ii 236).

One of Shakespeare's most important modifications of Cinthio's novella is the invention of Roderigo. Cinthio centres almost all of his narrative on the relationship of the Moor and the ensign, and the destruction of Disdemona. The corporal and the ensign's wife are quite marginal figures. When Shakespeare chose to structure his play around six major characters he had, mathematically, the opportunity to develop fifteen relationships for on-stage interaction among them. The fact that he chose not to activate five of those relationships at all and three of them in only a sketchy way helps us to understand how he went about the business of making a difficult story credible and compelling. The limitation imposed on Roderigo's interactions is a central example of Shakespeare's skill in developing an important character who is yet kept rigidly separated on stage from those in whose life he is enmeshed. He is in seven scenes of the play and on stage for almost 1000 of its lines. It is Othello's marriage he wants to help destroy, Cassio's reputation he ruins and Cassio's life he tries to take, but after speaking to Brabantio in the opening scene he utters less than a dozen words to characters other than Iago. In six of his scenes he is left on stage alone with

Iago for over 350 lines, which happens to be the second largest interaction, next only to that between Othello and Iago, observed by the audience in the play. For the other 600 lines Roderigo is on stage he is almost entirely mute. He never speaks one word to Desdemona the object of his desire, nor to Othello the object of his envy, and only one line to Cassio whom he is persuaded to murder. He is truly kept in the corner of Iago's jaw, first mouthed to be last swallowed. The fact that Shakespeare gives more on-stage life to the relationship between Iago and Roderigo than to that between Othello and Desdemona serves more purposes than showing how a villain can wind a pliable tool into his plot. Iago's contempt for his fellow men and the glib assertions of his cynical philosophy can be directed at Roderigo because, having so little regard for his 'snipe', he feels no need to hide his demonic nature. Cinthio devotes very little of his narrative to an exploration of the ensign's nature. In the interactions with Roderigo and in the soliloquies Iago speaks, Shakespeare allows the audience ample opportunity to try to understand the nature of his villain's power and the source of his grievances. We are allowed for almost one-sixth of the play to see Iago operating without his mask or with only the covering excuses to Roderigo for the villainy in which he ensnares him. Roderigo is, theoretically, a loophole in Iago's plot because he knows that Cassio was treacherously undone as the Moor's lieutenant. In spite of his knowledge of villainy, the disappointment of his hopes, and his threats to reveal what he knows Roderigo only speaks up on his death-bed.

In the Senate-scene the origin and nature of the relationship between Othello and Desdemona is discussed at length, yet Shakespeare radically limits the on-stage spoken interaction between them. Othello speaks to the senators, the Duke and Iago, she speaks to Brabantio and the Duke. They state their cases separately. Othello directs three lines to her and she speaks not a word to him. We hear the Moor's detailed account of their courting but we see nothing of it, and their married life in Venice is 'but an hour / Of love, of worldly matters and direction' (I iii 298–9). The romantic wooing has been conducted in the nine months Othello has spent in Venice. The basis of the attraction which draws Desdemona to Othello is no doubt more than what Iago will come to call bragging and fantastical lies, but their marriage is certainly not given the maturing of time and experience indicated in Cinthio's story. There they are allowed months of happily married life in Venice and the ensign and his plotting are not introduced until after the Moor and his wife are settled in Cyprus. But Iago can assure Roderigo and himself that as soon as Desdemona comes to know her new husband she will grow tired of him and that sanctimony and a frail vow will hardly be sufficient to hold them together.

The audience has a need of more explanations than are offered to Roderigo for the venomous revenge the ensign promises. Iago obliges: 'it is thought abroad that 'twixt my sheets / Has done my office. I know not if't be true; / But I, for mere suspicion in that kind, / Will do as if for surety' (I iii 381–4). The implication for the audience to take is that Iago is not so much acting from a motive, but rather amusing himself by looking for one. Roderigo is called a 'snipe', a game bird hunted in marshy areas. But Iago has us within his gunsights too. We are sitting ducks distracted by the decoy motivations he sends sailing our way. We are told that Othello 'will as tenderly be led by th' nose / As asses are' (I iii 393–6) even as we ourselves are being led by the nose. Iago has a considerable capacity for self-dramatization. He has an air of *grand guignol* as he reaches out for the trapping of Satanism to terrorize the audience and to give himself a sense of importance: 'Hell and night / Must bring this monstrous birth to the world's light' (I iii 397–8). Though Othello looks down for cloven feet on Iago at the end of the play he knows it is a fable. The ensign's invocation of satanic powers is another method of trailing his coat and piecing out motivations which will satisfy himself and his dupes, including us.

The tension which Shakespeare generates in this play is partly a result of the fact that the characters ensnared in nets are cut off from contact with us while Iago is not. The soliloquies remind me of the hypnotist's trick of turning to banter with the audience when he has frozen someone into an absurdly undignified posture on stage. The narrator of Thomas Mann's story *Mario and the Magician* is an average, decent, middle-class citizen who tries to understand why he feels compelled to stay at a performance in which a crippled grotesquely evil hypnotist, Cipolla, degrades his fellow human beings. It is clear that the magician gains ascendancy not only over his victims who perform his humiliating commands but also from those who passively watch them. At the climax of the show the magician humiliates Mario, a hotel waiter, by forcing him in trance to kiss him on the cheek as if he were his beloved. But when Mario wakes up he shoots the magician dead. The narrator then perceives that he was waiting for that fatal end as a liberation from the horror he had stayed to witness. We cannot, in *Othello*, escape an awareness that we are a source of Iago's power in acting as helpless listeners to his progress reports on his acts of villainy. We are compelled to wait for Emilia to wake from her trance and speak the truth though it costs her her life.

In Cinthio's narrative the Moor and Disdemona sail together over tranquil seas to Cyprus on business which has nothing to do with the danger or strife of war. Shakespeare builds tension out of a series of arrivals from the storm-wracked seas which have separated Othello and Desdemona. The protean Iago plays the role of court jester for the anxious Desdemona. Iago, like Thersites, regards the world as a kind of absurd theatrical spectacle designed to affirm his own cynical evaluation of human nature. It is his rooted conviction that he is in a world of players. Cassio is 'most apt to play the sir' (II i 172–3). Women are players in housewifery who 'rise to play, and go to bed to work' (II i 115). His remarks merely illustrate how undelectable he is as a villain to Desdemona, Cassio and Emilia when he plays blunt, honest soldier. The proportions within the scene are typical of the general design. We have to endure his vulgar slanders, his fusty jests, and his hideous 'asides' on Cassio's courtesy for 70 lines (II i 100–76). In all of the exchanges Shakespeare is working up to the joyful moment when Othello, reunited with Desdemona, expresses in an aria of love the sense that he has reached the very peak of his emotional experience. It is a heart stopping moment but it is only seventeen lines long (II i 180–97). We will remember this flash of ecstasy for the rest of Othello's muddied course. We do not at this point know it but, in this brief exchange, Othello speaks more than half the lines he will direct to Desdemona before he becomes irrecoverably lost in the toils of suspicions that she has cuckolded him.

We see Iago at the extreme point of insolence when he attends to the task of reinterpreting the innocent Cassio's solicitous courtesy to Desdemona in a sinister and fantastic light for the crestfallen Roderigo. The poor trash of Venice soon accepts a role in a plot to eliminate his rival on evidence he has seen neither with his own eyes, nor, in any degree of conviction, with Iago's. That, however, is not the most remarkable example of gullibility in this scene. How can Iago best convince the audience to share his vision of a corrupt world? By showing, as he does in the soliloquy following Roderigo's departure, how easily he can swallow his own lies. He believes Cassio loves Desdemona. Come to that he loves her himself. He suspects Othello of cuckolding him with Emilia and, as an afterthought, suspects Cassio with his nightcap too (II i 280–306). The leisure allowed to him to strike such teasing postures oppresses the audience. We have much more of Iago than we ever want or need. He has over two-thirds of the more than 200 lines of soliloquies and asides in the play. By the time Othello is first alone on stage musing in torment (III iii 242–3, 258–77) Iago has already delivered six of his soliloquies. Nothing bewilders us more about the unfathomable nature of evil than Iago's playful attempts, in his dance of the seven motives, to explain himself to himself.

While Cassio performs the role of stage-drunk in Iago's undeclared play, the ensign, a wizard at doubling, undertakes a bewildering variety of roles: convivial fellow-officer encouraging Cassio to celebrate his general's marriage (II iii 12–43, 60–113); enthusiastic author and director explaining to us how industrious he has been in setting the lieutenant up for catastrophe (44–59); concerned spectator revealing Cassio's lamentable weakness to Montano (114–39); stage-manager directing Roderigo in Cassio's tracks. His plot reaches a swift climax (140–58) and, once he has ensured that the bell arouses Othello, he is the only trusty unbiased reporter available. The review he gives of the theatrical triumph he has improvised modestly conceals the array of talents he has displayed in it.

The only exchange Othello has with Cassio, the subject of Iago's report, is a mere four lines long. Othello will not interact directly with Cassio again on stage until the very end of the play. The two characters between whom Iago forges a monstrous antagonism are involved in direct speech on stage for a mere 40 lines. He is able to keep his victims apart and work on them separately in isolation. He does not even have to hunt them down. In asking for the ensign's advice, as Cassio does, they make themselves available for roles in the improvised plots he is forever hatching. Following upon his success as a drunk Cassio accepts the role, though he knows it not, of adulterous cuckolder of his general. Because Iago's contempt for us is equal to his contempt for those on stage he can cockily begin to sell to us the plausibility of his new work-in-progress:

> And what's he then that says I play the villain,
> When this advice is free I give and honest,
> Probal to thinking, and indeed the course
> To win the Moor again?
>
> (II iii 319–22)

Iago demands that we acknowledge his acting skills as trusted counsellor. Shakespeare had already presented a stage-villain hissing diabolism in the role of Lucianus in *The Murder of Gonzago* with his 'Thoughts black, hands apt, drugs fit, and time agreeing' (*Hamlet*, III ii 245). Iago pours a different kind of poison in everyone's ears but no one on stage can ever share the kind of irritation Hamlet feels at the self-indulgent showiness of an actor mugging villainy: 'Begin murderer. Leave thy damnable faces and begin' (III ii 242–3). That irritation is the privilege of the audience of *Othello*. The *performance* of villainy is reserved for us in private shows, as here when Iago gives us, in what amounts to an insolent flourish of his cape, a touch of fire and brimstone villainy (II iii 333–6).

In Cinthio's narrative the initial events which lead to the Moor's jealousy are not organized by the ensign. The corporal falls from grace without any help. Nor does the ensign have any part in advising the corporal as to how he might repair his fortunes. The corporal does not even have to ask Disdemona to plead for him since she does it of her own accord. Shakespeare has Iago set on Cassio to sue to Desdemona, urge Emilia to persuade Desdemona to undertake the suit and promise to draw Othello out of the way while they work out their strategy. Desdemona with an admirable and predictable zeal, which nevertheless distresses the audience, explains how sincerely she will perform her role as suppliant (III iii 21–6).

Shakespeare invents many details as additions to Cinthio's story to justify the separation and breakdown in the relationship of the Moor and his wife. He amplifies the political context by inventing a crisis in the Venetian state which involves a battle with the Turks. He occupies Othello with the business of ensuring that peace is kept in Cyprus. Cinthio's entirely domestic story is set in a more public arena and in a severely telescoped time-frame. Shakespeare radically alters the weighting of interactions to overcome what he may have perceived to be implausible developments in the original story. Much of the success of Iago's plot depends on the scant knowledge Othello has acquired of Desdemona. His initial romantic courting has not had any time to yield place to the daily give and take of marriage. Shakespeare indicates an absence of experienced knowledge between the two in a variety of ways – the wooing, the elopement, the crisis which interrupts their wedding night and sends them in separate ships to Cyprus, and the further interruption because of Cassio's rowdiness.

But he achieves his aim mainly by allowing them so little time on stage together. When Iago finally turns on Othello alone to begin the first long assault in his campaign (III iii 93) we have to that point seen Desdemona and her husband on stage together on five occasions, but they have shared, almost equally, less than 90 lines of direct interaction in a play which has already run over 1500 lines. At no point have we seen them alone on stage. We will, in fact, only ever see them alone together on two occasions and the second one is the murder scene. In the second half of the play Shakespeare brings husband and wife together on five occasions for some 270 lines of direct interaction, three-quarters of the stage-life they spend together which serves at every point to confirm the suspicions Iago has aroused in the Moor.

An effective contrast to the brief glimpses we have in the first half of the play of Othello and Desdemona together are the extensive interactions Iago shares with several characters as he prepares to destroy their relationship. We see him talking to Roderigo on four occasions in interactions which take up three times as many lines as those given to the moments between the Moor and his wife. The sequence devoted to the cheering up of the dismissed Cassio by Iago takes up 70 lines, and Iago, in jesting with Desdemona at the landing in Cyprus, shares almost as many lines with her as she has with Othello in their various exchanges up to the mid-point of the play. When Iago tells his general that he does not know his wife well our experience in the play dovetails at all points to make the suggestion plausible.

In Cinthio the Moor is familiar with the ways of Venice and he resides there long enough to establish domestic felicity in his marriage. Othello, by contrast, asserts that he has no experience of the social mores of domestic and civilian life (I iii 81–7). Shakespeare inventively enlarges on Othello's exotic nature in many of his speeches and in Iago's private analyses of the 'honest fool' he is misleading. Shakespeare had long trained his audiences to take for granted the theatrical nature of the world with its multiple levels of illusion. He develops

Othello as a character to whom this European idea is alien and repellent, a quality for which there is no hint in Cinthio. Iago introduces Othello to the idea that acting is a basic practice of Venetian society manners:

> I would not have your free and noble nature,
> Out of self-bounty, be abused. Look to't.
> I know our country disposition well:
> In Venice they do let God see the pranks
> They dare not show their husbands; their best conscience
> Is not to leave't undone, but keep't unknown.
>
> (III iii 199–204)

Of all Iago's strategies of separation this is the most crucial, for it moves Othello into an area of which he has neither knowledge nor experience where the certain truth he seeks is, by definition, elusive. We are inclined not to impute simple gullibility to Othello as the cause of his fall because of the way everyone trusts Iago's honesty. But there are more particular reasons why Othello, who is induced to distrust Venetians, can nevertheless trust Iago. The ensign is, in the manner that Othello thinks of himself, a rough, blunt-spoken soldier who has lived on battlefields where the sophisticated role playing of civilian society has little opportunity to flourish. Iago is a man without polish more to be relished in the soldier than in the scholar. Soldiers in every age need little persuasion to look on civilians with their mannered courtesy and complex codes of behaviour as soft, effete and unreliable. Iago has shared the dangers of war with Othello when he has 'seen the cannon / When it hath blown his ranks into the air / And, like the devil, from his very arm / Puffed his own brother' (III iv 134–7). Othello is admirable in that he seems to have found in Desdemona a gentleness that he has placed no value on hitherto. But he is aware that there is some risk in abandoning his simple bachelor habits (I ii 24–8). When Iago asserts that Othello has stumbled into a theatre of illusions whose conventions he does not understand, Shakespeare has ensured, in every detail, that Othello has no accumulation of experience that would allow him to dispute it. The whole world becomes changed from

what it once was and Iago offers to act as critic and commentator to help Othello spy out some flaws in the disguises
adopted by those around him. Othello relies on the figure he
has known and trusted longest for he 'knows all qualities, with
a learned spirit / Of human dealings' (III iii 259–60).

In Shakespeare we feel Iago to be older and more experienced than Cassio. Cinthio makes no such distinction nor does
he give any evidence that the ensign has known the Moor
longer and shared many battle experiences with him. Shakespeare's Moor has developed a friendship with the young
Cassio who came a-wooing with him. He is mentor and patron
to one who, according to Iago, has 'never set a squadron in a
field' and who has made his mark in training as a theoretician.
Cinthio's ensign is superior in rank to the corporal so there is
no bitter resentment about any promotion. We may surmise,
without uncritically accepting Iago's views, that he was passed
over by Othello because he was so much taken for granted:
'And I (of whom his eyes had seen the proof / At Rhodes, at
Cyprus, and on other grounds / Christian and heathen) must
be belee'd and calmed' (I i 28–30). The more he relies on the
friend he has so long taken for granted the more he is separated
from any comfortable acceptance of the new friends who come
from the treacherous Venetian world of which he has such
limited experience.

The advantage Iago gains in persuading Othello that he is
in a world of tricky, skilful actors is that it gives him an
unchallengeable excuse for the shortage of unambiguous evidence of Desdemona's infidelity: 'Where's satisfaction? / It is
impossible you should see this, / Were they as prime as goats,
as hot as monkeys' (III iii 401–3). When Othello presses hard
for 'ocular proof' Iago can only offer the next best thing – a
report of a dream, a mere imitation of an action, Cassio miming
and rehearsing his act of love in his sleep. This is as close as
you can get to evidence in catching out the clever Venetian
actors in their sins. Well, that is not quite true. There is the
handkerchief. Commentators frequently point out how flimsy
Iago's plot is but fail to note that were it not so flimsy it could

not succeed. If at any point Iago offers Othello a fact which
breaches the completely theatrical, illusionary façade he has
created then he gives him a means of tearing it down. Iago
cannot take Othello behind the scenes because there is no
behind the scenes. Othello is separated from a world that does
not exist. A piece of linen is not much but we see very clearly
that, with only slightly altered circumstances, it would be
enough to destroy Iago's plot.

Shakespeare invents an exotic history of associations for
which Othello values the handkerchief, makes Iago's use of it
daring to the point of folly, and complicates the dangers associated with the talisman far beyond anything Cinthio imagines.
In the novella the ensign's wife has no contact with it, rather it
is the ensign himself who, without anyone's knowledge, steals
the handkerchief from Desdemona as she is distracted in the
enjoyment of playing with her child. There is never, in Cinthio,
any chance that this link in the plot could fail. The handkerchief completes its journey from the ensign's hand to the
corporal's lodging where the Moor is brought to observe a
sempstress in the window copying its design. Shakespeare
organizes Iago's use of the handkerchief as a lucky, stumbling
run across a minefield. The audience knows, as he does not
when he receives it from Emilia, that the handkerchief Iago
claims he has seen Cassio wiping his beard with earlier in the
day was only minutes past in Othello's hand or pressed to his
forehead by Desdemona. Though Othello has failed to register
its very distinctive embroidery the audience momentarily retains hope that the napkin can be rescued from its deadly
significance. When Desdemona comes on hunting for it (III iv)
we know that she was unaware of using it to soothe Othello's
horn-mad brow. As Emilia fails to reveal knowledge of its
whereabouts we know that this trifle light as air will become
confirmation strong as proofs of holy writ. It takes only 150
lines to make the flimsiest link in Iago's plot its lynch-pin.

In embroiling Emilia in the handkerchief's varied journey
Shakespeare indicates to us her ignorance of the really vicious
nature of her husband. His method of increasing the density of

character involvement in the handkerchief's journey not only allows Iago to survive several transits of thin ice, it also allows many opportunities for Othello to convince himself that he is ensnared by Venetian actors. The napkin passes from Desdemona's hand to Othello's to the floor, to Emilia to Iago. After it has been dropped in Cassio's lodging we see him give it to Bianca and we and Othello see her in jealousy throw it back at him. When Othello challenges Desdemona about the loss of his handkerchief she insists, as the wife does not in Cinthio, that they talk about returning Cassio to favour, refusing to let this red herring put her from her suit. It can only seem to Othello that the Venetian actress Iago has warned him of has extraordinary nerve in treating him as a cuckolded fool to his face when he talks of the evidence which makes her pretence invalid.

Shakespeare made significant changes in the peeping-Tom incident, where Othello attends to Iago's conversation with Cassio (IV i 100–66), as it appears in Cinthio. Cinthio's Moor does not overhear and misconstrue an actual conversation. He watches from a distance as the ensign talks to the corporal and interprets guilt simply from the corporal's gestures. Only afterwards does he hear from the ensign, who has complete freedom to invent, the actual contents of the conversation. In Shakespeare this painfully vivid scene demonstrates Iago's extraordinary luck in the risky improvisations he attempts. In addition to the good performance Iago gets from Cassio he receives the unexpected bonus of Bianca, as a self-recruiting member of his repertory company, bringing on the will-o'-the-wisp handkerchief as a final touch, and an addition to Cinthio, that stones Othello's heart. The Moor sees that a slut is his wife's chief competitor for Cassio's affections. It is the placing of this scene which gives it such potency. In Cinthio the sequence comes much earlier in the story just after the ensign has spread his lies and before the Moor has been told about the handkerchief or challenged his wife about its loss. When the Moor there, with no other 'evidence', accepts the ensign's report of a conversation conducted out of his hearing, he is

certainly buying a pig in a poke. Shakespeare's peeping-Tom
scene seems to Othello the cast-iron, solid evidence he has
been looking for, a behind-the-scene's glimpse of the Venetian
without his mask condemning himself out of his own mouth.
Othello has already heard about lecherous dreams, about
his handkerchief, and reports by Iago of Cassio's private
admissions of adultery. He has listened to his wife's denial of
the loss of the handkerchief and to her pleading for Cassio; he
has been driven to the point of seizure by his inability to catch
out these Venetians. So by the time Othello hears Cassio
laughing contemptuously about the 'bauble' who so dotes on
him, the precious handkerchief the Moor accidentally cast
aside as 'too little' has grown to monstrous proportions.
Tossed around so casually by the Venetians, it becomes the
very symbol of the illusory world of feckless duplicity that Iago
has created. Othello interacts directly with Cassio in only
three of the nine scenes in which they share the stage together
for a total of some forty lines. Here Othello observes Iago
talking for almost seventy lines with Cassio. The scene is a
vivid picture of the way Iago has separated Othello from those
he trusted.

Othello makes it clear in his behaviour to Desdemona
during the welcoming of Lodovico that he is no longer taken
in by Venetian performers. He believes her response to his
striking of her are the crocodile tears of 'well-painted passion'
and that she is 'obedient' only to the task of sustaining her role
(IV i 246–53). He wants, nevertheless to force a direct admission of guilt from this 'cunning'st pattern of excelling
nature'. Shakespeare adds to the intolerable pressure brought
to bear on the audience by linking to our experience of Iago as
such a good actor our experience of Othello as such a bad one.
Only now, in the brothel scene (IV ii), when Othello is almost
completely alienated from Desdemona, does Shakespeare
allow them for the first time in the play a direct interaction in
which they have the stage to themselves. By contrast, up to
this moment in the play Iago and Othello have shared almost
500 lines of interaction alone together. The Moor intends to

catch out these Venetian actors. He will force Desdemona to be what she is by becoming an actor himself. He will pretend to be like the Cassio he thinks he has seen, a regular inhabitant of the secret, backstairs world of purchased lust. He has seen Cassio's light, frivolous behaviour with his whore but he cannot imitate it. He is so maddened by Desdemona's 'performance' as bewildered innocent that he has to abandon his role as a customer in order to assault her wildly in his own proper person as a despised husband. The cunning whore of Venice acts him off the stage. The audience has waited a long time for this scene, for it has to maintain one last hope that if Othello and Desdemona are left alone together long enough they might discover the truth. Othello spends some 60 lines alone with his wife here but we see at once that the more vehemently she denies his accusations the more he is convinced they are correct. Othello, giving money to the madame, Emilia, for his 'course', leaves the bawdy house of his imagination as he is leaving his marriage at the heavy cost of receiving none of the pleasures for which he contracted.

In his bad acting, his inability to mask his cuckold's fury, the unsubtle Othello poses an increasing threat to Iago's plot. In Cinthio the ensign's wife knows the whole nature of her husband's villainy but reveals her knowledge only long after the deaths of Disdemona and the Moor, and just after the death by torture, in connection with other plots, of the villain. Shakespeare makes the person closest to Iago ignorant of his villainy but allows her to stumble all around the truth without uncovering it in time. This allows him to develop Emilia's unambiguous loyalty and steady companionship to the gentle and increasingly isolated Desdemona. The chief harvest he reaps by altering the nature of the ensign's wife he found in Cinthio is the 'willow scene'.

It is the only scene in the play, save for the transitional II ii and III ii, in which Iago makes no appearance. It is the only calm scene of normal domestic behaviour. This bedroom chatter, a pause at the brink of a headlong plunge to chaos, is entirely free of any role-playing deception, or the nightmare illusions which have filled the stage for so long. In the almost 100 lines they share alone the women sustain a longer interaction than any that we see between Othello and his wife. The affection displayed between the women here prepares us for Emilia's loyalty when she returns to the bedchamber later. All of her jests about disloyalty to husbands correspond to the picture of Venetian wiles that Iago has shown to Othello. Desdemona, unlike Othello, cannot bring herself to believe that such devious behaviour is possible. Since Iago first set to work to poison Othello's mind (III iii 93), we have seen Othello on stage for over 800 lines, but during all the corrosive decline in the Moor's faith we have seen Desdemona with him for less than a quarter of those lines. She still has no explanation for his bewildering behaviour and resists all the suggestions of jealousy Emilia shrewdly intuits.

The more Iago is caught up in the inexorable mechanism he has set in motion the less opportunity Shakespeare gives him to strut in soliloquy, superior and separate from his victims. In the attempted murder of Cassio, he has time only for a hasty explanation to us of his problem before the juggling act of keeping everyone in separate compartments begins to break down. Iago knows that both of his wounded dupes must die, but he bungles the job. He has an urgent need to be off stage so that he can re-enter in the role of detached, innocent bystander. He takes the risk of stabbing Roderigo in front of others but leaves Cassio as a loose end in his villainy.

Othello's calmness in approaching murder is a vivid contrast to Iago's hole-and-corner ambush. We can ascribe the Moor's calm nobility (V ii 1–22) to the fact that he is at last master of the stage. Because Desdemona is, initially, asleep he is not enraged by another of her 'performances' of pretended innocence. For a moment he sees himself as the embodiment of justice and recaptures the essence of that magisterially calm figure who described his whole course of love to the Venetian senate. But the delay incurred in affirming his calm resolution allows Desdemona to awake and he is soon forced back, as her words indicate (V ii 37–8; 43–4), into his posture of enraged cuckold. This is the final turn of the screw in the pressure Shakespeare applies to the audience. He allows husband and wife as long an interaction as any they have had hitherto. Othello reveals the identity of the man he suspects, Cassio, and the nature of his evidence, the handkerchief, but he grows more and more convinced of Desdemona's guilt the longer he spends with her. If we had once wished for them to be alone to uncover Iago's lies, we now wish for someone to interrupt them before they are acted upon. Shakespeare arranges matters so that everyone else is drawn into the streets because of Iago's bungled attempt at murder. We can hope that Emilia, on her way to report it, will arrive in time. She had knocked at the door of truth several times but she finds it only seconds too late behind the bedroom door. The final irony of Othello's confused response to Desdemona's mask occurs in her momentary revival after Emilia's entry. Her final line in which she claims to have killed herself is her one piece of deceptive acting in the play. It must seem to him one last outrageous attempt to outface him and deny him the certainty of justice in his own actions, perhaps even one final attempt to corrupt him into joining her world of lies. If her death were reported as an inexplicable suicide then her adultery and dishonour need never be uncovered, for 'their best conscience / Is not to leave't undone, but keep't unknown'. Othello rejects the mask his dying wife offers him and admits his guilt (V ii 130–1). It is at least partly because Othello cannot be two-faced that the Janus-headed Iago is exposed.

Shakespeare achieves the ironies and the tension by changing completely the nature of the murder as Cinthio writes it. The ensign hiding in the closet, the Moor leading his wife thither, the ensign jumping out to bludgeon her to death with a stocking full of sand, the pulling down of the roof to make it look like an accident – all of the detail is the stuff on which sensational journalism feeds. Shakespeare casts it all aside to capitalize on a rich paradox of his scenic structure. In producing a psychological and physical separation between Othello and Desdemona Iago never lets the Moor out his sight for very long.

Shakespeare, however, has Iago trust Othello to undertake the murder unaided in order to provide himself with an alibi for the villainy he confidently believes is undetectable. Iago has found roles for everyone in his plots and has provided for them all, with one crucial exception, adequate motivation for his actions and for their own. He took Emilia's filching of the handkerchief for granted and gave her no excuse for his need of it. The flaw in his theatre of illusions is a failure to act his own part completely. It is to some extent his contempt for women which allows him to engineer his plot, and it is contempt for his wife which supplies the gap in his fabrications through which the truth can rush. Emilia's loyalty to her dead mistress beyond fear of or duty to her husband does not surprise us. We have seen Emilia interacting for more lines with Desdemona than with her husband and of all Iago's interactions the one given least stage-life, less even than his talks with Desdemona, is the relationship with his wife.

At the end Othello is baffled with ignorance and we, kept for so long abreast of all the nasty manoeuvres and motives at the instant of their conception, are baffled by knowledge. We can understand why Iago will remain silent. He no longer has an audience he can tease with its helplessness to interfere as a source of his power. Many explanations have been given for the recovered stature which Othello achieves at the end. In spite of all the bizarre behaviour Iago has induced in him the dignity of his ending is impressive and that is partly because our sense of detachment is undercut. When Othello shares the knowledge we have been burdened with for so long we share the amazement of his response. When he asks 'Will you, I pray, demand that demi-devil / Why he hath thus ensnared my soul and body?' (V ii 301–2) there is no one in the audience, let alone on stage, who can provide a satisfactory answer. In tragedy we can bear to watch characters suffering because we gain understanding in *Othello* that certain things are unknowable.

It has often been asserted that Othello is simply a credulous fool, but if Shakespeare had indeed presented him so then our only recourse would be to get busy and put money in our purses. It is Iago's intention to convince us that the world is full of fools to be practised upon. Many theatregoers and critics are so convinced. It is remarkable that such people fail to recognize their kinship with Roderigo. Roderigo, with an advantage denied to Othello, sees Iago without his mask, believes he can be part of an evil plot and yet invulnerable to it, and is even willing to pay money to be convinced of the gullibility of Othello while ignoring his own. Iago has the audience on the hip because of the masterly ingenuity with which Shakespeare varies his techniques of character inter-action and separation. He keeps characters apart when we want them to be together, he brings them together when we want them kept apart. He makes us aware that we are separated from the action and yet makes our torment so real that we almost wish we could talk to the characters. The one character we would like to get away from is allowed to thrust himself upon us whenever he feels like it. The more we are put in the picture the more we understand how others are kept out of it. Othello has been forced to be an audience when he wanted to be an actor, he has been an actor when he thought of himself as an audience. He has been on stage when he thought himself behind the scenes. Our eagerness to accept his rehabilitation at the end is explicable in terms of the theatrical modes of action Shakespeare juggles with. It is a bewildering irony of his technique that Othello can get himself out of this world of theatrical illusions by deceiving those around him into thinking that he is weaponless. Iago has divided Othello from himself, from his wife and from us. When the enigma of Iago recedes we are for a moment reunited with the Othello we initially encountered. When it is his cue to strike he knows it without a prompter. In his final speech and his suicide he is able, as he was before the Senate in Venice, to express his nobility and to manifest himself rightly.

Karen Newman

From 'AND WASH THE ETHIOP WHITE': FEMININITY AND THE MONSTROUS IN *OTHELLO*

. . . opposed to the representation of Othello's participation in the play's dominant sex/gender system is a conventional representation of black sexuality evoked by other characters and by Othello himself in his traveller's tales and through his passionate action. The textual allusions to bestiality, lubriciousness, and the demonic have been often noted. Iago rouses Brabantio with 'an old black ram / Is tupping your white ewe . . . / . . . the devil will make a grandsire of you' (I i 88–9, 91), and 'you'll have your daughter cover'd with a Barbary horse; you'll have your nephews neigh to you; you'll have coursers for cousins, and gennets for germans' (110–13). 'Your daughter and the Moor, are now making the beast with two backs' (115–16) and Desdemona is transported, according to Roderigo, 'to the gross clasps of a lascivious Moor' (126). Not until the third scene is the Moor named, and the delay undoubtedly dramatizes Othello's blackness and the audience's shared prejudices which are vividly conjured up by Iago's pictorial visions of carnal knowledge. To read Othello as congruent with the attitudes towards sexuality and femininity expressed in the play by the Venetians – Iago, Brabantio, Roderigo and Cassio – and opposed to Desdemona's desire is to ignore the threatening sexuality of the other which divides the representation of Othello's character.[1] Othello internalizes alien cultural values, but the otherness which divides him from the culture and links him to the play's other marginality, femininity, remains in visual and verbal allusion.

209

For the white male characters of the play, the black man's power resides in his sexual difference from a white male norm. Their preoccupation with black sexuality is not an eruption of a normally repressed animal sexuality in the 'civilized' white male, but of the feared power and potency of a different and monstrous sexuality which threatens the white male sexual norm represented in the play most emphatically by Iago. For however evil Iago reveals himself to be, as Spivak pointed out (1958, 415 ff.), like the Vice in the medieval morality, or, we could add, the trickster/slave of Latin comedy, Iago enjoys a privileged relation with the audience. He possesses what can be termed the discourse of knowledge in *Othello* and annexes not only the other characters, but the resisting spectator as well, into his world and its perspective. By virtue of his manipulative power and his superior knowledge and control over the action, which we share, we are implicated in his machinations and the cultural values they imply.[2] Iago is a cultural hyperbole; he does not oppose cultural norms so much as hyperbolize them.[3]

Before the English had wide experience of miscegenation, they seem to have believed, as George Best recounts, that the black man had the power to subjugate his partner's whiteness, to make both his 'victim' and her offspring resemble him, to make them both black, a literal blackness in the case of a child, a metaphorical blackness in the case of a sexual partner. So in *Othello*, Desdemona becomes 'thou black weed' (IV iii 69) and the white pages of her 'goodly book' are blackened by writing when Othello imagines 'whore' inscribed across them. At IV iii, she explicitly identifies herself with her mother's maid Barbary whose name connotes blackness. The union of Desdemona and Othello represents a sympathetic identification between femininity and the monstrous which offers a potentially subversive recognition of sexual and racial difference.

Both the male-dominated Venetian world of *Othello* and the criticism the play has generated have been dominated by a scopic economy which privileges sight, from the spectacular opposition of black and white to Othello's demands for ocular

proof of Desdemona's infidelity. But Desdemona *hears* Othello
and loves him, awed by his traveller's tales of the dangers he
had passed, dangers which emphasize his link with monsters
and marvels. Her responses to his tales are perceived as
voracious – she 'devours' his discourses with a 'greedy ear,'
conflating the oral and aural, and his language betrays a
masculine fear of a cultural femininity which is envisioned as a
greedy mouth, never satisfied, always seeking increase, a point
of view which Desdemona's response to their reunion at Cyprus
reinforces.[4] Desdemona is presented in the play as a sexual
subject who hears and desires, and that desire is punished
because the non-specular, or non-phallic sexuality it displays
is frightening and dangerous.[5] Instead of a specular imaginary, Desdemona's desire is represented in terms of an aural/
oral libidinal economy which generates anxiety in Othello, as
his account to the Senate of his courtship via fiction betrays.[6]
Othello fears Desdemona's desire because it invokes his monstrous difference from the sex/race code he has adopted, or,
alternatively, allies her imagined monstrous sexual appetite
with his own.

Thomas Rymer, a kind of critical Iago, claims the moral of
Othello is first 'a caution to all Maidens of Quality how, without their parents' consent, they run away with Blackamoors,'
an instruction which he follows with the version of his Italian
source, Cinthio: 'Di non si accompagnare con huomo cui la
natura & il cielo & il modo della vita disgiunge da noi' (1693
[ed. Springarn, 1957, 221).[7] Both Rymer and Cinthio reveal
how Desdemona is punished for her desire: she *hears* Othello
and desires him, and her desire is punished because it
threatens a white male hegemony in which women cannot be
desiring subjects. When Desdemona comes to tell her version
of their wooing, she says: 'I saw Othello's visage in his mind.'
The allusion here is certainly to her audience's prejudice
agains the black 'visage' that both the Senators and Shakespeare's audience see in Othello, but Desdemona 'saw' his
visage through hearing the tales he tells of his past, tales
which, far from washing the Moor white as her line seems to

imply, emphatically affirm Othello's link with Africa and its legendary monstrous creatures. Rymer's moral points up the patriarchal and scopic assumptions of his culture which are assumed as well in the play and most pointedly summoned up by Brabantio's often quoted lines: 'Look to her, Moor, have a quick eye to see: / She has deceiv'd her father, may do thee' (I iii 292–3). Fathers have the right to dispose of their daughters as they see fit, to whom they see fit, and disobedience against the father's law is merely a prelude to the descent into hell and blackness the play enacts, a fall, we might recall, Best's tale uncannily predicts. Desdemona's desire threatens the patriarchal privilege of disposing daughters and in the play world signals sexual duplicity and lust.

The irony, of course, is that Othello himself is the instrument of punishment; he enacts the moral Rymer and Cinthio point, both confirming cultural prejudice by his monstrous murder of Desdemona and punishing her desire which transgresses the norms of the Elizabethan sex/race system. Both Othello and Desdemona deviate from the norms of the sex/race system in which they participate from the margins. Othello is not, in Cinthio's words, 'da noi,' one of 'us,' nor is Desdemona. Women depend for the class status on their affiliation with men – fathers, husbands, sons – and Desdemona forfeits that status and the protection it affords when she marries outside the categories her culture allows.[8] For her transgression, her desire of difference, she is punished not only in a loss of status, but even of life. The woman's desire is punished, and ultimately its monstrous inspiration as well. As the object of Desdemona's illegitimate passion, Othello both figures monstrosity *and* at the same time represents the white male norms the play encodes through Iago, Roderigo, Brabantio.[9] Not surprisingly, Othello reveals at last a complicitous self-loathing, for blackness is as loathsome to him as to George Best, or any male character in the play, or ostensibly the audience.

At IV i, Iago constructs a drama which Othello is instructed to interpret, a scene rich in its figurations of desire and the monstrous. Cast by Iago as eavesdropper and voyeur, Othello imagines and thus constitutes a sexual encounter and pleasure that excludes him, and a Desdemona as whore instead of fair angel. Cassio's mocking rehearsal of Bianca's love is not the sight/site of Desdemona's transgression, as Othello believes, but its representation; ironically this theatrical representation directed by Iago functions as effectively as would the real. Representation for Othello is transparent. The male gaze is privileged; it constructs a world which the drama plays out. The aptly and ironically named Bianca is a cypher for Desdemona whose 'blackened whiteness' she embodies. Plots of desire conventionally figure woman as the erotic object, but in *Othello* the iconic centre of the spectacle is shifted from the woman to the monstrous Othello whose blackness charms *and* threatens, but ultimately fulfils the cultural prejudices it represents. Othello is both hero and outsider because he embodies not only the norms of male power and privilege represented by the white male hegemony which rules Venice, a world of prejudice, ambition, jealousy, and the denial of difference, but also the threatening power of the alien; Othello is a monster in the Renaissance sense of the word, a deformed creature like the hermaphrodites and other strange spectacles which so fascinated the early modern period. And *monstrum*, the word itself, figures both the creature and its movement into representation, for it meant as well a showing or demonstration, a *representation*.

HISTORICAL CONTINGENCY: REREADING *OTHELLO*

The position which a text occupies within the relations of ideological class struggle at its originating moment of production is ... no necessary indication of the positions which it may subsequently come to occupy in different historical and political contexts.

(Bennett, 1982, 229)

> His nose was rising and Roman, instead of African and
> flat: His Mouth the finest shaped that could be seen;
> far from those great turn'd Lips, which are so natural
> to the rest of the Negroes. The whole Proportion and
> air of his face was so nobly and exactly form'd, that
> bating his colour, there could be nothing in Nature
> more beautiful, agreeable and handsome.
>
> (Aphra Behn, *Oroonoko*, 1688)[10]

Behn's description of her black protagonist Oroonoko is startling in its congruence with Ridley's portrait of the black Othello
[in the Introduction to his 1958 edition] with which we began.
A black tragic hero of Othello's proportions, or Behn's noble
Oroonoko, is only possible if black is really white, if features
are 'classical,' that is European, and colour is merely an un-
fortunate accident. By the late seventeenth century, the role
and status of blacks in English society had changed, and the
discourse of racism was fully established. No longer 'spectacles
of strangeness' and monstrosity who occupied unstable, exotic
and mythic ideological roles, they were slaves, situated in a
growing capitalist economy which their exploited labour sustained. In the sixteenth and early seventeenth centuries, the
slave trade in England was desultory and the status of blacks
liminal rather than fixed. As Best's *Discourse* and the accounts
of early voyagers illustrate, blacks occupied mythic roles
rather than positions as mere chattel or economic linchpin. In
Elizabethan and Jacobean England, blacks were not only ser-
vants; they owned property, paid taxes, went to church.[11] But
with the establishment of the sugar industry in the Caribbean,
and the tobacco and cotton industries in America, the position
of blacks changed and their value as slave labour was fully
recognized and exploited. The Royal African Company, char-
tered in 1672, monopolized the African trade until 1698 when
the rapid expansion of the colonies dependent on slave labour
was so great that it was deprived of its exclusive rights and the
market opened to competition. Newspapers of the late seventeenth century testify to a changed view of blacks – advertise-
ments of slaves for sale, and more importantly, hue-and-cry

notices seeking runaways who were often described as wearing collars emblazoned with their owners' arms, or with inscriptions such as one reported in the *London Gazette* (1688): 'The Lady Bromfield's black, in Lincoln's Inn Fields'.

By the late seventeenth century, Englishmen had come to realize the significance of the slave trade to the British economy. In 1746, M. Postlewayt put that realization forcefully into words: 'the most approved Judges of the commercial Interests of these Kingdoms have ever been of Opinion, that our West-India and Africa trades are the most nationally beneficial of any we carry on ... the daily Bread of the most considerable Part of our British Manufacturers, [is] owing primarily to the Labour of Negroes.'[12] By the mid-eighteenth century, the *Gentleman's Magazine* claimed there were some 20,000 blacks in London. Their increasing numbers led to growing prejudice and fear that they threatened the position of white working people. In pamphlets and the popular press, blacks were represented increasingly as caricatures, bestial, apelike, inhuman, stripped of the exotic or mythic discourses of the sixteenth and early seventeenth centuries. By the time of Rymer's attack on *Othello*, Shakespeare's heroic and tragic representation of a black man seemed unthinkable. In his 'Short View of Tragedy' (1693), Rymer found Shakespeare's choice reprehensible, a transgression of both tragic and social decorum.[13] Rymer's attitude toward the 'blackamoor' is historically predictable; more surprising, perhaps, is his critical slippage, like Ridley's some 250 years later, from blackness to femininity.[14]

Rymer notoriously claimed that the moral of *Othello* was 'a warning to all good Wives that they look well to their Linnen' (1693, [1957, 221]). He devotes the last pages of his attack to the 'Tragedy of the Handkerchief,' claiming that 'had it been *Desdemona's* Garter, the Sagacious Moor might have smelt a Rat; but the handkerchief is so remote a trifle, no Booby on this side of *Mauritania* cou'd make any consequence from it ... Yet we find it entered into our Poets head to make a Tragedy of this *Trifle*' (1693 [1957, 251, 254]). Rymer takes issue with

Shakespeare's presentation of the handkerchief because he finds it too trifling a detail to sustain tragedy. His comment here reflects not only the changing generic expectations of neoclassicism, but also Rymer's cultural prejudices against women, their supposed materiality and preoccupation with the trivial.[15]

In the early modern period, the handkerchief was in fact a sign of wealth and status; by the early eighteenth century, however, it had become commonplace (Elias, 1978, 143–52). In *cinquecento* Venice, possession of a lady's handkerchief was considered proof of adultery and led to stringent punishments. In 1416, a certain Tomaso Querini received a stiff sentence of eighteen months in jail and a fine of 500 *lire di piccoli* for carrying out 'many dishonesties' with Maria, wife of Roberto Bono. Records from the case describe Tomaso's crime as having

> presumed to follow the said lady and on this public street took from her hands a handkerchief, carrying it off with him. As a result of this deed the said Tomaso entered the home of Roberto many times during the day and night and committed many dishonesties with this lady with the highest dishonor for ser Roberto.
>
> (Ruggiero, 1985, 61–2)[16]

Many critics and readers of the play have sought to save Shakespeare's handkerchief from Rymer's harsh judgement by demonstrating not its historical significance as a sign of adultery, but its symbolic significance and meaning. Their efforts have been limited by their own historical boundaries and by reigning critical preoccupations and practices which too often seek to work out equations which restrict the richness of *handkerchief* as signifier. The handkerchief in *Othello* is what we might term a snowballing signifier, for as it passes from hand to hand, both literal and critical, it accumulates myriad associations and meanings.[17] It first appears simply as a love token given by Othello to Desdemona and therefore treasured by her; only later do we learn the details of its provenance and design. In the Renaissance, strawberries signified virtue or goodness, but also hypocritical virtue as symbolized by the frequently occurring design and emblem of a strawberry plant with an adder hiding beneath its leaves (Ross, 1960, 225–40). This doubleness is, of course, appropriate for Othello's perception of Desdemona, for when the handkerchief is first given it represents her virtue and their chaste love, but it later becomes a sign, indeed a proof, of her unfaithfulness. Iago's description of the napkin as 'spotted' constitutes for Othello a new meaning to the handkerchief – the strawberries become signs of Desdemona's deceit.[18]

In psychoanalytic terms, the handkerchief which Othello inherits from his mother and then gives to Desdemona has been read symptomatically as the fetishist's substitution for the mother's missing phallus. Like the shoe Freud's young boy substitutes 'for the woman's (mother's) phallus which the little boy once believed in and does not wish to forego', the handkerchief is the fetish which endows 'women with the attribute which makes them acceptable as sexual objects' – that is, makes them like men (Freud, 1927 [1963, 215, 216]). For Othello, it both conceals and reveals Desdemona's imperfection, her lack. But the psychoanalytic scenario is problematic because it privileges a male scopic drama, casting the woman as other, as a failed man, thereby effacing her difference and concealing her sexual specificity behind the fetish. The handkerchief in *Othello* does indeed figure a lack, but ironically it figures not simply the missing penis, but the lack around which the play's dramatic action is structured, a desiring femininity which is described in the play as aberrant and 'monstrous' or a 'monster'.[19] The handkerchief, with its associations with the mother, witchcraft, and the marvellous, represents the link between femininity and the monstrous which Othello and Desdemona's union figures in the play. It figures a female sexual topography that is more than a sign of male possession, violated virginity, even deceit, and more than the fetishist's beloved object. It figures not only Desdemona's lack, as in the traditional psychoanalytic reading, but also her own sexual parts – the nipples, which incidentally are sometimes represented in the courtly love blason as strawberries, lips and even perhaps the clitoris, the berry of sexual pleasure nestled beneath phalanged leaves.[20]

The handkerchief, therefore, is significant not only historically as an indicator of class or transgression, or psychologically, because it signifies male fears of duplicity, consummation, and castration, but also politically precisely because it has become a *feminine* trifle. *Othello*'s tragic action is structured not around a heroic act or even object – a battle, as in *Antony and Cleopatra*, or kingship as in *Macbeth* and *King Lear* – but around a trifle, a feminine toy. Instead of relegating *Othello* to the critical category domestic tragedy, always implicitly or explicitly pejorative because of its focus on woman, jealousy and a triangle, we can reread *Othello* from another perspective, also admittedly historically bound, that seeks to displace conventional interpretations by exposing the extraordinary fascination with and fear of racial and sexual differences which characterizes Elizabethan and Jacobean culture. Desdemona and Othello, woman and black man, are represented by discourses about femininity and blackness which managed and produced difference in early modern England.

COLONIALISM AND SEXUAL DIFFERENCE

Was Shakespeare a racist who condoned the negative image of blacks in his culture? Is Desdemona somehow guilty in her stubborn defence of Cassio and her admiring remark 'Ludovico is a proper man'?[21] Or in a new critical vocabulary, in her 'erotic submission, [which] conjoined with Iago's murderous cunning, far more effectively, if unintentionally, subverts her husband's carefully fashioned identity' (Greenblatt, 1980, 244)? Readers preoccupied with formal dramatic features claim such questions are moot, that the questions themselves expose the limits of moral or political readings of texts because they raise the spectres of intention or ignore the touted transcendence of history by art. But as much recent poststructuralist and/or political criticism has demonstrated, even highly formalist readings are political, inscribed in the discourses both of the period in which the work was produced and of those in which it is consumed.

The task of a political criticism is not merely to expose or demystify the ideological discourses which organize literary texts, but to *reconstitute* those texts, to reread canonical texts in noncanonical ways which reveal the contingency of so-called canonical readings, which disturb conventional interpretations and discover them as partisan, constructed, made rather than given, natural, and inevitable. Such strategies of reading are particularly necessary in drama because the dramatic immediacy of theatrical representation obscures the fact that the audience is watching a highly artificial enactment of what, in the case of *Othello*, a non-African and a man has made into a vision of blackness and femininity, of passion and desire in the other, those marginal groups which stand outside culture and simultaneously within it.

Shakespeare was certainly subject to the racist, sexist, and colonialist discourses of his time, but by making the black Othello a hero, and by making Desdemona's love for Othello, and her transgression of her society's norms for women in choosing him, sympathetic, Shakespeare's play stands in a contestatory relation to the hegemonic ideologies of race and gender in early modern England. Othello is, of course, the play's hero only within the terms of a white, elitist male ethos, and he suffers the generic 'punishment' of tragedy, but he is nevertheless represented as heroic and tragic at a historical moment when the only role blacks played on stage was that of a villain of low status. The case of Desdemona is more complex because the fate she suffers is the conventional fate assigned to the desiring woman. Nevertheless, Shakespeare's representation of her as at once virtuous and desiring, and of her choice in love as heroic rather than demonic, dislocates the conventional ideology of gender the play also enacts.

We need to read Shakespeare in ways which produce resistant readings, ways which contest the hegemonic forces the plays at the same time affirm. Our critical task is not merely to describe the formal parameters of a play, nor is it to make claims about Shakespeare's politics, conservative or subversive, but to reveal the discursive and dramatic evidence for such representations, and their counterparts in criticism, as representations.[22]

NOTES

1. Homi Bhabha's notion of hybridity, which he defines as 'the revaluation of the assumption of colonial identity through the repetition of discriminatory identity effects' (1985, 154), is suggestive for my reading of *Othello*.

2. Casual assumptions about the Shakespearean audience are problematic, and the 'we' of my own critical discourse is equally so. Shakespeare's audience was not a classless, genderless monolith. The female spectators at a Globe performance, both the whores in the pit and the good English wives Stephen Gosson chastises for their attendance at the theatre in *The Schoole of Abuse*, view the play from different perspectives from those of the white male audience of whatever social and economic station. As women, if we are implicated in Iago's perspective and Othello's tragedy, we are unsexed, positioned as men; however, if we identify with Desdemona, we are punished. See the interesting work on female spectatorship in film theory by Laura Mulvey (1975) and Mary Ann Doane (1983) in *Screen*.

3. In Leo Africanus' *Historie of Africa*, the 'Portugals' are most often singled out as the destroyers of Africa and her peoples. From this perspective, the Iberian origins of Iago's name suggest that his destruction of Othello/Africa can be read as an allegory of colonialism. For detailed if occasionally dubious parallels between Leo's *Historie* and *Othello*, see Johnson (1985).

4. Compare Thomas Becon's lively description of a whore in his *Catechisme* (1564, XX, ii^v), typical of such representations in the period: 'the whore is never satisfied, but is like as one that goeth by the way and is thirsty; even so does she open her mouth and drink of everye next water, that she may get. By every hedge she sits down, & opes her quiver against every arrow.' Becon makes explicit what is only implied in *Othello*: the link between female orifices – ear, mouth, genitals – and the perceived voraciousness of females.

5. This alternative sexual economy suggests another trajectory of desire in *Othello* which cannot be explored further here. Iago's seduc-

tion is also cast in terms of the aural/oral, as for example when he claims to pour 'pestilence into his [Othello's] ear' (II iii 347). For an interesting discussion of *Othello* and the 'pathological male animus toward sexuality', particularly Desdemona's, see Snow (1980) 388.

6. I am grateful to Rey Chow and the other members of the Brown University seminar 'Cultural Constructions of Gender' (1987) at the Pembroke Center for Teaching and Research on Women for valuable discussion of the play's sexual economies.

7. For the status of blacks and moors in Renaissance Venice, see Fedalto (1976).

8. For an excellent discussion of gender and class in *Othello*, see Stallybrass (1986).

9. For a psychoanalytic reading of Othello's relation to 'the voice of the father', see Snow (1980) 409–10.

10. Quoted in Jordan (1968) 28.

11. See Walvin (1972) 13, and Shyllon (1977). It is worth noting that slavery between Europe and Africa was reciprocal. W. E. B. DuBois (1947, 52) points out that during the sixteenth century 'the [black] Mohammedan rulers of Egypt were buying white slaves by the tens of thousands in Europe and Asia'. Blonde women were apparently in special demand: quoted in Chandler (1985), who points out that the 'moors' were black, and that historians' efforts to claim their tawniness represent racial prejudice.

12. Postlewayt writes in order to justify the Royal African Company's attempts to regain its monopoly; his pamphlet is exemplary, but many others could also be cited. Quoted in Walvin (1972) 51–2.

13. Rymer's attack on Shakespeare in the age of growing Shakespeare idolatry prompted other critics to a different tack – to dispute Othello's blackness altogether rather than reprehend it.

14. This same slippage from blackness to femininity is implicit in the commonly believed notion that apes and negroes copulated, and especially that 'apes were inclined wantonly to attack Negro women'. For contemporary references, see Jordan (1968) 31.

15. Rymer's characterization of Emilia as 'the meanest woman in the Play' (1693, 254) requires comment. The moralism of his 'Short View' might lead most readers to award Bianca that superlative, but predictably Rymer cannot forgive Emilia her spunky cynicism toward men and her defence of women.

16. I am grateful to Jonathan Goldberg for this reference.

17. My argument about the handkerchief has much in common with Stallybrass (1986).

18. Boose (1975) argues that the handkerchief represents the lovers' consummated marriage and wedding sheets stained with blood, a

sign of Desdemona's sexual innocence. She links the handkerchief to the folk custom of displaying the spotted wedding sheets as a proof of the bride's virginity.

19. See, for example, I iii 402; III iii 111, 433.

20. Snow associates the spotted 'napkin' not only with Desdemona's stained wedding sheets, but also with menstrual blood. He argues that the handkerchief is therefore 'a nexus for three aspects of woman – chaste bride, sexual object, and maternal threat' (1980, 392).

21. For a discussion of critical attitudes toward Desdemona, and particularly this line, see Garner (1976).

22. For a discussion of the problem of representation and colonialist discourse, see Said (1978).

REFERENCES

Becon, Thomas (1564), 'Catechisme', in *Workes* (London).

Bennett, Tony (1982) 'Text and History' in Widdowson, Peter (ed.), *Re-reading English* (London: Methuen) pp. 223–36.

Bhabba, Homi (1985), 'Signs Taken for Wonders: Questions of Ambivalence and Authority under a Tree outside Delhi, May 1817', *Critical Inquiry*, 12, pp. 144–65.

Boose, Lynda (1975), 'Othello's Handkerchief: The Recognizance and Pledge of Love', *English Literary Renaissance*, 5, pp. 360–74.

Chandler, Wayne B. (1985), 'The Moor: Light of Europe's Dark Age', in *African Presence in Early Europe*, special issue of *Journal of African Civilizations*, 7, pp. 144–75.

Doane, Mary Ann (1983), 'Film and the Masquerade: Theorizing the Female Spectator', *Screen*, 23, pp. 74–87.

DuBois, W. E. B. (1947), *The World and Africa* (New York: Viking).

Elias, Norbert (1978), *The Civilizing Process: The History of Manners*, trans. Edmund Jephcott (New York: Urizen).

Fedalto, Giorgio (1976), 'Stranieri a Venezia a e Padova', in Arnaldi, Girolamo and Stocchi, M. P. (eds), *Storia della cultura veneta dal primo quattrocento al concilio de Trento* (Vicenza: N. Pozza) vol. 3, pp. 499–535.

Garner, S. N. (1976), 'Shakespeare's Desdemona', *Shakespeare Studies*, 9, pp. 232–52.

Johnson, Rosalind (1985), 'African Presence in Shakespearean Drama: *Othello* and Leo Africanus' *Historie of Africa*', *African Presence in Early Europe*, special issue of *Journal of African Civilizations*, 7, pp. 267–87.

Jordan, Winthrop (1968), *White Over Black* (Chapel Hill, N.C.: University of North Carolina Press).

Mulvey, Laura (1975), 'Visual Pleasure and the Narrative Cinema', *Screen*, 16, pp. 6–18.

Ross, Lawrence (1960), 'The Meaning of Strawberries in Shake-speare', *Studies in the Renaissance*, 7, pp. 225–40.

Ruggiero, Guido (1985) *The Boundaries of Eros: Sex Crimes in Renaissance Venice* (New York: Oxford Universtiy Press).

Rymer, Thomas (1693), 'A Short View of Tragedy', in Spingarn, J. E. (ed.) (1957), *Critical Essays of the Seventeenth Century* (Bloomington, Indiana University Press), vol. 2.

Said, Edward (1978), *Orientalism* (New York: Pantheon).

Shyllon, Folarin (1977), *Black People in Britain, 1555–1833* (Oxford: Oxford University Press).

Snow, Edward A. (1980), 'Sexual Anxiety and the Male Order of Things in *Othello*', *English Literary Renaissance*, 10, pp. 384–412.

Spivak, Bernard (1958), *The Allegory of Evil* (New York: Columbia University Press).

Stallybrass, Peter (1986), 'Patriarchal Territories: The Body Enclosed', in Ferguson, Margaret, Quilligan, Maureen, and Vickers, Nancy (eds), *Rewriting the Renaissance* (Chicago: University of Chicago Press).

Walvin, James (1972), *The Black Presence* (New York: Schocken Books).

SELECT BIBLIOGRAPHY

EDITIONS

Othello, ed. Alice Walker and J. D. Wilson (Cambridge University Press, 1957).
Othello, ed. M. R. Ridley, Arden Edition (Methuen, 1958). Uncontroversial scholarly edition, conveniently reprinting the source material.
Othello, ed. Kenneth Muir (New Penguin Edition).

CRITICAL STUDIES

Geoffrey Bullough (ed.), *Narrative and Dramatic Sources of Shakespeare* (Routledge, ongoing publication). Professor Bullough's monumental collection assembles, for every play, the source that Shakespeare is generally considered to have followed for his main story, plus any contemporary works on the same or similiar themes he might have read or heard about. Everything is printed in full and the reader now has the great convenience of having it all in one book. The *Othello* material is in volume VII.
George R. Elliott, *Flaming Minister: A Study of Othello as Tragedy of Love and Hate* (Duke University Press, 1953). An interesting and deeply felt study of the play as a tragedy on the theme of pride. This, the chief of the deadly sins because it makes all the other sins inflexible, intermingles with love and causes it to be changed, at white-heat, to hate.
Helen Gardner, 'The Noble Moor' in *Proceedings of the British Academy XLI* (Oxford University Press, 1955). A penetrating and eloquent account of the play which is also a spirited defence of the nobility and magnificence of the

hero's character against that tendency in twentieth-century criticism which has tried to present these qualities as flawed by self-deception and self-indulgence.

Robert B. Heilman, *Magic in the Web: Action and Language in 'Othello'* (University of Kentucky Press, 1956). A very detailed analysis – almost, at times, *too* exhaustive in its determination to cite all the evidence and leave no corner of the play unexamined, but full of good things, e.g. the best defence, if it needs one, of the apparent unrealism of Desdemona's return from death to utter her last words (pp. 215–16), or the brilliant analysis of Iago's 'Now I do love her too' soliloquy (pp. 200 ff.). Language, symbolism, theme, character – all are discussed, in conjunction and together, in a generously enthusiastic book that 'ne'er feels retiring ebb, but keeps due on'.

Marvin Rosenberg, *The Masks of Othello* (University of California Press, 1961). Subtitled *The Search for the Identity of Othello, Iago and Desdemona by Three Centuries of Actors and Critics*, this lively book gathers together what we know of the interpretations of these characters by great actors from the seventeenth century to the twentieth, and links them in a broad narrative fresco with the judgements of critics on these characters; it also offers a cogent statement of what Shakespearean interpretation owes, and must always owe, to the theatre.

W. H. Auden, *The Dyer's Hand* (Faber, 1963). Contains his (in my opinion) occasionally wrong-headed but stimulating and provocative study of Iago as 'the sole agent in the play' . . . 'a parabolic figure for the autonomous pursuit of scientific knowledge through experiment which we all, whether we are scientists or not, take as natural and right'.

Eldred Jones, *Othello's Countrymen: The African in English Renaissance Drama* (Oxford University Press for Fourah Bay College, 1965). By the middle of the sixteenth century, the English reader could learn about Africans from first-hand accounts as well as from Herodotus and other

ancients. Africans (commonly called Moors) were fre-
quent in the theatre; Mr Jones lists 45 dramatic works in
which they appear, and describes many of the non-
dramatic works from which playwrights probably took
their material. Convention generally showed the Moor as
villainous, like Shakespeare's early Aaron in *Titus Andro-
nicus*, but sometimes allowed him the simpler kinds of
nobility. Mr Jones compares Othello with Shakespeare's
other Africans, and points out that it is Iago who 'repro-
duces and exaggerates many of the unfavourable characteristics commonly credited to Moors'. He deals also with
the make-up and costume of Elizabethan stage Moors.

Shakespeare Survey, 21. Kenneth Muir (ed.) (Cambridge
University Press, 1968). This issue of the annual *Survey*
pays special attention to *Othello*, both in articles and
illustrations. Particularly arresting is Ned B. Allen's study
of the composition of the play, in which he argues that
Shakespeare wrote Acts III, IV and V some time before he
wrote I and II, so that many of the problems which have
exercised critics are simply the result of inconsistencies
between the first and second parts; Shakespeare 'made a
play by splicing together two parts not originally written
to go together'. Other contributors continue to treat
Othello as a single play rather than two discrete frag-
ments; Emrys Jones offers a useful sidelight in '*Othello*,
"Lepanto" and the Cyprus Wars', which argues that the
play is influenced by James I's heroic poem 'Lepanto',
especially in view of Shakespeare's position as chief
dramatist to the 'King's Men'. Dame Helen Gardner
contributes a terse but lucid survey of *Othello* criticism,
1900–67, while essays on Delacroix and Verdi illustrate
the play's impact on the continental European sensibility.

G. K. Hunter, '*Othello* and Colour Prejudice' in *Proceedings of
the British Academy LIII* (Oxford University Press, 1957).
An invaluable aid to setting this aspect of the play in
historical perspective.

Jane Adamson, *Othello as Tragedy: A Study in Judgement and*

Feeling (Cambridge University Press, 1980). A penetrating psychological study of the characters and their interaction, almost Bradleian in its detailed intensity, though making use of modern psychological concepts.

Martin L. Wine, *Othello* in the 'Text & Performance' series (Macmillan, 1984). A useful, down-to-earth student guide, aimed more or less at sixth-form and first-year students, which treats the play first as a printed text and then in performance, with a survey of the main productions and acting interpretations since the 1940s. The author has taken into account that many of his readers will be likely (more likely, perhaps) to have made their first acquaintance with Shakespearean production on the screen than in the theatre.

Patricia and Geoffrey Hartman (eds) *The Question of Theory* (Methuen, 1985). A show-case of recent theoretical criticism, employing the methods and demonstrating the preoccupations of feminism and the new historicism.

Terry Eagleton, *William Shakespeare* (Basil Blackwell, 1986). An interesting thematic analysis which the author describes as 'centred on the interrelations of language, desire, law, money and the body'. It has six short chapters; I find the sixth, dealing with the last plays or 'romances', particularly helpful, but the fourth, 'Nothing', which opens with a treatment of *Othello* and goes on to deal with *Hamlet* and *Coriolanus*, is also very rewarding.

NOTES ON CONTRIBUTORS

JOHN BAYLEY. Thomas Warburton Professor of English Literature, Oxford University. His books include studies of Tolstoy, Pushkin and Hardy.

A. C. BRADLEY (1851–1935). English critic. Taught at the universities of Oxford, Liverpool and Glasgow and then became Professor of Poetry at Oxford in 1901.

ANTHONY BRENNAN. Professor of English Literature, MacMaster University, Ontario. His publications include *Shakespeare's Dramatic Structures* (1988) and *Onstage and Offstage Worlds in Shakespeare's Plays* (1989).

NEVILL COGHILL (1899–1980). Anglo-Irish critic, producer, teacher, Oxford don (was Auden's tutor), preceded Dame Helen Gardner as Merton Professor of English Language and Literature. Produced much theatrical work, including co-authorship of a successful adaptation from Chaucer, *The Canterbury Tales* (1968). Books include *Geoffrey Chaucer* (1966) and *Shakespeare's Professional Skills* (1964), *The Collected Papers of Nevill Coghill: Shakespearean and Medieval*, (ed.) Gray, published in 1988.

T. S. ELIOT (1888–1965). Major poet and critic. American-born, settled in England in 1915 and took British nationality in 1927. Nobel Prize for Literature, 1948.

WILLIAM EMPSON (1906–1984). Professor of English Literature, University of Sheffield, 1953–71. One of the rare academic critics to be generally acknowledged as a man of genius. His brilliant career, launched by the publication of *Seven Types of Ambiguity* in 1930, continued without a break for half a century, except that he voluntarily gave up writing for five years to work for Allied propaganda during the Second World War. His books, too numerous and too well known to be listed in full, include *Essays on Shakespeare* (1986), *Collected Poems* (1984), and a posthumous sampling of miscellaneous critical writing, *Argufying* (1988). He was knighted in 1979.

G. WILSON KNIGHT.   English critic, producer, actor, teacher. Taught at the University of Leeds, 1946–62. Pioneered modern Shakespearean criticism with a brilliant cluster of books, *Myth and Miracle* (1929), *The Wheel of Fire* (1930), *The Imperial Theme* (1931) and *The Shakespearean Tempest* (1932).

F. R. LEAVIS (1895–1978).   Cambridge critic (Fellow of Downing College) who influenced a whole generation. Founder-editor of *Scrutiny*, a critical review with specific educational interests. His books include *Revaluation* (1936), *The Great Tradition* (1948) and *Anna Karenina and Other Essays* (1969).

KAREN NEWMAN.   Professor of Comparative Literature and English at Brown University, and the author of *Shakespeare's Rhetoric of Comic Character* (1985).

CHRISTOPHER NORRIS.   Professor in the School of English Studies, Communication and Philosophy, University of Wales, Cardiff. Publications include *Deconstruction: Theory and Practice* (1982), studies of Jacques Derrida and Paul de Man, and a forthcoming book on Spinoza.

INDEX

230